Faith in a Hard Ground

ST ANDREWS STUDIES IN PHILOSOPHY AND PUBLIC AFFAIRS

Founding and General Editor:
John Haldane, University of St Andrews

Values, Education and the Human World
edited by John Haldane

Philosophy and its Public Role
edited by William Aiken and John Haldane

Relativism and the Foundations of Liberalism
by Graham Long

Human Life, Action and Ethics: Essays by G.E.M. Anscombe
edited by Mary Geach and Luke Gormally

The Institution of Intellectual Values: Realism and Idealism in Higher Education
by Gordon Graham

Life, Liberty and the Pursuit of Utility
by Anthony Kenny and Charles Kenny

Distributing Healthcare: Principles, Practices and Politics
edited by Niall Maclean

Liberalism, Education and Schooling: Essays by T.M. Mclaughlin
edited by David Carr, Mark Halstead and Richard Pring

The Landscape of Humanity: Art, Culture & Society
by Anthony O'Hear

Faith in a Hard Ground: Essays on Religion, Philosophy and Ethics by G.E.M. Anscombe
edited by Mary Geach and Luke Gormally

Subjectivity and Being Somebody
by Grant Gillett

Faith in a Hard Ground

Essays on Religion, Philosophy and Ethics by G.E.M. Anscombe

Edited by
Mary Geach and Luke Gormally

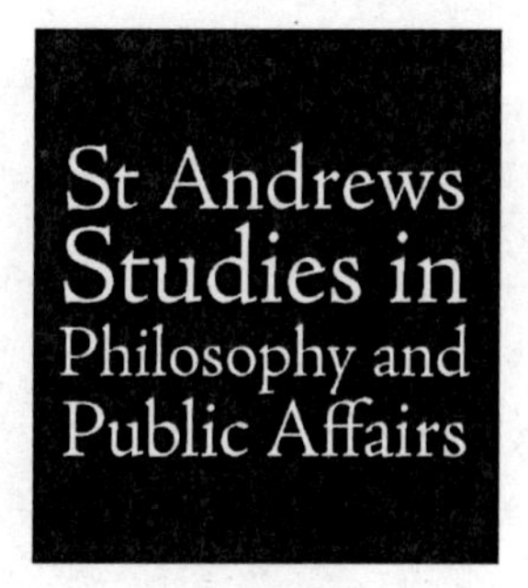

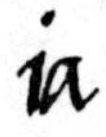

IMPRINT ACADEMIC

Published in the UK by Imprint Academic
PO Box 200, Exeter EX5 5YX, UK

Published in the USA by Imprint Academic
Philosophy Documentation Center
PO Box 7147, Charlottesville, VA 22906-7147, USA

ISBN 9781845401214 (paper)
ISBN 9781845401436 (cloth)

A CIP catalogue record for this book is available from the
British Library and US Library of Congress

Cover Photograph:
St Salvator's Quadrangle, St Andrews by Peter Adamson
from the University of St Andrews collection

And his faith grew in a hard ground
Of doubt and reason and falsehood found,
Where no faith else could grow.

G K Chesterton, *The Ballad of the White Horse*

For

Becky and Tom

Contents

Preface

The present volume is a successor to *Human Life, Action and Ethics*[1] as part of the project to collect in book form hitherto uncollected and unpublished papers by the late Professor Elizabeth Anscombe. The papers in this volume for the most part concern questions about religious belief, and more particularly about teachings of the Catholic Church, which exercised Elizabeth Anscombe or audiences she was invited to address. A reviewer of the previous volume[2] thought "readers should bear in mind that, with the exception of her celebrated essay 'Modern Moral Philosophy' ... she did not include these essays in her collected works." Her failure to do so was in the case of most essays in that volume hardly surprising since only three of the twenty three papers in it were written or published prior to the process of selecting papers for publication in her *Collected Philosophical Papers*.[3] Of the twenty five papers in the present volume, however, at least eight were written prior to the selection of papers for the three volumes of collected papers which appeared in 1981. Anscombe kept all of them (with the exception of No.7) on file. Some of them are of interest for their philosophical exploration of questions arising from statements of religious belief; others elucidate what she thought important in the living of a Christian life and in the life of the contemporary Church, apt as it is to succumb to the influences of a secularist culture. They all contribute to a rounded understanding of her work.

---

[1] *Human Life, Action and Ethics. Essays by G E M Anscombe*, edited by Mary Geach & Luke Gormally (Exeter & Charlottesville, VA: Imprint Academic, 2005).

[2] Professor Sir Michael Dummett, in *The Tablet* 9 July 2005.

[3] *The Collected Philosophical Papers of G E M Anscombe*. Volume 1: *From Parmenides to Wittgenstein*; Volume 2: *Metaphysics and the Philosophy of Mind*.; Volume 3: *Ethics, Religion and Politics*. Three papers from Volume 3 are reprinted in the present volume (Nos.2, 10 and 11) to fill what would otherwise be lacunae in the picture of Anscombe's thinking the present collection aims to present on the range of topics it covers.

No doubt her selection of papers for the 1981 volumes was influenced by what Anscombe thought would command attention among her contemporaries in Anglo-American philosophical circles. But she stood out from those circles not merely for her philosophical originality but also for her defence of what the Catholic Church taught. This led to her being in increasing demand to address Catholic audiences, especially about some of the moral issues which have exercised Catholics in the past half century.[4] Some of those audiences were philosophically sophisticated, others were not. Anscombe pitched her exposition to suit the level of understanding she could assume in her audience. What she did assume in Catholic audiences, which she was not entitled to assume elsewhere, was acceptance of authoritative Church teaching. Some of the papers in the present volume make no such assumption, but many do. Readers will need to be sensitive to this kind of difference, as well as to the differing levels at which exposition is pitched.

I have attempted to establish the dates and the original audience/readership of the papers in this volume. This proved to be a somewhat time-consuming part of the editing process, since there were no indications on file. It was eventually possible, within the time available, to provide precise details of dates and audience/readership for some papers, and approximate details for a related group of three papers, but no information was found about a number of papers. Features of their physical format suggested that the group of three ('Prophecy', 'The immortality of the soul', and 'On being in good faith', Nos. 3, 9 and 12) were all given in the late 1950s and early 1960s to the Philosophical Enquiry Group which met each year between 1954 and 1974 at the Dominican Conference Centre at Spode House in Staffordshire. It was Fr Columba Ryan OP, then teaching philosophy at the adjoining Hawkesyard Priory in the 1950s, who originally proposed inviting a number of Catholics who were professional philosophers to meet on a regular basis at Spode

---

[4] Two published papers which addressed topics assigned to her and which Anscombe struggled to find engaging have been omitted from this volume: 'Gradualness in a law and a law of gradualness', *Anthropos [Anthropotes]* 2 (1986), pp. 183–6; and 'Why have children?', *Proceedings of the American Catholic Philosophical Association* 63 (1990), pp. 48–53. Her little paper 'Philosophy, Belief and Faith', *Priests and People* 9 (1995), p. 387, is too slight to warrant inclusion. One other published paper, 'Contraception and Natural Law', *New Blackfriars* 46 (1965), pp. 517–21, would have merited inclusion were it not for the fact that the points it makes are more fully made in a number of papers in the present collection. The paper was a response she made at a meeting of the Philosophical Enquiry Group at Spode House in 1964 to a paper by Fr Herbert McCabe OP.

House. Among the first invitees were Elizabeth Anscombe and Peter Geach, and both remained leading figures in the Group for the following twenty years. A number of distinguished twentieth century philosophers were participants in these meetings. The meetings focused on philosophical issues related to Christian belief and practice. The Group eventually expanded its membership to include non-Catholic Christian philosophers.

I owe some of these details to informative conversation with Fr Columba Ryan OP, now in his nineties but happily continuing to exhibit an undimmed mind and wit. Others to whom I am grateful for kindly responding to my enquiries about various papers are: Dr Judith Champ, the Reverend Dr Dermot Fenlon Cong. Orat., Professor John Finnis, Sir Anthony Kenny, and Monsignor Roderick Strange.

The hitherto unpublished papers in this collection were notably short on bibliographical references; I have supplied a number flagged by asterisks. In similar fashion brief notes are supplied on some of the persons to whom the author refers and who are unlikely to be familiar to the majority of readers. Nearly all references flagged by Arabic numerals were supplied by Professor Anscombe; I have often amplified these to provide fuller information. In the initial footnote to each paper, where information is provided about the source and date of the paper, the distinction between 'manuscript' and 'typescript', as the names suggest, is between handwritten and typed documents.

There are a *very few* places at which typescripts of papers are corrupt or were not corrected by the author, and to avoid unintelligible wording I have replaced it with wording which seemed demanded by the context; the replacement wording is in square brackets.

I undertook the work of editing these papers since retiring from paid employment. So I am very grateful for a substantial grant for 2008 which I received from the Earhart Foundation to carry out this work and the associated work of organising Elizabeth Anscombe's papers. In this connection I have reason to be thankful to those who supported my application for funding: John Finnis, Robert George, John Haldane, Alasdair MacIntyre, and Anselm Müller. Additional gratitude is owed to John Haldane for welcoming this volume into the series of which he is general editor.

I am indebted, as with previous editorial work, to the assistance of Davide Lees—now Fr Davide Lees, priest of the Diocese of Rome.

It has been gratifying to again collaborate with my wife in editing this volume of her mother's papers. It is a joy to dedicate the volume to our children who, when they were younger, were hardly in a position to begin to appreciate the mind of their grandmother, but now are better placed to profit by some of what she wrote which is published here.

Luke Gormally

June 2008

Introduction

In one of the papers here, Elizabeth Anscombe argues that since analytical philosophy is more a matter of styles of argument and investigation than of doctrine, it ought not to surprise anyone that a practitioner of that philosophy should be a Catholic Christian. Some people, however, have found it surprising that Peter Geach and Elizabeth Anscombe (my parents) should have been distinguished members of the analytic school, while at the same time believing and practising the Catholic religion. I was told of one American philosopher who belonged to that school saying 'They're good philosophers, aren't they? But they're Catholics. They must compartmentalize.' On the other hand, a graduate student at an English university told me that her supervisor had said that Anscombe's philosophy was narrowly concerned with arguments to support her Catholic positions.

The paper 'Twenty opinions common among Anglo American philosophers', which is in this volume, shows that she by no means compartmentalized, but was very well aware of the doctrinal implications of philosophical beliefs. She sees these 'twenty opinions' as objectionable on philosophical grounds, beside being contrary to the Catholic faith, but she does not in this paper argue against them, she just sets them forth. As for the suggestion that she would only think about a philosophical topic in order to support some Catholic position, I think the supervisor cannot have read her writings. She held it philosophically objectionable, for instance, to maintain that we are not mere members of a biological species, but *selves.* She also thought this contrary to the Catholic religion, for human beings—living human bodies—are viewed by that religion not as mere vehicles for a thinking part, but as having, qua human beings, the dignity that belongs to a rational nature. To be alive and to have a soul are the same, the soul being the form of the body. However, anyone who had actually read her essay on 'The First Person'[1] would know that there is none of this in that essay, and that she had treated the matter in the careful way she had been taught by Wittgenstein, who said to her that you cannot go too carefully about a philosophical error, you do not know how much truth there may be in it. She saw the truth in the notion of self-consciousness: that first person knowledge cannot be paraphrased away by putting some other expression in place of the pronoun. She only denied that it follows from this that there is an entity—the self—the referent of 'I', or that we should understand the pronoun as being 'a name I call myself', as the song says.

Did she consider philosophical questions simply for the sake of the theology? Sometimes she would do just the opposite. She devised a method, which she recommended to me, of mining Aquinas for helpful philosophical points: this was to prospect for philosophically usable bits in the *Summa theologiae* by considering to what Catholic doctrine her particular philosophical problem was relevant. (The demonstrative 'this', for example, is relevant to Eucharistic doctrine.)

The papers here were some of them never published and were given at Spode House[2], among other Catholic philosophers. In such company she no doubt felt freer to say things which might give a wrong impression elsewhere: for instance, she frankly says in the paper on 'Immortality' that she cannot for the time being make sense of the concept of immaterial substance.[3] She does not deny the existence of God and the angels, but thinks of the word 'substance' as being a useful word for a category, members of which are kinds of thing. One should remember here—and perhaps the matter came up in discussion at Spode—that where a degenerate Cartesian (but not Descartes himself) would suppose that God and we were of a kind, as in number 19 of Anscombe's list of inimical opinions, Aquinas did not think that God belonged to any kind at all. An angel also, in the thought of Aquinas, is necessarily the only one of his kind, because of not being material, while the human soul is not a substance, being the form of the human body. If Aquinas is right, then Anscombe was at least on to something in our culture when she spoke of immaterial

[1] Reprinted in her *Collected Philosophical Papers, Volume II: Metaphysics and the Philosophy of Mind* (Oxford: Basil Blackwell, 1981), pp. 21–36.

[2] See Luke Gormally's Preface.

[3] Her later thought on the subject of the soul is to be found in *Human Life, Action and Ethics. Essays by G E M Anscombe* edited by Mary Geach and Luke Gormally (Exeter & Charlottesville, VA: Imprint Academic, 2005); see Index references under 'soul'.

substance as a confused concept. Perhaps also at the Spode meeting, someone pointed out the traditional use of the concept 'substance', or 'being', which we find embedded in a phrase like 'consubstantialem Patri'. At all events, she did not publish the paper.

What then was the relation of faith and reason in her mind? It might help to have some picture of her as a religious and philosophical person.

Anscombe was converted to the Catholic religion when she was still at Sydenham High School, and was instructed and received into the Church when she went up to Oxford, by the Dominican, Fr Richard Kehoe. The reading which had accompanied her conversion had given her a passion for philosophy which remained with her until near the end of her life. She had started doing philosophy on paper when attempting to improve an argument for the existence of God which she found in a work on natural theology. (I suspect that the way in which geometry was taught in those days meant that young people received an ideal of proof without being given explicit instruction in logic. Geometry was her favourite branch of mathematics.) In this book she had encountered, and rejected, the idea that God has knowledge of what sins dead people would have committed if they had lived longer. She saw that there was not in general any such thing to be known. She consciously became a Catholic, but her treatment of this book shows that she was a philosopher, with good philosophical instincts, before she knew that she was one.

Intellectually, she was exceptionally diligent. Mary Warnock describes her as 'dedicated to the dialogue which is central to philosophy'[4], but it was not only with philosophers that she was always ready to take up a problem and give her mind to it. She was, in some ways, a more attentive parent than most: children rarely, I think, receive so many and such considered replies to their questions. She was good at thinking at the level of the person she was speaking to, and some of the papers we have reproduced here are capable of being understood by any reasonable person, being designed for non-philosophical audiences – the paper 'On the hatred of God', for instance, and the one on 'Christians and nuclear weapons designed for the destruction of cities'.

Her favourite child, she said, was the one who was six: she admired the thought of six-year-olds, so in us her children reason sprang up in the light of an appreciative and powerful intellect,

---

[4] Mary Warnock (ed) *Women Philosophers* (The Everyman Library) (London: J M Dent, 1996), p. 204.

whose influence may be measured by the fact that all seven of us have remained believing and practising Catholics to this day. She also used to pray for each of us that was absent, naming us individually in family prayers, which generally took place morning and evening. Thus she not only provided the necessary example of prayer, which she mentions in the paper here on 'The moral environment of the child', but also obtained as an answer to her petitions a continuation of faith in us. It should be remarked that her prayer had a manifest sincerity (which in this paper she mentions as important) partly because she was ready to ask God for mundane things which she cared about, like favourable weather and good exam results. She told me that when she had asked Richard Kehoe what it was all right to pray for, he had said 'Anything it is all right to want'.

In her mind, faith came first, and this is why we kept the faith. Philosophy was in a sense her life, as farming or music might be the life of another person: their love and not just their living, and just as for such another person there might come a time when they have to make a choice between their worldly avocation and the continued following of Christ, so a moment of choice came to her in the form of an intellectual temptation. She told me how one day – I think it was as an undergraduate – she had come across a passage in Russell to the effect that an argument from the facts about the world to the existence of God could not be valid, as one could not deduce a necessary conclusion from a contingent premiss.[5] She had not at the time been able to see what was wrong with the notion that necessities can only be deduced from necessities, but she had known that to deny the possibility of moving by reason from the facts about the world to a knowledge of the existence of God was to deny a doctrine defined as of faith by an ecumenical council.

She went then to church and made an act of faith; I suppose it was the standard one 'My God I believe in thee and all thy Church doth teach, because thou hast said it and thy word is true'. She realized later that of course one can derive necessary conclusions from contingent premises. If she had relied on her own understanding, she would have lost her faith for a falsehood. If anyone distorted his

[5] My father, Peter Geach, told me that the passage in question is in Russell's *Philosophy of Leibniz*. A second edition of this was published in 1937, when Anscombe was an undergraduate. This fits in with my impression that it was while browsing in Blackwell's that she came across the book. It is in paragraph 109 that Russell says, as a step in his proof that there is 'formal vice' in Leibniz's cosmological argument, 'But as the premiss is contingent, the conclusion also must be contingent'.

thought for the sake of his dogmatic position, it was Russell, whose failure even in his mature years to sort out the logic in this passage is astonishing in so great a logician.[6] He appears here as an example of the hatred of God of which Anscombe speaks in her Latin sermon, a translation of which is included among these papers.

Faith, she says in a paper published here, is believing God, but this story shows how public she believed the voice of God could be, speaking as it has done in the teaching of the Church. To proceed on the assumption that this teaching is true is seen by some as a limitation on one's freedom, but this is only the case if the Church does not have the teaching authority she claims to have. Philosophers nowadays accept on authority much that they do not themselves have the expertise to know firsthand, and they do not see it as a limitation on their freedom that they are expected e.g. to believe that the blood circulates. We accept this sort of thing on the authority of the scientists, and if they are right this acceptance is not a limitation on our freedom. The part that human faith like this plays in our knowledge is considered in the first paper in this book, 'What is it to believe someone?'. This problem, of what it is to believe *someone*, which we do all the time, is obviously one which is interesting independently of questions having to do with divine faith. The sort of problems that divine faith raises, when considered as Anscombe here considers it, as a topic in itself, are intrinsically interesting problems, like that of the message from someone which informs one of his own existence: is one believing him in believing that part of the message? The subject of believing someone was vital to Anscombe because of her

---

[6] He allows that from a complex proposition there may follow a necessary conclusion which is 'presupposed' in it, but thinks an argument absurd which proceeds from a proposition to its presuppositions. However, from a contingent conjunction of the form 'All a's are b's and all b's are a's' we get a necessary conclusion of the form 'All a's are a's', which follows here neither because it is a necessary proposition presupposed by the premises, nor because, being necessary, it is implied by all propositions, but by the application to a contingent premise of rules (&e and Barbara) which we all use to deduce contingent propositions from one another. 'Formal vice' does not belong to such an argument, which is thus a counterexample to any general rule that formal vice belongs to arguments with contingent premises and necessary conclusions. To say then as Russell does that since the premiss is contingent, the conclusion drawn from it must be, is entirely unjustified, and Russell ought in his second edition to have removed the sentence which said this. He could point out in reply to my example that though the syllogism may have a necessary conclusion, it does not prove that conclusion's necessity, but he does not make any such distinction in this passage, not troubling to linger over a topic so likely to rouse him from dogmatic slumber.

religion, but this is just one of the very many instances there are of topics vital for faith and philosophically important in themselves, which mean that even if only these topics interested a philosopher, he would still be concerning himself with the great questions that there are.

Anscombe was kept, in her youthful encounter with the sophisms of Russell, from accepting a step (contingent premises, therefore contingent conclusion) which was, logically, a wrong one: kept by what was once called her 'theological straightjacket': by her acceptance, that is, of the authority of the Church.

This expression was used by her colleagues Bernard Williams and Michael Tanner in a letter to *The Human World*[7], in which they attacked her views on chastity and accused her of preaching 'impoverishment of life'. She agreed, saying 'That one must be prepared to lose one's life to save it, that 'being poor in spirit' is blessed, that what looks like deprivation and mutilation may be the path of life, the alternative death: all this Christianity has indeed taught.' When I asked her once why she had accepted the Catholic religion, she said because she believed the teaching of Christ. She did not say to me that Christ's teaching was borne out by her own experience, but so it was. She had laid down, for the sake of the faith that was in her, her philosopher's inclination to rely on her own understanding, and had gone on to become, as the unbeliever Mary Warnock put it, 'The undoubted giant among women philosophers'[8], a favoured student of Wittgenstein, a thinker known for the freshness of her thought, a pioneer of philosophical pathways which many have followed, a forger of expressions which have become part of the currency of philosophy. Her book on intention[9] has made by its originality and its truth a lasting difference to philosophy, a difference which caused the best known of the American action theorists to aver that the book was the greatest work on the subject since Aristotle.[10] She lived faithful to philosophy, and rejected bad arguments, even for Catholic

[7] Issue 9, Nov 1971, pp. 42–8. The quotation from Anscombe is from her reply (pp. 48–51) at p. 51.

[8] *Women Philosophers* (see footnote 4 above) p. 203, a volume in which appears Anscombe's inaugural lecture on 'Causality and Determination'. In private communication with Anscombe, Warnock had said she wanted something which was not about ethics, as there was a lot of ethics in the anthology anyway.

[9] G E M Anscombe, *Intention* (Oxford: Basil Blackwell, 1957).

[10] This extravagant saying of Donald Davidson's (quoted on the front of the Harvard paperback edition of *Intention*) reflects the tendency, common among twentieth-century Anglo-Saxon philosophers, to make the unexamined, or

positions.[11] She remains in the minds of many as a subtle unfolder of difficult and intricate truths. She kept her ability to look at a question in a way which was free from what she used to call 'syndrome thinking'. In all this we see borne out the teaching of Christ that 'He who loses his life for my sake, the same shall save it': for her life, as I have said, was philosophy.

The tale of Anscombe's adherence to the teaching of the first Vatican Council, even though this meant surrendering her philosopher's reliance on her own understanding, will appear to many as consonant with her defence of the encyclical *Humanae Vitae*. However, she never, as far as I know, had any temptation to doubt the church's teaching on contraception.[12] Those who think of the Church as being like a political party, in which every good member keeps to the party line, will be surprised at the mental independence shown by the papers in this book: by, for example, her paper on 'Simony in Africa' (which was given at the Beda, a college for mature men studying for the priesthood) shows her as clearly not a party line woman. She forebears to make judgements about the economics of a distant place, but simply objects to the sale of sacraments as the sacrilege that it is, and confutes the idea that what is involved is not a sale, but only a contribution for the support of pastors.[13] The question of when a mutual provision of goods constitutes a sale or mercantile exchange, is an interesting one in itself: does a family which provides a party for a child for whom presents are bought thereby enter into such an exchange?

Indeed, her support of Catholic teaching on contraception was itself evidence of this independence: she was defending that teaching before the encyclical came out, at a time when change was expected and people with a 'party line' mentality were becoming uncertain about the matter.

---

ill-examined, assumption that hardly anything worth reading was written in philosophy between the time of the Stoics and that of Descartes.

[11] Thus she attacked the argument of C S Lewis against the position he called 'naturalism', thus causing him to write an improved version of the relevant chapter of his book *Miracles*. In the paper 'Two theologians' published here she attacks the argument of Vermeersch on the subject of lying, though he defends the Catholic position that all lying is sinful but not all is gravely so.

[12] Before she read it publicly, she read her first paper on the subject to me, as we used to spend a lot of time talking together in her study.

[13] The Code of Canon Law, agreeing with what Aquinas says in the article cited by Anscombe, allows customary contributions for the support of the clergy. Aquinas distinguishes between these and customary payments for sacraments, which can never be right, but as he suggests, an important question is whether the payment is made a condition of one's having the sacrament administered.

Anscombe's argument in 'Contraception and Chastity', and in her earlier, pre-encyclical, paper on the same topic[14], is largely—but not entirely—a sort of argument from authority: she points out that no sense can be made of traditional Catholic teaching about sex if contraception is permissible. Thus she followed ecclesiastical authority, but her understanding of what was authoritative teaching and what not was affected by her knowledge that at one time the very doctrine of the Trinity had been held by 'Athanasius contra mundum', and that in some places then it had been the laity, and not the bishop, who had upheld orthodoxy[15]. She had learned somewhere, and told me, that once during that bad period the Pope had spoken in a way which was susceptible of an interpretation that accorded with the contemporary heresy.

I remember my parents recalling a silly idea which had been current in the reign of Pope Pius XII—the idea that one should 'think papally': that when considering some subject one should find out what the Pope thought about it, and then think that. This mindset would have contributed to the muddled thinking of those who believed the teaching on contraception was about to change, but Anscombe was too hard-headed to go in for this hypothetical bit of 'Papal thinking': she hewed to the old teaching, not uncritically but faithfully, and so was ready to welcome *Humanae Vitae* when it came out. She had feared that the teaching would lapse, like the teaching on usury (for which she offers here a reasoned defence), though she says in one of the papers here that she had been sure that if a decree was made on the subject of contraception it would condemn contraceptive intercourse. She also saw more in the encyclical, as time went by, than the hard core which ratified the old teaching which she had been defending: for one thing, Paul VI had stressed the necessity of consent by both parties in the marriage act. We include here a number of her papers on contraception, each of which has its own interest. She gave so many because people would ask her to come and talk on the subject.

---

[14] 'You can have sex without children. Christianity and the new offer', the text of a lecture delivered in 1966 and reprinted in Anscombe's *Collected Philosophical Papers, Vol.III: Ethics, Religion and Politics* (Oxford: Basil Blackwell, 1981), pp. 82–96.

[15] She described to me, however, an occasion when she had mentioned this at some gathering, and had been applauded, after which applause someone had asked her if she intended to express some view denying the lawful authority of bishops, which she had rejected with horror.

She had, as far as I know, no general theological theory of her own about the relation of ecclesiastical authority to individual thought, though she does make it clear in the paper on faith that she did not think that faith meant writing a blank cheque for the Pope to fill out. Also there is included in this collection a careful consideration of the difficulties some people have with the concept of authority in morals. Wittgenstein's warning about philosophical error is clearly heeded here. Thus she does not only point out the sophistry of arguing that since we necessarily have to be guided by our own conscience we cannot be guided by authority in ethical matters: she also acknowledges the necessity of making your own judgements in this field, since, like maths, virtue cannot be understood unless it is practised, so that in applying precepts, even those learned from authority, one has at some point to make one's own decision as to how precepts are to be applied. There has to be the possibility of connatural knowledge of what is right, the knowledge which comes from virtue; without such knowledge one cannot understand ethical propositions, so as to know how to apply them, so ethics cannot be a matter of knowing that things are bad because God has revealed the fact that they are forbidden.

She showed the seriousness of her belief in Catholic teaching by adhering to that teaching as an individual thinker. For instance, she upheld, in face of a very widespread Lutheranism about the Blessed Sacrament, the doctrine that the substances of bread and wine do not remain after the consecration. She knew enough about the meaning of the word 'substance' to realize what this means: that the bread and the wine themselves cease to exist when consecrated. She believed in the authority of the Council of Trent on this matter. The practice of referring to the sacred species as 'the bread and wine' was one which she never adopted or ceased to deplore. She told me that when her parents, in a vain attempt to keep her from becoming a Catholic, had sent her to an Anglican ecclesiastic to discuss the matter, this reverend gentleman had said to her that he believed the sacrament to be the body of Christ. 'Is it bread?' she said toughly, and he had to admit he thought it was, thus showing that there was a real difference between his belief and the Catholic teaching which she had learned to hold. He wrote to her parents advising them to let her join the Church, as he had never encountered anyone so convinced of the Roman Catholic 'version' of this doctrine. Her Catholic Truth Society pamphlet on this subject, which is included in this volume, shows that the watering-down of the teaching, which was being attempted by many in the years following Second Vatican Council, did not alter her belief in the slightest. She had a marked reverence for the sacrament, so that when Professor Gonzalo Herranz saw her at Mass in Pamplona, not knowing who she was, he thought from the simple piety of her behaviour that it was some poor peasant woman kneeling there.[16] The child she describes at the beginning of the pamphlet 'On Transubstantiation' was her own eldest child Barbara, informed at a very tender age by the manifest faith of her mother. This pamphlet shows her view of the relation of faith and reason: she does not try to use reason to explain how transubstantiation is possible, but sees the task of reason as being to reply to reasoned arguments for the impossibility of that substantial change.

She drew from the doctrine of the infallibility of the Church the logical conclusion that what has been infallibly taught in the past is still right, even if it is not fashionable to say so. This attitude no doubt contributed to her belief that the teaching which condemned usury was correct. However, as she had been converted as a teenager by reading the works of the distributist Chesterton, it is possible that she had been turned against usury before becoming a Catholic. At any rate, she argues here, without relying on authority, for the wrongness of lending money for interest. She had no objection to dividends, however, and so cannot be dismissed as anti-capitalist. People nowadays, including Catholics, do assume that there is nothing immoral about interest, and to say that there is is to suppose that a large proportion of the more vocal members of the Church may for a time get things seriously wrong about morals, and that the bishops may systematically fail to resist something in society which is intrinsically evil. Of course, money is very elusive in its nature, being a sort of social construct. The whole matter needs thinking out anew in a way which makes it clear whether mortgage payments are really a kind of rent, or whether the large rents people are expected to pay are iniquitous in the same way that usury is.

However, even in matters less elusive than usury, Anscombe was more prepared than most bishops to condemn the way of the world, as her paper on 'Christians and nuclear weapons designed for the destruction of cities' makes clear: she thought that Catholics should avoid any participation in the bomb-wielding wickedness of defence departments who are ready to envisage the destruction of whole cities as one of the things they may do under certain circum-

[16] She was also less careful about her clothes than most women, and would go on wearing garments which some people might regard as too old.

stances. It would have been good for her to write a book about co-operation, for the facts about shared guilt are made most clear as instances of the facts about intention which she understood so well. However, this paper is very simple and plain, without the irony of her radio talk 'Does Oxford Moral Philosophy Corrupt the Youth?'[17] in which she mentioned the idea, to her abominable, that Christians should be prepared to act against their ideals lest their scruples exclude them from positions of power where they might be an influence for the good.

What she has to say about ethics in general should be of interest to those who are exercised by the question of whether it makes a difference to one's practical conclusions whether or not one takes general ethical propositions to be true in virtue of people's sentiments, tastes and choices. The difference between objective and subjective ethics comes out in a practical way when one considers the different attitudes people may take towards the concept of mistaken conscience. Especially in cases where feeling is likely to be affected by the desire to be like others, it can make a difference to be able to ask oneself 'But is this feeling right? Am I making a mistake about the ethics here?'

One way in which moral advisers may fail people who have doubts about whether to commit respectable sins, is telling them that they must follow their consciences. That sounds unexceptionable, since we are indeed obliged to follow our consciences. But would you say 'follow your conscience' to a man whose code of honour obliged him to kill his father's killer, for example? If people are advised by the clergy in this sort of way, the teaching authority of the Church is rendered ineffectual, and *carte blanche* is given to self-deceiving wilful ignorance of moral truth.

The view that an erroneous conscience always excuses means that belief in objective morality does not have the practical effect it should have. It becomes an idle wheel in the mental machine. The view of Aquinas is that one's conscience may be culpably mistaken, and that if such a culpably mistaken conscience leads us to act in a way which is contrary to the moral law, then we are guilty without knowing it. If it is true that the practical difference between objectivist and subjectivist positions is to be found here, this is not just an odd opinion of Aquinas: it or something like it is a vital part of any objectivist morality in which the concept of right action is to have any practical importance.

---

[17] Reprinted in *Human Life, Action and Ethics*, pp. 161–7.

My mother always accepted this teaching of Aquinas, and therefore rejected one common interpretation of the widely believed doctrine that in order for a man to be guilty of mortal sin there must be 'full knowledge, full consent… .' These expressions are in any case ambiguous—knowledge of what? Consent to what? She taught me that the full knowledge in question was knowledge of what sort of action one was performing, under a description its answering to which rendered it culpable, and that one might sin mortally by knowingly performing an action belonging to a certain kind, when one did not know that kind of action to be mortally sinful, or to be a sin at all. However, as she tells in the paper 'Morality'[18], she came later to realize that ignorance of the moral law is not the only kind which is culpable. She discusses different ways in which ignorance may be wilful. Any ethicist should be interested in the cases she considers, where part of the evil choice is the failure to engage one's mind as it should be engaged. The man who finds he has sold petrol instead of paraffin[19] and vaguely thinks (being too lazy to do anything about it) 'Oh, they're sure to notice' is not fully aware that he is seriously endangering their lives, but it is his fault that he is not aware. What we find in Anscombe is a serious discussion of the ways in which we may not be in good faith, of the ways in which the silence of our consciences may be evidence not of virtue but of vice.

A case Anscombe does not mention, which brings out the nature of the problem, is that of Ahab, who complains to his wife Jezebel that Naboth is stubbornly refusing to sell his ancestral vineyard.[20] So Jezebel says 'Who's king around here anyway? I'll fix it for you!' Later she comes to Ahab and says Naboth is dead and Ahab can occupy the vineyard, so Ahab takes it over. A very little reflection on Ahab's part would have made him realize that it was likely, given Jezebel's attitude, that unless he stopped her she was going to engage in some illegitimate exercise of royal power: also, that when Naboth was dead this was probably because of some dirty work on her part, to which he would be a sort of accessory after the fact if he took occupation of Naboth's ancestral patch. What she had done was use threats to have Naboth framed and then executed: but the king did not have full knowledge of, or full consent to, what his wife was doing; so it would appear, from the doctrine that these are required

[18] See also the earlier paper 'On being in good faith' and the later (1989) McGivney lectures on 'Sin'.

[19] i.e. kerosene

[20] See I *Kings* 21 and 22. 38.

for mortal sin, that he had not committed one. It was for this sin, however, that the dogs licked up the blood of Ahab where they had licked up that of Naboth, and who does not find that this direful end befits the direful deed? People in power are surely often guilty in the blind sort of way that Ahab was guilty. Dare we say that the wilful ignorance of government lets them off the hook morally? If a ruler's confessor took this line, would that not prevent the man from doing his job conscientiously?

The Old Testament is full of morally wise stories like this, so that the man envisaged by Anscombe in her paper 'On Prophecy', who is impressed by the Jewish scriptures to the point of taking them for a guide, is indeed a possible figure. We used sometimes to read Scripture together as a family, and we never learned to make the conventional but groundless distinction between the God of the Old Testament and the God of the New. To begin with the Old, and to see in it the proof of the New, to begin as a Jew and to see in Christ the promised Messiah: this my mother called 'the royal road' to the Catholic faith. It is in the light of the orthodox Catholic tradition concerning the divine inspiration of the Old Testament and the unique status of the Jews that one is to understand the paper 'Paganism, Superstition, and Philosophy', which begins with a very unfriendly description of the Jews by Tacitus. I heard that when she read this paper one Japanese philosopher was fearful about the reaction of any Jews who might be present, but I think that a Jew would know in what spirit Anscombe was reading the passage: she was presenting it as an example of the heathen raging and the gentiles imagining a vain thing; she is like Newman presenting a picture of the early church through the hostile eyes of its contemporaries. The point of the paper is to draw a contrast between, on the one hand, the intransigent intolerance of pagan superstition and idolatry which Anscombe sees as essential to the Judaeo-Christian tradition, and, on the other, various foggy pagan attitudes. One of these is a sort of worldly tolerance, as in the Roman empire; another, the Hindu attitude that all the gods are manifestations of the one god, another, the rather similar assumption, made by followers of Wittgenstein, that religious truth is only really to be found in the spirituality of the individual, that this is the place where religions touch internally, and that the common truth in all religions is this human spirituality. The question she leaves us with is why this spirituality should matter.

All these positions may involve more or less compromise with the world against which Anscombe stood so uncompromisingly, condemning its murderousness and idolatry. But the wickedness of the nations, and the sense that Israel is unique, that God has not dealt thus with other nations,[21] leaves a question: what light is there for the other nations? In the final paper she argues both from Scripture, and from the failure of Quine to avoid ontological commitment to more than what he would allow to exist, that the divine wisdom is the light which enlightens every man coming into this world.

Mary Geach

June 2008

[21] Once I took a Jewish friend of mine to the Easter Vigil, and she said afterwards to my mother that she now understood that Christianity was a making available to the Gentiles the riches which belonged to Israel. Rather to my surprise, Anscombe agreed.

1*

What Is It to Believe Someone?

> There were three men, A, B and C, talking in a certain village. A said 'If that tree falls down, it'll block the road for a long time.' 'That's not so if there's a tree-clearing machine working', said B. C remarked 'There *will* be one, if the tree doesn't fall down.' The famous sophist Euthydemus, a stranger in the place, was listening. He immediately said 'I believe you all. So I infer that the tree will fall and the road will be blocked.'
>
> Question: What's wrong with Euthydemus?

Believing someone is not merely a neglected topic in philosophical discussion; it seems to be unknown. I have found people experiencing difficulty in grasping it from the title – found them assuming, for example, that I must really mean 'believing *in* someone'. How do I mean, believing someone? If you told me you had eaten sausages for breakfast, I would believe you. The thing itself is extremely familiar. Does it deserve the attention of a philosophic enquiry? I hope to show that it does. It is of great importance in philosophy and in life, and it is itself problematic enough to need philosophical investigation.

If words always kept their old values, I might have called my subject 'Faith'. That short term has in the past been used in just this meaning, of believing someone. (Of course that term had also other meanings like *loyalty*, etc.) This old meaning has a vestige in such an expression as 'You merely took it on faith' – i.e., you believed someone without further enquiry or consideration. This is only actually *said* as a reproach – but it is often true when it is not blameworthy.

* First published in C F Delaney (ed) *Rationality and Religious Belief* (Notre Dame, IN: University of Notre Dame Press, 1979), pp. 141–51. Reprinted by permission of the University of Notre Dame Press.

At one time there was the following way of speaking: faith was distinguished as human and divine. Human faith was believing a mere human being; divine faith was believing God. Occurring in discussion without any qualifying adjective, the word 'faith' tended to mean only or mostly 'divine faith'. But its value in this line of descent has quite altered. Nowadays it is used to mean much the same thing as 'religion' or possibly 'religious belief'. Thus belief in God would now generally be called 'faith'—belief in God at all, not belief that God will help one, for example. This is a great pity. It has had a disgusting effect on thought about religion. The astounding idea that there should be such a thing as *believing God* has been lost sight of. 'Abraham believed God, and that counted as his justification.' Hence he was called 'the father of faith'. Even in this rather well-known context where the words appear plainly, they are not attended to. The story itself has indeed remained well known even to ignorant intellectuals mainly because of the thoughts of the fictitious author Johannes de Silentio.[1] Interesting as these thoughts are we should notice that the author gets into the territory of his interest by cunningly evading the first point of the story, that *Abraham believed God*. He knows it is there, but he does not confront it. This has had its effect; for in matters of intellectual fashion we tend to be like sheep. And so, even though the words appear plainly, they are not, it seems, reflected on. Rather, we are deluged with rubbish about 'believing in' as opposed to 'believing that'. Like the chorus of animals in Orwell, there is a *claque* chanting 'believing in goo–ood, believing that ba–ad'.

Naturally anyone thinking on those lines won't take an interest in belief with a personal object. For that is necessarily always also 'believing that'. It is indeed convenient, and for my purposes all but necessary, to coin the form of expression: believing *x* that *p*.

I am not interested here in any sense of 'believing in—' except that in which it means 'believing that—exists'. This belief, with God as an argument, could not be 'divine faith'. This comes out quite clearly if we use my suggested form: believing *x* that *p*. It would be bizarre to say that one believed N that N existed. Let us consider the most favourable case for this being possible: an unheard-of relation, who writes to you out of the blue to apprise you of his existence and circumstances. Believing that he does indeed exist is accepting the letter as genuinely what it purports to be, and hence that the writer is

[1] *Fear and Trembling*, to be obtained from booksellers by citing the author S. Kierkegaard.

who he says he is. If you do accept that, you may believe more things—as, that he has a sheep farm in New South Wales—on his say-so. That will be believing him. But the actual existence of the ostensible *he*, whose say-so this is, cannot be believed in the same manner. 'He says he exists, and I suppose he knows and doesn't mean to deceive me.'

My topic is important not only for theology and for the philosophy of religion. It is also of huge importance for the theory of knowledge. The greater part of our knowledge of reality rests upon the belief that we repose in things we have been taught and told. Hume thought that the idea of cause-and-effect was the bridge enabling us to reach any idea of a world beyond personal experience. He wanted to subsume belief in testimony under belief in causes and effects, or at least to class them together as examples of the same form of belief. We believe in a cause, he thought, because we perceive the effect and cause and effect have been found always to go together. Similarly we believe in the truth of testimony because we perceive the testimony and we have (well! often have) found testimony and truth to go together! The view needs only to be stated to be promptly rejected. It was always absurd, and the mystery is how Hume could ever have entertained it. We must acknowledge testimony as giving us our larger world in no smaller degree, or even in a greater degree, than the relation of cause and effect; and believing it is quite dissimilar in structure from belief in causes and effects. Nor is what testimony gives us entirely a detachable part, like the thick fringe of fat on a chunk of steak. It is more like the flecks and streaks of fat that are distributed through good meat; though there are lumps of pure fat as well. Examples could be multiplied indefinitely. You have received letters; how did you ever learn what a letter was and how it came to you? You will take up a book and look in a certain place and see 'New York, Dodd Mead and Company, 1910'. So do you know from personal observation that that book was published by that company, and then, and in New York? Well, hardly. But you do know it *purports* to have been so. How? Well, you know that is where the publisher's name is always put, and the name of the place where his office belongs. How do you know that? You were taught it . What you were taught was your tool in acquiring the new knowledge. 'There was an American edition' you will say, 'I've seen it'. Think how much reliance on believing what you have been told lies behind being able to say that. It is irrelevant at this level to raise a question about possible forgery; without what we know by testimony, there is no such thing as what a forgery is *pretending* to be.

You may think you know that New York is in North America. What is New York, what is North America? You may say you have been in these places. But how much does that fact contribute to your knowledge? Nothing, in comparison with testimony. How did you know you were there? Even if you inhabit New York and you have simply learned its name as the name of the place you inhabit, there is the question: How extensive a region is this place you are calling 'New York'? And what has New York got to do with this bit of a map? Here is a complicated network of received information.

With this as preamble, let us begin an investigation.

'Believe' with personal object cannot be reflexive. Since one can tell oneself things, that may seem odd. We shall see why it is so later.

One might think at first blush that to believe another is simply to believe what he says, or believe that what he says is true. But that is not so, for one may already believe the thing he says. (If you tell me 'Napoleon lost the battle of Waterloo' and I say 'I believe you' that is a joke.) Again, what someone's saying a thing may bring about, is that one forms one's *own* judgment that the thing is true. In teaching philosophy we do not hope that our pupils will *believe us*, but rather, that they will *come to see* that what we say is true—if it is.

A witness might be asked 'Why did you think the man was dying?' and reply 'Because the doctor told me'. If asked further what his own judgment was, he may reply 'I had no opinion of my own—I just believed the doctor.' This brings out how believing x that p involves relying on x for it that p. And so one might think that believing someone is believing something on the strength of his saying that it is so. But even that is not right. For suppose I were convinced that B wished to deceive me, and would tell the opposite of what he believed, but that on the matter in hand B would be believing the opposite of the truth. By calculation on this, then, I believe what B says, on the strength of his saying it—but only in a comical sense can I be said to believe *him*.[2]

Now we have the solution to the puzzle which I set at the head of this essay. Euthydemus' utterance is crazy. But why? If logic is concerned only with what follows from what, his logic is impeccable. The conjunction of A's and B's remarks implies that there will be no machine working; from that and C's contribution we derive that the tree will fall. Why then is Euthydemus' remark so off-key? The

[2] This case was described to me in discussion by Mary Geach.

answer is, that he cannot be telling the truth when he says 'I believe you all'. He cannot be believing A at that stage of *that* conversation, unless A still purports to believe what he said. But A does not purport so to believe if he gives no sign, and if what B said is not merely true, but also as pertinent as it must be if what C said is true. The assumption that A privately sticks to what he said, indeed, makes it questionable what he meant, i.e. what thought lay behind A's saying 'If the tree falls the road will be blocked'. (It might for example be the conviction that the tree *will* fall and block the road.) Now Euthydemus makes no check on A; he does not wait a moment to see how A reacts to what B and C say. The natural way to understand B's remark is to take it as casting doubt on what A said, and that is what makes Euthydemus' 'I believe you all' so insane. For *insane* is just what Euthydemus' remark is and sounds—it is not, for example, like the expression of a somewhat rash opinion, or of excessive credulity.

We also see why one cannot 'believe oneself' when one tells oneself something. To believe N one must believe that N himself believes what he is saying.

So far we have considered cases of believing people who are perceived. But often all we have is the communication without the speaker. This is so almost any time we find something out because it is told us in a book.

Of course we may be handed the book by a teacher who tells us something about the author. Then we have a communication with a perceived person communicating; and this is about another communication where the communicator is unperceived. It is interesting that when we are introduced to books as sources of information in our childhood it does not usually go like that. We are taught to consult books like oracles, and the idea of the author is not much brought to our attention at first. In any case, after a time we come to receive communications in books without anyone introducing them to us, and we are apt to believe—as we put it—what the book says about itself; for example that it was printed by a certain printer.

To believe a person is not necessarily to treat him as an original authority. He is *an* original authority on what he himself has done and seen and heard: I say *an* original authority because I only mean that he does himself contribute something, e.g. is in some sort a witness, as opposed to one who only transmits information received. But his account of what he is a witness to is very often, as in the example of there being an American edition, heavily affected or rather all but completely formed by what information *he* had received. I do not mean that if he says 'I ate an apple this morning' he is relying on information that that was an apple; if he is in the situation usual among us, he knows what an apple is—i.e. can recognise one. So, though he was 'taught the concept' in learning to use language in everyday life, I do not count that as a case of reliance on information received. But if he says he saw a picture by Leonardo da Vinci, that *is* such a case. He has necessarily depended on some tradition of information. Thus a speaker may be a total original authority for the fact that he gives, as would usually be the case if one of us said he had eaten an apple, or *an* original authority, but not a total one, as if he says he saw some of Leonardo's drawings; or he may not be an original authority at all, as if he says that Leonardo made drawings for a flying machine. In this latter case he almost certainly knows it from having been told, *even* if he's seen the drawings. (It is true that he *might* have 'discovered it for himself'. If so, then all the same he has relied on information received that these are Leonardo drawings; and he has noticed—*here* he is an original authority—that *these* drawings are drawings of a flying machine; that *Leonardo* made drawings for flying machines will then be inference on his part.)

When he knows it just from being told (as most of us do) then, as I say, he is in no way an original authority. But that does not mean that there is no such thing as believing *him*. Much information is acquired from teachers who are not original authorities, and their pupils who acquire it believe *them*. As opposed to what? As opposed to merely believing that what they say is true. Consider belief reposed in what an interpreter says—I mean the case of believing the sentences he comes out with. If you believe those communications, probably—i.e. in the normal case—you are believing his principal: your reliance on the interpreter is only belief that he has reproduced what his principal said. But *he* is not wrong if what he says is untrue, so long as it does not falsely represent what his principal said. A teacher, on the other hand, even though in no way an original authority, *is* wrong if what he says is untrue, and that hangs together with the fact that his pupils believe (or disbelieve) *him*.

These various considerations draw attention to the further beliefs that are involved in believing someone. First of all, it must be the case that you believe that something is a communication from him (or 'from someone') and second, you have to believe that by it he means to be telling you *this*. It is important for us that natural noises and visual phenomena do not usually sound or look like language, that the question whether someone is speaking or whether this is a bit of written language is hardly ever a difficult one to answer. Someone who saw the markings of leaves as language and strove to decipher them as messages, possibly directed to himself, would strike us as demented. And this brings out another aspect: that the communication is *addressed* to someone, even if only 'to whom it may concern', or 'the passer-by' or 'whoever may happen in the future to read this'.

We see, then, that various questions arise: (1) Suppose that someone gets hold of written communications, but they are not addressed to him at all, not even meant to reach him. Can he be said to believe the writer if he believes what they tell the addressee? Only in a reduced or extended sense, though the matter is perhaps not one of any importance. (2) Suppose someone gets a written communication which is addressed to him, but the actual writer – I mean the author – is not the ostensible communicator. For example, I write letters to someone as from a pen-friend in Oklahoma. Can the recipient be said to believe (or disbelieve) either the actual author or the ostensible communicator? Surely not the former, except in a very special case and in a roundabout way: I mean, he might himself discern that this comes from the actual writer, myself; and judge that I was trying to tell him something. But otherwise not. This case, where there is intervening judgment and speculation, should alert us to the fact that in the most ordinary cases of believing someone, there is no such mediation. In order to believe NN, one 'must believe' that, e.g. this is a communication from NN; but that is not believing in the sense of forming a judgment. If one learned it was not a communication from NN, one would straightway cease to say one was believing NN. Now can the recipient, if he *is* deceived, be said to believe or disbelieve the ostensible communicator? Here we have to consider two distinct cases, according as the ostensible communicator exists or not. If he does not exist, then the decision to speak of 'believing him' or 'disbelieving him' is a decision to give those verbs an 'intentional' use, like the verb 'to look for'. 'The child had an imaginary companion whom he called Efelin and who told him all sorts of things – he always believed Efelin.' And so one might speak of someone as believing the god (Apollo, say), when he consulted the oracle of the god – without thereby implying that one believed in the existence of that god oneself. All we want is that we should know what is called the god's telling him something.

If on the other hand the ostensible communicator does exist, then a third party may be less likely to use the verb 'believe' 'intentionally', i.e. to say 'So, thinking that NN said this, he believed him'. But it is an intelligible way of speaking. And NN himself might say 'I see, you thought I said this, and you believed me'. If the recipient, however, says 'Naturally I believed *you*', NN might reject this, saying 'Since I didn't say it, you weren't believing me'. Thus there is an *oscillation* here in the use of the notion of believing and disbelieving a person.

(3) This comes out in another way where the recipient does not believe that the communication *is* from NN. This, it seems, lets him off the hook of any reproach from NN about his not having believed him, not having done what he asked, and so on. But may not NN have a complaint at the very doubt whether a communication *is* from him, really is so? It depends on the circumstances; but NN may well regard it as an evasion, if the recipient seizes on the possibility of treating the communication as not coming from him when it did. NN may call it a refusal to believe him.

(4) If X is to believe NN, something must be being taken as a communication, and since X must be believing something 'on NN's say-so', there is also involved the belief that *this* communication says such-and-such. This may seem absurd: surely I may simply believe *your words*, and not have a different version of their meaning and say that what you said meant *that*. On the other hand I ought to be able to elaborate upon anything that I believe: to be able to say who is being referred to, or what time, or what sort of action if I am told, and believe, e.g. 'John's daughter eloped at Christmas'. Nor are one's beliefs tied to particular words; one reproduces the gist of what one has been told in various ways, and so there is, after all, room for the belief that *that* communication told one such-and-such. So when someone says that he believes such-and-such because he believes NN, we may say 'We suspect a misunderstanding. What did you take as NN's telling you that?'

Now, therefore, instead of speaking of the 'actual writer'—by whom in the case of the pen-friend I understood the author—we can speak of the immediate producer of what is taken, or makes an internal claim to be taken, as a communication from NN. Such a producer may be a messenger, anyone who 'passes on' some communication, or an interpreter (translator) of it. And the recipient can at any rate *fail to believe* (as opposed to disbelieving) NN out of a variety of attitudes. He may not notice the communication at all. He may notice it and take it as language and make something of it but not take it as addressed to himself. Or he may notice it and take it as language and yet, whether or not he takes it as addressed to himself, he may make the wrong thing of it. And he may take it as addressed to himself and not make the wrong thing of it but not believe that it comes from NN. Only when we have excluded all the cases – or, more probably, simply *assumed* their exclusion – do we come to the situation in which the question simply is: Does X believe NN or not? That is to say: there are many presuppositions to that question as we ordinarily understand it.

It is an insult and it may be an injury not to be believed. At least it is an insult if one is oneself made aware of the refusal, and it may be an injury if others are. Note that here the difference between disbelief and suspension of judgment is of less importance than where the object is only a proposition and not a person. And failure of some of the presuppositions allows scope for reproach. If A has not believed that something was a message from NN when it was, or has given it some false interpretation, NN may (perhaps justly) see in this a readiness on A's part not to believe him. And even if A has falsely believed that something *was* a message from NN and has disbelieved it, while NN cannot say (except in an extended sense) 'You disbelieved me!' he may be able to say 'You showed yourself very ready to disbelieve me'. Or: 'You showed yourself ready to credit me with saying something that could not be worthy of belief'. For it would be a megalomaniac who complained of not being believed, when he agrees that the thing that was not believed was, anyway, not true. Compare the irritation of a teacher at not being believed. On the whole, such irritation is just—in matters where learners must learn by believing teachers. But if what was *not* believed should turn out to be false, his complaint collapses.

Let us suppose that all the presuppositions are in. A is then in the situation—a very normal one—where the question arises of believing or doubting (suspending judgment in face of) NN. Unconfused by all the questions that arise because of the presuppositions, we can see that believing someone (in the particular case) is trusting him for the truth – in the particular case.

I will end with a problem. I imagined the case where I believed what someone told me, and got the information from his telling me, but did not believe *him*. This was because I believed he would tell me what he thought was false, but also would be clean wrong in what he thought. Now I *may*—it is not the normal case, but it certainly occurs—have to reflect on whether someone is likely to be right and truthful in a particular case when he is telling me that p. If I conclude that he is, I will then believe him that p. I think it is clear that this could not be the case for learners, at least elementary learners or young children. But someone might say: 'What is the difference between the two cases, culminating in belief that *p* because NN has told one that *p*?' In both cases there is calculation; in one, you believe what the man says as a result of a calculation that he is a liar but wrong, and in the other, you calculate that he is truthful and right. (No belief in his *general* truthfulness is involved.) The difference between the two cases is only as stated. When you say that in the first case you do not believe the *man*, only what he tells you, and in the second case you believe the man, that is just a bit of terminology: you are only willing to *call* it believing the man when you believe he is right and truthful in intent.

It appears to me that there is more to be said than that about the priority of rightness and truthfulness in this matter, but I am not clear what it is.

2*

Faith

In the late 1960s some sentence in a sermon would often begin: 'We used to believe that ...'. I always heard this phrase with an alarmed sinking of the heart. I had alternative expectations. The more hopeful one was for some absurd lie. For example: 'We used to believe that there was no worse sin than to miss Mass on Sunday'. The worse one was of hearing something like 'We used to believe that there was something special about the priesthood'; 'We used to believe that the Church was here for the salvation of souls'.

Now there was a 'We used to believe ...' which I think could have been said with some truth and where the implied rejection wasn't a disaster. There was in the preceding time a professed enthusiasm for rationality, perhaps inspired by the teaching of Vatican I against fideism, certainly carried along by the promotion of neo-thomist studies. To the educated laity and the clergy trained in those days, the word was that the Catholic Christian faith was *rational*, and a problem, to those able to feel it as a problem, was how it was *gratuitous*—a special gift of grace. Why would it *essentially* need the promptings of grace to follow a process of reasoning? It was as if we were assured that there was a chain of proof. First, God. Then, the divinity of Jesus Christ. Then, *his* establishment of a Church with a Pope at the head of it and with a teaching commission from him. This body was readily identifiable. Hence you could demonstrate the truth of what the Church taught. Faith, indeed, is not the same thing as knowledge—but that could be accounted for by the *extrinsic* character of the proofs of the *de fide* doctrines. The knowledge which was contrasted with faith, would be knowledge by proofs *intrinsic* to the subject matter, not by proofs from someone's having *said* these things were true. For matters which were strictly of 'faith' intrinsic

* Text of the Fifth Wiseman Lecture delivered on 27 October 1975 at Oscott College, the Seminary of the Archdiocese of Birmingham, England.

proofs were not possible, and that was why faith contrasted with 'knowledge'.

This is a picture of the more extravagant form of this teaching. A more sober variation would relate to the Church that our Lord established. In this variant one wouldn't identify the church by its having the Pope, but otherwise; and one would discover that it had a Pope and that was all right. This more sober form had the merit of allowing that the believer was committed to the Christian faith, rather than suggesting that he had as it were signed a blank cheque to be filled out by the Pope in no matter what sum.

A yet more sober variant would have avoided trading on the cultural inheritance for which the name of Jesus was holy so that it was easy to go straight from belief in God to belief in Jesus as God's Son. In this more sober variant one would be aware of the dependence of the New Testament on the Old: one would be clearly conscious of the meaning of calling our Lord 'Christ'.

The 'sober variants' would have a disadvantage for the propagandists of the rationality (near demonstrability) of faith—though a great advantage in respect of honesty and truthfulness. The disadvantage was that that no one could suppose it quite easy for anyone to see that what Jesus established was matched by the Catholic Church that we know. If it was just a matter of his having founded a Church with a Pope, then it was easy indeed! But otherwise it was *obvious* that learning and skill would be required to make the identification. And the considerations and arguments would be multifarious and difficult to be sure about. Hence the problem most commonly felt, amongst the more intellectual enquirers, as to the character of the *certainty* ascribed to faith. The so-called preambles of faith could not possibly have the sort of certainty that *it* had. And if less, then where was the vaunted rationality?

But there was a graver problem. What about the 'faith of the simple'? They could not know all these things. Did they then have some inferior brand of faith? Surely not! And anyway, did those who studied really think *they* knew all these things? No: but the implication was that the knowledge was there somehow, perhaps scattered through different learned heads, perhaps merely theoretically and abstractly available. In the belief that this was so, one was being rational in having faith. But then it had to be acknowledged that all this was problematic—and so adherence to faith was really a matter of hanging on, and both its being a *gift* and its *voluntariness* would *at this point* be stressed.

I sometimes hear accounts of the times of darkness before Vatican II which strike me as lies. I hope that I have not been guilty of lying in what I have said here. This at least is my recollection of how it was in some presentations, some discussions, some apologetic.

Was, and is no longer, not necessarily because better thoughts about faith are now common; there is a vacuum where these ideas once were prominent. But all these considerations, proofs, arguments and problems are now out of fashion, for various reasons which I won't discuss.

The passing away of these opinions is not to be regretted. They attached the character of 'rationality' entirely to what were called the preambles and to the passage from the preambles to faith itself. But both these preambles and that passage were in fact an 'ideal' construction—and by 'ideal' I don't mean one which would have been a good development of thinking, if it had occurred in an individual; I mean rather 'fanciful', indeed dreamed up according to prejudices: prejudices, that is, about what it is to be reasonable in holding a belief.

The right designation for what are called the 'preambles' of faith is not that but at least for part of them, 'presuppositions'. Let me explain this in a simple example. You receive a letter from someone you know, let's call him Jones. In it, he tells you that his wife has died. You believe him. That is, you now believe that his wife has died because you believe *him*. Let us call this just what it used to be called, 'human faith'. That sense of 'faith' still occurs in our language. 'Why', someone may be asked, 'do you believe such-and-such?' and he may reply 'I just took it on faith—so-and-so told me.'

Now this believing Jones, that his wife has died, has a number of presuppositions. In believing it *you* presuppose (1) that your friend Jones exists, (2) that his letter really is from him, (3) that that really is what the letter tells you. In ordinary circumstances, of course, none of these things is likely to be in doubt, but that makes no difference. Those three convictions or assumptions are, logically, presuppositions that *you* have if your belief that Jones' wife has died is a case of your believing Jones.

Note that I say they are *your* presuppositions. I do not say that your believing Jones entails those three things; only that your believing Jones entails that you *believe* those three things.

In modern usage 'faith' tends to mean religion, or religious belief. But the concept of faith has its original home in a particular religious tradition. If a Buddhist speaks of 'his faith', saying for example that his faith ought not to be insulted, he means his religion, and he is borrowing the word 'faith' which is really alien to his tradition. In the tradition where that concept has its origin, 'faith' is short for 'divine faith' and means 'believing God'. And it was *so* used, among the Christian thinkers at least, that faith, in this sense, could not be anything but true. Faith was believing God, as Abraham believed God, and no false belief could be part of it.

I want to say what might be understood about faith by someone who did not have it; someone, even, who does not necessarily believe that God exists, but who is able to think carefully and truthfully about it. Bertrand Russell called faith 'certainty without proof'. That seems correct. Ambrose Bierce has a definition in his *Devil's Dictionary*: 'The attitude of mind of one who believes without evidence one who tells without knowledge things without parallel'. What should we think of this?

According to faith itself faith is believing God. If the presuppositions are true, it is, then, believing on the best possible grounds someone who speaks with perfect knowledge. If only the presuppositions are given, Bierce would be a silly fellow and Russell would be confused. But is there even the possibility of 'believing God'? This is hard to grasp: it is itself one of the 'things without parallel'.

Anyway, in general, 'faith comes by hearing', that is, those who have faith *learn* what they believe by faith, learn it from other people. So someone who so believes believes what is told him by another human, who may be very ignorant of everything except that *this* is what he has to tell as the content of the faith. So Bierce's Devil may be right. One who has not evidence believes one who has not knowledge (except of that one thing): at least, he believes what the latter says and he gets what he believes from the latter; yet, according to faith he believes God. If so, then according to faith a simple man—a man with no knowledge of evidence—may have faith when he is taught by a man ignorant of everything except that these are the things that faith believes. More than that, according to faith this simple man and his teacher have a belief in no way inferior to that of a very learned and clever person who has faith.

If faith is like that, even if it is believing God, then it follows that the Bierce definition is right after all. For everyone is to have faith and few can be learned, and their learning doesn't give them a superior kind of faith. Everyone is to run: and few are road-sweepers.

It is clear that the topic I introduced of *believing somebody* is in the middle of our target. Let us go back to Jones, and investigate *believing*

Jones, when you read in his letter that his wife has died. You can't call it believing Jones just if Jones says something or other and you do believe that very thing that he says. For you might believe it anyway. And even if it's someone's saying something that *causes* you to believe it, that doesn't have to be believing *him*. He might be just making you realize it, calling it to your attention—but you judge the matter for yourself. Nor is it even sufficient that his saying it is your *evidence* that it is true.[1] For suppose that you are convinced that he will both lie to you, i.e. say the opposite of what he really believes, and be mistaken. That is, the opposite of what he thinks will be true; and he will say the opposite of what he thinks. So what he says will be true and you will believe it because he says it. But you won't be believing him!

Ordinarily, of course, when you believe what a man says, this is because you assume that he says what he believes. But even this doesn't give us a sufficient condition for your believing to be believing *him*. For here again one can construct a funny sort of case—where you believe that what he believes will be true, but by accident, as it were. His belief is quite idiotic; he believes what he's got out of a Christmas cracker for example. In fact, unknown to him but known to you, what has been put in the crackers for their party are actual messages with some practical import. You know that the messages in the blue crackers are all true, and the ones in the red crackers all false. *He* believes any of them. And now he tells you something, and you believe it because he says it and you believe he is saying what he believes, *and* because you know that this thing that he believes comes out of a *blue* cracker. That wouldn't be believing *him*. But when you believe your history teacher, for example, it *is* enough that you believe what he says because he says it and you don't think he's lying and you think what he believes about that will be true. I mean that is enough for you to be believing *him*.

So the topic of believing *someone* is pretty difficult. Of course if you could put in that you believe the person *knows* what he is telling you, these difficulties don't arise. You believe what he says because he says it and you believe that he knows whether it is so and won't be lying. That's why this particular problem won't normally arise about that letter from your friend Jones telling you his wife has just died.

Now there is another question about what it is to believe someone, which concerns the presuppositions. I said that *you* presuppose that

---

[1] I asked Mary Geach to construct a case to show this. She responded with what follows.

Jones exists, did write the letter, and did say that in it, if you believe *him* to the effect that that was so. I didn't say that the mere fact of your *believing Jones* presupposed those things. Now what in fact are we to say here? Suppose someone has a hoax pen-friend—I mean, the pen-friend is really a contrivance of his school-fellows who arrange for their letters to be posted from Chicago to England and make the non-existent correspondent tell their friend all sorts of things. And suppose he believes the things in the usual sort of way in which people believe things they are told. Is he *believing the pen-friend*? What are we to say? Wouldn't we say that some ancient believed the oracles of the gods? And wouldn't it then be right to say he believed the god whose oracle it was?

If you insist on saying that the deluded victim does not 'believe the pen-friend' because the pen-friend doesn't exist, you will deprive yourself of the clearest way of describing his situation: 'he believed the non-existent person'. And, somewhat absurdly, you will have to say that his own expression of belief 'I believe her', is *not* an expression of belief, or not a proper one. What then would be the proper one? We had better settle for saying that the victim believes the pen-friend, and that the ancient was believing Apollo—who does not exist. And doesn't the same point hold for the case where the letter-writer does exist, but you have misunderstood what he wrote, or mistakenly supposed that *this* letter is from him? Especially if the mistakes were quite reasonable ones.

Now let us think some more about the presuppositions. Ordinarily the presuppositions of believing N simply do not come in question. I get a letter from someone I know; it does not occur to me to doubt that it *is* from him. Suppose that the doubt *does* occur for some reason. The letter perhaps *says* it is from him—the very thing to raise a doubt! Now I take it as obvious that, if I decide to believe that the letter *is* from him, I won't do so on the grounds on which I believe *him* when the letter says his wife is dead. For I believe his wife is dead because *he* says so. But the reason why I believe the letter is from him is not that *he* says so. *His* credibility is not my warrant for believing that the letter is from him. Even if the letter begins 'This is a letter from your old friend Jones' and I just believe that straight off and uncritically, I believe the sentence, and I believe that the letter is from Jones because the sentence says so, but I could never say I believed it because I believed *him*. This is the sense in which the presuppositions of faith are not themselves part of the content of what in a narrow sense is believed by faith.

Now let us change the case. Suppose a prisoner in a dungeon, to whom there arrives a letter saying: 'This letter comes from an unknown friend, N'.* It proposed to help him in various needs which he is invited to communicate by specified means. Perhaps it also holds out hope of escape from the prison. The prisoner doesn't know if it is a hoax or a trap or is genuine, but he tries the channels of communication and he gets some of the things that he asks for; he also gets further letters ostensibly from the same source. These letters sometimes contain information. We will suppose that he now believes that N exists and is the author of all the letters; and that he believes the information as coming from N. That is, his belief in that information is a case of believing N. His belief *that* N exists and that the letters come from N is, just as in the more ordinary case, not an example of believing something on N's say-so. On the other hand, as we are supposing the case, he does not have *prior* knowledge of N's existence. And it could happen that he, like the man who uncritically accepts the letter beginning 'This is from Jones', believes the opening communication 'This is from an unknown friend—call me N' straight off: just as he'd likely believe straight off that a whispered or tapped communication purporting to come from the next cell is a communication from another prisoner. Even so the beliefs which *are* cases of believing N and the belief *that* N exists are logically different. This brings out the difference between presuppositions of believing N and believing such-and-such as coming from N. 'Pre-suppositions' don't have to be temporarily prior beliefs.

Suarez said that in every revelation God reveals that he reveals. That sounds like saying: every letter from N to the prisoner informs him that the information in the letter is from N, and every bit of information from N is accompanied by another bit of information that the first bit was from N. Put like that there is an absurdity, an infinite regress. But it should not be put like that. Rather: in every bit of information N is also claiming (implicitly or explicitly, it doesn't matter which) that he is giving the prisoner information.

* The original publication of this paper had the following curious footnote at this point: 'This development of a case which I considered (see 'What is it to believe someone?' in Volume II) of a letter from an otherwise unknown person, is taken from Peter Geach. See *The Virtues* (Cambridge, 1977).' 'What is it to believe someone?' did not appear in Volume II of the *Collected Philosophical Papers*. It appears as the first paper in the present volume. The reference to Peter Geach's *The Virtues* is to pp. 38–9 of that volume.

And now we come to see the difficulty. In all the other cases we have been considering, it can be made clear *what* it is for someone to believe someone. But what can it mean 'to believe God'? Could a learned clever man inform me, on the authority of his learning, that the evidence is that God has spoken? No. The only possible use of a learned clever man is as a *causa removens prohibens.* There are gross obstacles in the received opinion of my time and in its characteristic ways of thinking, and someone learned and clever may be able to dissolve these.

Forgetting that about 'hearing'—i.e. from teachers—should we picture it like this: a man hears a voice saying something to him and he believes it is God speaking, and so he believes what it says—so he believes God? But what does he believe when he 'believes it is God speaking?' That God has a voice-box? Hardly. In relation to the belief that it is God speaking, it doesn't matter how the voice is produced. There is a Rabbinical idea, the Bath Qol, the 'daughter of the voice'. You hear a sentence as you stand in a crowd—a few words out of what someone is saying perhaps: it leaps out at you, it 'speaks to your condition'. Thus there was a man standing in a crowd and he heard a woman saying 'Why are you wasting your time?' He had been dithering about, putting off the question of becoming a Catholic. The voice struck him to the heart and he acted in obedience to it. Now, he did not have to suppose, nor did he suppose, that that remark was not made in the course of some exchange between the woman and her companion, which had nothing to do with him. But he believed that God had spoken to him in that voice. The same thing happened to St Augustine, hearing the child's cry, 'Tolle, lege'.

Now the critical differentiating point is this. In all those other cases it is clear what the one who 'believes X' *means* by 'X speaking', even when we judge that X doesn't exist; for example, what the believer in the oracle means by 'Apollo speaking'. But it is not clear what it can mean for God to speak.

For Apollo, or Juggernaut, is simply the god of such and such a cult. Note, I am not here following those who explain deity as 'the object of worship'. That definition is useless, because they have to mean by 'worship' 'the honour paid to a deity'. Divine worship is the special sort of honour intended to be paid, the special sort of address made, to a deity. This may be offered to what is not divine, to a stone or another spirit or a man; or to what doesn't exist at all.

So when I say 'Apollo was the god of such-and-such a cult', I am calling attention to the question: what would it mean to say 'These were not—none of them were—the temples and oracles of Apollo'—precisely *of* the temples and oracles of Apollo? What would it mean to say that Shiva was not the god of destruction? Shiva is the god of this worship, which is the cultus of a god of destruction.

In this sense, God is not the god of such-and-such a worship. This is something that can be seen by an atheist too, even though he holds that there is in any case no such thing as deity. For he can see, if he thinks about it, that 'God' is not a proper name but is equivalent to a definite description (in the technical sense). That is, it is equivalent to 'the one and only true god', 'the one and only real deity'. The point of putting in 'true' and 'real' is that those who believe there is only one deity have so much occasion to speak of deities that they do not believe to exist. We then speak of Apollo, Shiva and Juggernaut as gods who are not gods. An atheist believes that God is among the gods who are not gods, because he believes that nothing is a deity. But he should be able to recognize the identity of 'God' with 'the one and only god'.

It is because of this equivalence that God cannot be formally identified as the god of such-and-such a cult or such-and-such a people. To say that God is the god of Israel is to say that what Israel worshipped as god was 'the one and only god'. So it *could* significantly be denied. And it *could* be seen to be true—even by one who believed that the description 'the one and only god' is vacuous.

And so we can say this: the supposition that someone has faith is the supposition that he believes that something—it may be a voice, it may be something he has been taught—comes as a word from God. Faith is then the belief he accords that word.

So much can be discerned by an unbeliever, whether his attitude is potentially one of reverence in face of this phenomenon or is only hostile. But the Christian adds that such a belief is sometimes the truth, and that the consequent belief is only then what *he* means by faith.

3*

Prophecy and Miracles

My problems are contained in three documents:

1. The decree of the Vatican Council that the prophecies and miracles of Moses and the prophets and Christ supply solid external arguments for the truth of Christianity.**
2. The warning in *Deuteronomy*:

   If there rise in the midst of thee a prophet or one that saith he hath dreamed a dream, and he foretell a sign and a wonder, and that come to pass which he spoke, and he say to thee: Let us go and follow strange gods, which thou knowest not, and let us serve them, thou shalt not hear the words of that prophet or dreamer. (*Dt* 13. 1–3)

3. Lessing's 'On the proof of the Spirit and of Power'.*** Lessing says 'It is one thing to experience the fulfilment of prophecy; fulfilled prophecies of which I know only as a matter of history that others are supposed to have experienced them, are quite another thing.' And the same for miracles. The 'proof of the Spirit and of power' of which St Paul speaks in *I Corinthians*, he says, was to work miracles and to prophesy. Origen could refer to such a proof because of the known existence of such things in his own time. But reports of fulfilled prophecies are not fulfilled prophecies, reports of miracles not mira-

* From the undated typescript of a paper, probably delivered in 1957 (see p.33) to the Philosophical Enquiry Group which used to meet at the Dominican Conference Centre at Spode House, Staffordshire. (See Editor's Preface.)

** Vatican Council I, Dogmatic Constitution 'Dei Filius', chapter 3 'De fide'. See H Denzinger & A Schönmetzer (eds) *Enchiridion Symbolorum Definitionum et Declarationum de rebus fidei et morum*, 36th edition (Barcelona-Freiburg-Rome: Herder, 1976), §3009 (p. 589).

*** There is an English translation in *Lessing's Theological Writings.* Selections in translation with an Introductory Essay by Henry Chadwick (London: Adam & Charles Black, 1956), pp. 51–6. The translations in the paper seem to be Anscombe's own.

cles. 'Those that take place before my own eyes have their effect in an *immediate* way; the others are supposed to have their effect through a medium that deprives them of all power.'

Note that unlike *Deuteronomy* Lessing does not impose any restrictions on what effect (on my beliefs) witnessing fulfilled prophecy may be permitted to have, other than that one could not believe the prophet if he contradicted part of one's own experience that was as certain as one's observation of his performance.

He goes on to say that he does not in the least doubt that Christ worked miracles and fulfilled prophecies; but this can only be as certain as any historical event.

> We all believe that there was such a person as Alexander, who conquered almost all Asia in a short time. But who would stake something of great and permanent importance, whose loss was irreplaceable, on this belief? Who, in consequence of this belief, would forswear for ever all knowledge that should conflict with it? Certainly I should not. I have at present nothing to object against Alexander and his conquests; but it would after all be possible that they were founded on a mere poem of Choerilus who accompanied Alexander, just as the ten year siege of Troy is founded on nothing but Homer.

Similarly:

> That Christ, against whose resurrection I have no significant historical objection, gave himself out as the son of God on account of it; that his disciples believed he was that on account of it; this I readily believe. For these truths, as truths of one and the same class, follow quite naturally one from the other.
>
> But now, leap from that historical truth to a quite different class of truths, and to demand of me that I should transform all my metaphysical and moral concepts accordingly; to expect me, because I can set no trustworthy evidence against the resurrection of Christ, to alter all my fundamental ideas of the deity—if that is not a *metabasis eis allo genos* then I don't know what Aristotle meant by that term.
>
> Of course [he says], you say: this Christ, who rose from the dead—which you admit as an historical fact—this Christ said that God had a son of the same nature as himself and that he was that son.—Splendid! If only the fact that Christ *said* this were not equally merely historically certain.

He goes on, very surprisingly, to counter the argument that the authors are inspired and so cannot err, by saying that it is only historically certain that these authors were inspired. Of course one would expect him to say: but that's only certain to one who already believes the Christian religion. That he says such an extraordinary thing must come of the background against which he wrote. Conceivably he meant: that these texts we have before us are the texts which were supposed to be inspired, is only historically certain. This is indeed a rather strong point as far as concerns an unlearned man's arguments from a single passage; for all he knows, it is a doubtful bit of the text, and so *not* part of the canon as received in the early times of the Church.

The most central part of his argument comes in the following passage:

> Who denies it—I do not—that the reports of those miracles and prophecies are just as trustworthy as any historical truth can be?—But now: if they are *only* so trustworthy, why are they so used as suddenly to make them infinitely more trustworthy? How? By building quite different things, and more things, on them, than one is entitled to build on historically evidenced truths. If no historical truth can be demonstrated, then neither can anything be demonstrated *by* historical truths. *That is: accidental historical truths can never become the proof of necessary truths of reason.*

I do not know much about the history of ideas; but I suspect that Lessing, in this and in other writings about religion and religious controversy, has been very influential: so many things that, in a distorted and vulgarised form, were for long commonplaces, are to be found in him with a seeming stamp of originality and freshness.

His argument in this paper is, I think, more intricate than it seems to be. I will try to separate out various points he makes.

1. In the argument about Alexander, it at first seems strange that he should use the fact that we *might* have known of Alexander only through a poem of Choerilus, to prove that we cannot base anything with perfect certainty on the existence of Alexander. But there are two reasons for this remark.

(a) I think there is certainly a dig at the fact that we know of Christ's words and actions ultimately only through one source—the *New Testament*. 'This one book' he calls it elsewhere. It is of course several books, not one; but this point may not seem important, as all were written by members of a close knit group of men.

(b) But the main reason for this argument becomes apparent when he talks about accidental historical truths not becoming the proof of necessary truths of reason. What is to be believed about God, about what can be ascribed to God, he thinks of as a 'necessary truth of reason', a metaphysical truth, I suppose; and a metaphysical truth, like a mathematical truth, could not possibly *follow* from a historical fact: if it could follow, then the historical fact would have to be as certain as metaphysical truths are supposed to be; but a historical fact *could* be quite uncertain, as Alexander would be if we only knew of him through a poem of Choerilus. I think that is the argument; it is not at this point an argument from the *actual* uncertainty of Alexander. I think it is not worth attention, because the assumption that anything believable about God must be 'a necessary truth of reason' is worse than doubtful; it is incoherent. It possibly derives from Leibnizian notions of 'necessary being', which I hope we can regard as exploded: and it goes with Lessing's idea, which has become so widespread, that the truths of religion must all be such that the human race could in the end have thought them out for themselves.

2. From the point of view of the Vatican decree, Lessing's insistence that historical truths can never be quite certain may be unimportant. For there is nothing there about a *demonstration* of the truth of Christianity; only about 'solid external arguments'; it is even, I believe, heresy or near heresy to hold that the mysteries of faith can be *demonstrated* (No one says 'Jesus is Lord' but by the Holy Ghost, St Paul says; but you can follow a demonstration without the Holy Ghost); hence high probability—which Lessing is quite willing to concede—may be enough to constitute 'solid external arguments'. Of course in view of the point we have already considered, he would object to a merely *probable* argument for 'necessary truths of reason'. But while that need not detain us, there is of course the central objection against faith itself: it is *certain*, its grounds—if it has grounds—at best probable: what excuse can one have for it, then? The excuse, someone might say, must be something that makes the things called 'probable grounds' utterly irrelevant. A person may have what strike him as probable grounds, and embrace Christian faith, and then discover that his probable grounds were nothing but gimcrack arguments and historical errors; but he is supposed to hold on to faith just the same. So his 'grounds' were nothing but the ladder which he kicked away, important only psychologically; and it must be a mistake to think that any such ladder *rightly* leads to faith—unless *any* ladder will do. There is probably something of this

in Lessing's remark about 'building things on historical truths which one is not entitled to build'; and this remains, even if one discards his view that anything to be believed about God must be a necessary truth of reason.

3. Quite apart from Lessing's central criticism of the contemporary *argument* for Christianity from prophecy and miracle, it is important to notice that his position is certainly incompatible with Christian belief at all. In this essay he *appears* to be arguing only against a certain argument, not against Christian beliefs: he appears to be saying 'If you hold them, it is on other grounds, not these'; he even ostensibly holds them—for other reasons; namely, their admirable content. But it is very clear that the Christian religion is false if, say, Christ is a myth. The role of Christ is not, as some people, who I suppose are in some line of descent from Lessing, would say: to show how noble a human being *might* be, and so inspire us. And that Christ was not a myth but a real person is historical fact. Therefore the Christian religion is incompatible with the falsehood of certain historical statements. But Lessing's position about what can be believed about God would not merely show that it could not be derived from any historical knowledge, but also that it could not be incompatible with any antecedently possible historical statements. And in fact I imagine he might have admitted this. It is very clear that he regarded Christ just as a teacher: and in a teacher it is the teaching that is important; it really does not matter whether the alleged teacher existed or not, so long as the teaching is there. Lessing was one of those who distinguished between the 'religion of Christ' (which he explained as 'the religion which he practised and acknowledged') and 'the Christian religion' (mainly characterised by the belief that Christ was the son of God): it may be that he was one of the originators of this long commonplace distinction. He was, of course, too informed to deny that the 'Christian religion' occurred in Christ's reported utterances, but insisted on distinguishing between what was hopelessly obscure and what was marvellously clear in these; the 'Christian religion' occurred only in what was obscure, not in what was clear. He dignified what was clear by the name 'the religion of Christ'. He himself draws the analogy I have used earlier between religious and mathematical truths: what would it matter if, historically, some fraudulent procedure led to a mathematical truth, he asks.

4. The proof of the Spirit and of power is in *contemporary* miracles and prophecies. I think Lessing greatly exaggerates the certainty

(from an external, impartial point of view) which Origen may have had about these. Here it is useful to be a Catholic, since Catholics don't say as others do and Lessing did 'there are no more miracles now'. I don't know Origen's biography; but it seems very likely that he knew of them as much from hearsay as we usually do now; even if, as seems the case, miracles were ever so much more common then, they were all the same thoroughly astonishing events; and presumably unbelievers regarded them with as much incredulity and lack of interest as unbelievers now show in regard to such things, which Catholics accept. Signs and wonders, even in Apostolic times, and done by Christ himself, are rare enough for *most* people only to hear of them. But perhaps all this is only for the sake of argument, and Lessing was in fact quite sceptical about all miracles and prophecies: I don't know.

* * *

These points are merely by way of preamble, to clear the ground before considering Lessing's central argument against the arguments for Christianity from miracles and prophecies fulfilled. Of course, this boils down to its being reasonable to say 'But these things *may* not be true, so how can I use them to support Christianity?' Put like that, Lessing's argument appears quite strong. And, put like that, it is fairly clearly in conflict with the decree of the Vatican Council. His argument is valuable, because it does not confuse the issue by attacking the truth of the recorded miracles and fulfilments of prophecy.

What makes the Vatican decree of extraordinary interest, I think, is that it is probably common among us to believe in fulfilled prophecies and miracles *because* we believe the Catholic religion and they are part of our doctrines. Besides, the passage from *Deuteronomy*, as well as reasonable reflection on the requirements of faith, would incline us to say that a prophet or wonder-worker is to be judged in the light of the Christian religion. If prophecies and miracles offer 'solid external arguments', they would seem to need to be established as prophecies and miracles *before* belief in Christianity is introduced: but isn't there a *theological* element in calling something a fulfilled prophecy, and even more, a miracle?

Returning to Lessing, I will try to say what seems right and what wrong about his contentions. First, as to miracles: I think that it must be conceded him that the reports of them could not be expected to appeal to an external judge as certainly true. The most famous – and the only one, I believe, still used in apologetic – is Christ's resurrection. Lessing concedes that it is as certain as any historical fact. I do not agree. In fact, this concession is one which I think it important, not merely for philosophical but for apologetic purposes, to oppose. In arguments on the subject, doubters are usually pressed for an alternative explanation. Why should they have one? What is unreasonable about saying 'Heaven knows what happened to produce this belief; I do not. And I know much too little about what may go on in human minds in the origins of embracing a new religious belief, to draw any conclusions (as I am so often pressed to do) from the subsequent careers of the Apostles (supposing them to be truly related in the main) or from the sudden appearance and growth of a new religion, which after all is all I am really perfectly certain of. I do know one thing: new religions sometimes spread like wildfire. How this works, and how it gets established in them is obscure. I concede that this is an impressive religion too; but then it had a very impressive religion behind it: that of the Old Testament. Remember that beliefs in miraculous events in connexion with the founders and heroes of religion are quite common. The most I can grant is that the record is quite as *if* these things had happened: the manner is not legendary, though the matter is!'

Lessing appears to me certainly wrong in saying 'that no historical certainty can be strong enough to be absolute'; hence, *if it is strength of certainty that is really in question*, it is not true that historical certainty is always too weak to *base* absolute certainty upon it. I do not here say that strength of certainty *is* what is in question; but Lessing certainly treats it as what is important in some of what he says, though of course there is a hint of something else in his talk of jumping to a different *class* of truths. But for the moment I will concentrate on strength of certainty. I should not mind staking anything whatever on the existence of Alexander, or forswearing for ever any proffered appearance of knowledge that conflicted with it. It is indeed not open to me to stake salvation upon it; but that is because Alexander has never been given any such role.[1] If he were to be given such a role, then, so far as the certainty of his existence is concerned, it would be possible.

How many people who ostensibly at least knew people who knew Alexander have left writings about what he did? I neither know nor need to know in order to be certain he existed. It may be said that

[1] Having written this I let it stand; but I had forgotten that the career of Alexander is described at the beginning of the books of Maccabees: so I must and do stake my salvation on it after all.

direct or near direct knowledge of him in our sources is unimportant: he is like Stalin—very widely known *of* in his own time, and in the wideness of the knowledge of him in his own time, he is superior to Christ, whose position is perhaps more comparable, as far as that is concerned, to that of Joanna Southcott, or perhaps of John Wesley, or someone half-way between them.

The question gets a bit more complicated if I wonder whom I mean by 'Alexander'. Do I rule it out, say, that the heir of Philip's throne died and an imposter took his place half-way through his victorious career? I do rule it out: it is so *vehemently improbable*. And here Lessing is on to me: this is where probability comes in, as opposed to plumb certainty. But I wish to say it does not begin to come in before this: that is to say, I object to his lumping together everything historical as of inferior certainty to my own experience. I am more certain that there was a great conqueror Alexander (and for that matter, more certain that there was a female religious imposter Joanna Southcott) than that I met Dom Illtyd Trethowan* here last year—and that, without having gone into the evidence in either case. This is so, though I am *very* certain that I did meet Dom Illtyd here last year; so that I should look for some strange explanation, or think that I had got completely bemused in some way, if it turned out that the monk of that name was in Australia at that time so that I could not have met him. But it *could* turn out that he had been; whereas things making it remotely probable that there was no Alexander are inconceivable; there could be no reason to think one knew what any historical evidence suggested at all, if a great range of things in history were not quite solid. Experience, unless it is made right by definition, is not more but less certain; and what I judge from experience may, some of it, more easily be wrong.

Now, that Christ claimed to be the Son of God, and that he rose from the dead, is not solid in *this* fashion. What is solid in this fashion is that he existed, preached, like an Old Testament prophet, and was at least ostensibly crucified under the Roman authority; and that believers took him for the Messiah and the Son of God and believed he had risen from the dead. Something—as it might be a report in Tacitus—suggesting something else, e.g. that they thought he had

* Dom Illtyd Trethowan (1907–1993) was a monk of Downside Abbey where he taught philosophy and theology for many years. The author of a substantial body of both philosophical and theological writings, he was a participant in a number of the annual meetings of the Philosophical Enquiry Group that met at Spode House.

gone into hiding, would never die, and came in secret to visit believers, would *not* seem to be evidence suggesting that we are misinformed as to the beliefs of Christians then; it would be evidence that Tacitus gave ill-informed accounts of things. Tacitus actually says that the Jews worshipped a donkey because one had led them to find water in the desert; we do not take this as evidence for the beliefs of Jews in his time. What we know about this is, on the contrary, a standard for judging what Tacitus said. Similarly, if we found some reference (in some Rabbinical tradition, let us say as a fancy for the sake of example) suggesting that the Son of Mary and Joseph, the putative parents of the pseudo-Messiah worshipped by the Christians, was simply an artisan turned thief who got himself crucified by the Romans, and never preached a word; no one would judge it to be evidence of anything but Jewish spite. As for the actual death, disappearance from the tomb, and reappearance of Christ, and also the claim to be the Son of God, these belong to the very large realm of historical assertions which it would indeed be absurd to claim certainty for, but the time for disproving which is past. I think that Lessing is unconscious of the existence of this class of historical assertions too; with them there is no danger of running up against a disproof of them, and the greater part of them must be true: but of any particular one, we cannot say it is perfectly certain. We may note that the death of Christ would be refuted, in normal circumstances, just by his reappearance alive.

Sticking to things that are absolutely solid (since Lessing's argument requires us to do this) we can say in the same way: that Christ predicted the siege and destruction of Jerusalem and the dispersal of the Jews is not solid in this fashion; but it is solid that it was anciently written down *as* a prophecy that Jerusalem would be trodden underfoot by the Gentiles until the time of the Gentiles was up; and in fact Jerusalem has been in the hands of the Gentiles from the Roman siege until now. The prophecy would be falsified, or at any rate deprived of any particular sense, if the Jews had possessed, or now came to possess, Jerusalem without any noteworthy and permanent change in the status or condition of the Gentiles. If Lessing tells me that the ancientness of the prediction is something I know 'only historically', I reply that this sort of historical certainty is as good as any certainty.

Now prophecies whose ancientness, priority, and fulfilment are really clear and certain to a quite detached observer are necessarily few. This is chiefly because of a point that Lessing makes elsewhere:

in order to say 'This was predicted, and it happened' we have to judge that the thing that happened, not merely was describable in the words occurring in the prediction, but was *what* was predicted: otherwise 'fulfilment' equals 'applicability of these words'; and can't this just be an accident? Thus the fact that the words 'they pierced my hands and my feet' occur in a psalm; and the words 'he who would touch the unjust must be filled with iron and the shaft of a spear' in the last words of David, could be seen as prophetical by believing Christians, or by pious Jews awaiting the 'consolation of Israel', who, having Christ preached to them 'searched the scriptures daily to see whether these things should be so', like the synagogue of Berea when St Paul came there; but can just be noted as mysterious utterances in ancient texts by anyone else. This holds true of a large number of the passages of the Old Testament which automatically make a Christian think of Christ.

There are however special difficulties about the notion of the applicability of prophetical words as *accidental*. If someone says something true about the past, and it then turns out that he knew nothing of those events, then it was just an accident that his words applied. But it is impossible to know the future of the world and of human affairs; so this test for accident cannot be made. This point needs stressing: someone who believes in a possibility of 'precognition' comparable to 'memory' is thereby rendered incapable of understanding the nature of prophecy at all.

Since we can't test whether a prophet *meant* such and such future events by whether he knew of them, then if like Lessing we are going to demand that it should be clear that *this is what he meant*, we thereby restrict the range of *possible* prophecy very severely. I think we restrict it to predictions containing proper names and predicates with a very definite sense, like the death of a man or the desolation of a site. If I say: 'Father Ryan will be dead before the year is out' that is clear enough; the trouble about such predictions, of course, is that we hardly ever know of their priority with certainty. If I say Chicago will be desolated by an earthquake, will be abandoned, and never again inhabited; it will be all ploughed fields where Chicago was, and there will never be a city there again; then that is definite too. We have such a prophecy in Isaiah concerning Babylon, whose priority and fulfilment have the absolute certainty about which Lessing disputes; priority, because Babylon did not become desolate until after the establishment of Seleucia in the second century B.C.; and certainty, since the prophet is extremely explicit, so that it would be safe to say that the present day establishment of any town on the site of Babylon would be a falsification of the prophecy. 'The Arab will not pitch his tent there', the prophet said: nor will he: he believes the place to be devil-haunted. Other cases are: the final destruction of the great city of Tyre (not unequivocally accomplished until the fourteenth century) and the prophecy that Egypt should never again be a great nation after being conquered by Nebuchadnezzar, and should have its cities scattered among ruined and abandoned cities. Apart from cities and countries, peoples have proper names; and the prophecies concerning the Jews, their being scattered all over the world, their sufferings, down to horrid details like being driven to eat afterbirths (verified in the Roman siege and again in Hitler's camps), the downfall of their enemies, and their return to Palestine—all this appears to have been fulfilled or (I hope) to be being fulfilled. But here, of course, it would be possible to argue that what the prophets 'meant' was the scattering over the known world at the Exile and the return under Cyrus: possible, that is, to the impartial unbeliever, who can write off the association of their return with the advent of a conquering and triumphant Messiah as a fantastic hope for the immediate future on the part of the writers. Thus, if you want to be able to say 'This is what the prophet meant', you are under very severe restrictions. Even a prophecy with an attempt at dates in it—which you might suppose to be rather definite—is necessarily obscure unless you have a certain chronology and a certain *terminus a quo*. The example for this is the prophecy in David, that forty-nine and 434 years after the going forth of the order to build up Jerusalem, Messiah the Prince should be killed. What did the *terminus a quo* mean to the writer? The Edict of Cyrus? The permit of Darius? The first permission of Artaxerxes? The later edict of Artaxerxes? The fact that if we take one of these it brings us out to the time of the crucifixion, and that no other yields any result even by a rough approximation may by impressive; but not to someone who *first* wants to know just what was in the writer's mind. Now if the writer was writing after the event to which the words are taken to have applied, the whole question falls to the ground: but if before, then there is no such thing as his having *that* event in mind: for future events aren't there to have in mind, except in so far as they lie in their causes which are present; but that is not the case for such events.

To show the character of prophecies without proper names, take the prophecy in *Daniel*, that after Nebuchadnezzar's should come two great empires, and then a fourth 'iron' empire, very great and powerful, which should split up into many states getting their character from it, but never able to coalesce. If someone says this here and now, in the past tense, the reference to the Roman Empire is clear and the description commonplace. If—to mention something that Lessing, who was so great a dramatic critic, would have appreciated—in a modern play words describing history known to the audience are put in the mouth of someone supposed to be speaking in an earlier time, the impression created is necessarily bogus; everyone knows what the author means. But if such words are really found to have been uttered in a former time, then they at once become vague and problematic. This is a logical point: of the many, many utterances we might make now about the present or the past, which have a good sharp sense, by far the greater number would look hopelessly obscure if said earlier, of the future: even ones with proper names: e.g. 'Suez was unnavigable for sunken ships': we all know what that means; 'Suez will be unnavigable for sunken ships' as a prophetical utterance written in 1850, would have been hopelessly unintelligible. Now let us take an unfulfilled (eschatological) prophecy of Zechariah: 'I will gather all the nations to Jerusalem to battle', about which one feels pretty vague; and imagine the effect on those words of a set of events which fitted the whole chapter and included an attack on Jerusalem by a United Nations expeditionary force! That is the kind of effect that the history of the Roman Empire and of its break-up into many states has on Daniel's prophecy. These considerations result in an interesting point: the critical principle that prophetical writings must have been clearly intelligible in their own times is *itself* a denial of the possibility of all but prophecy of a very restricted type.

That is to say: for almost all prophecies, to see them fulfilled is to interpret them; and this is because of the difference between past and future. To ask whether a prophet had *these events* in mind is senseless. The most we can do is to distinguish between cases where the prophet—professing to prophesy—utters words which have a natural application, considering his whole context, to the events we think they prophesied; and cases where all that can be said is that one can see how someone might apply those words, ripped out of context and taken by themselves, to this event. For example, the application of Jeremiah's prophecy about Rachel mourning for her children to the slaughter of the Innocents is of the second kind. Prophecies like 'They pierced my hands and my feet', and that of Isaiah addressed to the disobedient among the Jews 'I shall call my servants by another name' are of the first kind, as is the prophecy of Daniel. Prophecies like Zechariah's 'They shall look upon one whom they pierced' are of the first kind in their most obvious application, namely to the *second* coming of Christ, as St John uses them in the Apocalypse; and of the second in the application St John makes of them in the Gospel: there the words are reft out of their context and applied in isolation; but of course the reference of the 'piercing' to the Crucifixion is of the first kind; that is why I can adduce this example, even though the 'looking upon' intended by the prophet is eschatological.

But the question arises: why on earth should one be impressed by prophecy at all? Why should it even interest one? We have almost certainly all heard anecdotes of old prophecies in some sense verified: I can supply one, which I know sufficiently directly to know that it is true. There was a row of heads of English monarchs being placed in Llandaff Cathedral: the prediction, told as such in the early thirties, was that when the last place was filled, a disaster would befall the country. The last head was Edward VIII's; after that, a landmine hit the Cathedral in the second world war. What has one for such stories but a shrug and a smile, even when one actually knows them to be true (which of course is usually not the case)?

Now a prophecy fulfilled, or a miracle done, is supposed to *attest* something. In the story I have told, nothing is attested except the prediction itself, since it turned out true in some sense: but to say it was attested is to say *nothing* but that it turned out true. But let us take an example where there might be thought to be something to attest. It is widely reported—the story comes, I believe, from Walter Starkie—that a gypsy woman said of Leslie Howard just before he was killed in an air crash: 'I will not stay in the room with that man: there is death in his face'. Naturally, I do not know whether this story is true, since I neither was there nor know the author of it. You have to know a man, and to know him extremely well, to judge his truthfulness about that sort of story: a point which I think makes ridiculous the argument that we have to believe what the earliest Christians said they had observed, or said they had from people who had observed them. People love wonderful stories. However, let us suppose that I *knew* the story to be true, say from having witnessed it myself; for I can say in the manner of Lessing that I have nothing against it. Then it might be suggested that it attested the gypsy. But in what sense? That it attested *other* predictions she might make? But why should she always be right; or even if she was always right in sincere prophecies, *why* should she never lie? What possible good reason could I have to say that it attested her in any way: let alone that it attested, say, her religion (for there is a Romany religion, which might be hers) or her advice? I should say: none. Now if someone says: there must be some explanation; at least such events prove that gypsies have strange powers of telling the future, I reply that such events, if they occur specially among gypsies, prove that such events occur specially among gypsies, and nothing else at all. Nor do I agree that there must be an explanation. But if there must, then if we are to deal in occult matters at all, one can offer a different explanation: namely, that God permits the devil to prompt people who would like to claim such powers to make such utterances in the presence of people who may thereby be tempted to occultism. If you 'must' have an explanation when you are outside the sphere of natural knowledge, there can be no 'must' about the explanation you offer. This point is neglected by psychical researchers who are ready to speak of 'what only so-and-so could have known'—in the natural course of events—as evidence that it was so-and-so who imparted it—in a quite abnormal way, but if it could be imparted in a quite abnormal way, then the argument from 'only so-and-so could have known it' falls heavily to the ground.

There is a sense of the term 'accidental' other than that in which Lessing used it. As we saw, he called the fulfilment of prophecy accidental if the words of the prophecy had a natural enough application, but the event was not in fact what the prophet meant; and as we also saw, this restricts the kind of prophecy that is possible at all very considerably, because it is *not* possible to 'mean' any but a very restricted range of future events in the way in which one can 'mean' present [or] past ones; if we are going to allow prophecy a wider range than that, the only criticism on the ground that it was not what the prophet 'meant' would be that it can be told from the context that that was not the *kind* of thing the prophet meant—as, if somebody now said that there would be a parliament in Saudi Arabia too, and later some witches' assembly issued edicts there, we could say it wasn't the kind of thing he had meant. Now supposing that I seriously, not just as a philosophical example, say here and now 'Johannesburg will be captured by Ghana', and it goes on record that I say it in 1957; and in 1990 it happens. To say 'this was accidental' is to *say* 'this was not a prophecy'; that is, this is itself a theological remark. If I said it as a philosophical example, then it has some sense to say 'the fulfilment was accidental': if I uttered it as a prophecy—i.e. a prediction not based on judgment of future events from their present causes, and not, of course, as an expression of intention on my own part—then to say 'it was accidental that it was fulfilled' can only mean (a) the 'fulfilment' wasn't the *kind* of thing she meant, or (b) we do not allow this to be prophecy, where 'prophecy' has a *theological* meaning. Except in the following types of case where one can say: this is the very sort of thing for that man, or these men, to have said; e.g. if I hated a politician and say: he will come to a bad end—and he does come to a bad end—then it might well be said, hating him so, this was the very thing for me to say. So if it is part of the Jewish religion to believe that there will never cease to be Jews, or of the Christian religion to believe that 'this gospel' will be preached all over the world, and 'this church' never fail, this seems no more prophetical than Horace's '*Exegi monumentum aere perennius*'. Thus though the disappearance of the Jews would refute both Judaism and Christianity, the fact that it would refute Christianity is more impressive, since Christianity would still be there to be refuted, if they did disappear, and the belief in their remaining does not seem to be 'the very thing' for Christians to profess.

* * *

Now if all this is so, the impartial, indifferent observer is confronted quite certainly only with a few scattered prophecies relating to cities and peoples; and with *reports* of miracles and of fulfilments of prophecies which it is absurd to pretend he must regard as certainly true. So what becomes of the 'solid external arguments' of the Vatican decree? I will sketch my answer to this, very briefly. It can be summarised in one sentence: Only if a man is impressed by the Old Testament, to the extent of being inclined to take it as his teacher, has the argument from prophecies and miracles any serious weight. And that is why the argument is not found at the present day; since with the exception of an occasional Jew, that is a very uncommon position for a man to be in, though an entirely solid and reasonable one.

To describe this position, I will invent a character. I will suppose a man who believes in God and despises the worship of idols and the fear of spirits; I won't suppose him to be a 'seeker after God' like Enoch, but already to acknowledge God as the author of seasonal benefits; and to suppose that it is 'impious' e.g. to commit great injustices. I will suppose this man to have heard little of Christianity; and to happen to have his interest caught by the Old Testament, for one reason or another, sufficiently to read it with attention and to come to admire the Mosaic Law, both in its public, juridical character and in its prescriptions for private persons. He skips the ceremonial and purificatory prescriptions as of no interest to him. He does not admire this Law just because it prescribes things that accord with his own views; it does that in part, no doubt; but in part he finds it instructive. For example, it greatly heightens his own notion of the paramountcy of God; it absolutely forbids superstition, 'seeking truth from the dead', concern with omens, soothsaying; if we suppose him acquainted with, say, Arabian tribes of the fiercer sort, we can also suppose that he is struck by the prescriptions tending to check the licence and bloody revenge natural among such people; the arrangements tending to make impossible the casual jettisoning of wives and the killing of those who have suddenly or accidentally killed your relations. For while revenge was *forbidden* as a matter of *personal ethic*, it is also made *difficult* as a matter of *public law* by the establishment of the cities of refuge. He notes the prohibition on punishing any but the offender—remember that even Roman law, as codified by a Christian Emperor, permitted the destruction of the family and close associates of a man found guilty of treason against the state; but the Mosaic law forbade it. He notes the restriction on stripes as a punishment to forty 'lest thy brother become vile in thy sight'*—equally astonishing when you think of Roman floggings, or floggings in the British navy up to quite recent times. There is no torture in the Mosaic law: remember again that the Code of Justinian retained the *requirement* to torture slaves as witnesses. He notes the fact that if you so much as knocked out the tooth of a slave, he was to go free; the asylum to runaway slaves from the nations round about, the prohibition on man-stealing; the provision whereby you could not send a slave or bondman away if he had married in your house and chose to remain; the provisions forbidding persecution of poor debtors. He sees the contrast between the estimation of offences against property (the penalty being n-fold restitution, n ranging from 2 to 6, to be worked off if it could not be paid off) and offences against the person and sexual offences. He sees the death penalty prescribed for idolatry, blasphemy, murder, sodomy, bestiality, adultery, and even fornication by or with a betrothed virgin: and this indeed strikes him as perhaps rather doubtful, so much death penalty for some rather common offences; but in every other regard he is impressed by the law and the ethic as something incomparably superior to what is usually found in codes of law, which usually

* *Deuteronomy* 25.3

seem designed in some way at least to flatter avarice and power and for the respect of persons and the oppression of many of those subject to them and above all for the glorification of those who have supreme power. I have given only the roughest outline, since there is no time here to refer to the many details and institutions, which have an extraordinary particularity about them, seemingly designed to circumvent the natural meanness and cunning of human beings. The Hebrew ethic has for so long been upon the whole just 'morality' to the West that it was difficult to see and admire it. So much against the shedding of innocent blood – who could find that remarkable in the last few centuries? Now with the West abandoning this ethic, it becomes possible to see it again. *Ave atque vale.*

I will suppose this man to be so impressed by this law, which is so ancient, that he begins to regard the Old Testament as a source of instruction and to form his mind in accordance with it, and even to say to himself that he can entertain the idea that the law really was given by God, and the prophets sent by God to re-teach it. (Here one may ask: how has he come to regard these books as a unity? For of course they are just a lot of separate books. Bind up Homer, a few Greek tragedies, comedies and histories, and a few dialogues of Plato into one volume and call this the Greek message – it is possible that this volume would, so to speak, have a physiognomy. I will suppose my man to be aware that there are a lot of separate books and to discover, with astonishment, that they have more than a physiognomy, but are really one in doctrine and in point.) Now if he is in this frame of mind, he may begin to wonder about the many other things to be found in these books. We can suppose him first to have read the earliest stories as legends of origin, and not to concern himself with what it can be supposed to mean that someone received commands from God to sacrifice his son, or be circumcised, or slaughter a lot of people. But what he next notices is the promises and prophecies relating to an eternal Golden Age under a just ruler, not only for the people of the books, but for everyone. Such promises and prophecies could not especially interest him at first otherwise than by appealing to natural longings for a Golden Age, and so appearing as the expression of such longings; but once he is, so to speak, converted to the veneration of the law and the prophets, he may begin to take them more seriously.

It is at this stage, and, I think only at this stage, that the fulfilment of the prophecies that I have mentioned can begin to have any weight. If he notes them, and allows himself to entertain the idea that the whole range of books is a revelation; if he begins to hunt for what the promised Messiah is, in more detail (for so far he has of course no impression beyond that of the conquering just king of the Golden Age)—then he will find a great many puzzles; a great deal that seems contradictory and incomprehensible. It is at this stage that I will suppose him to encounter the New Testament, having soaked himself in the Old in the kind of way I have described, and to find in the New both a manifest continuation of what he has already read, and *a* solution of much that seems inexplicable; principally in the teaching concerning the *two* comings of the Messiah, first to suffer and to die, and then to rule in power, which immediately makes clear a great many extreme obscurities in the Old Testament; and concerning the divinity as well as the humanity of the Messiah, which is again and again implied and indicated in the Old Testament, but only set forth as doctrine in the New.

That is to say: when St Augustine said that the fulfilment of the prophecies in Christ was the greatest proof of his divinity, what he said was true; but the proof requires a very special position on the part of someone who is to consider it. That is why the kind of apologetic that Lessing argued against, which did not assume that position, was so vulnerable and stupid.

The role of the miracles, which I have contended cannot possibly be accepted as certainly true occurrences by the indifferent historian, seems to me to be this: if one is seriously entertaining the truth of the whole revelation in the way I have hinted at, the miracles are consonant. That God attested Christ by miracles is possible, if Christ is Christ—i.e. is the Messiah promised in the Old Testament. Then the problem, how on earth these seemingly factual records came to be written, of such incredible things, is resolved by the hypothesis that they happened. If they did happen, what would one expect the records of them to look like? And if they did happen, do they not support the teaching? But I repeat, it is not reasonable to ask an indifferent historian to solve this problem, of how such records came to be written; he *can* reasonably just leave it unsolved.

With this we come to the problem of the notion of divine attestation at all. The mere fact that someone is a wonder-worker, or utters prophecies that are fulfilled, certainly does not show he is divinely attested.

So far as I can see there has to be a thesis of natural theology, as I might call it, that if someone works 'a sign and a wonder' or utters a prophecy which gets fulfilled, in God's name, then he is divinely attested. Now what does this rest on? It might rest on faith. In *Deuteronomy*, when the Jews were forbidden to consult soothsayers and necromancers, and omens, they were promised prophets 'like Moses' whom they were to attend to instead. But, the passage goes on, they'll want to know how to tell a prophet. And the answer is: if the prophet foretells something, and it doesn't happen, then that was just his presumption. The implication seems to be that if a prophet of their people, apparently teaching according to the Law, foretells something and it does happen, he is attested.

That is to say: the teaching of the prophets must first be such as would reasonably be thought to belong to the truth as revealed by Moses; only if that is so does the question even arise. *Then*, if he foretells something and it happens, and if he does not try to lead them into idolatry after that, he is attested.

This might be taken as matter of faith. But if [what] constitutes divine attestation is only learned by faith, then what becomes of the 'solid external arguments' of the Vatican decree?

Are we to say God wouldn't let a prophecy be fulfilled or a wonder be done, if it was done in his name, except by someone he was attesting? I think we should be chary of arguments about what God wouldn't do.

I think the argument must be rather that if a prophet who is apparently teaching the truth, dares to foretell something contingent, then this is presumption of him unless he has it from God and must say it. Now if he teaches a lie straight away afterwards, or if the thing does not happen, then he is proved presumptuous. But if he is not proved presumptuous, then we ought not to dare not to believe and obey him: so long as what he says does not conflict with the known truth.

There is a well known, I believe well authenticated, story of a man, John Lee of Buckfastleigh, in our own time, who was convicted of murder on very good evidence. In prison, he said that he would not hang because he had an assurance of this from God (in a dream, or something of the sort) because he was innocent. He did not hang, because the trap would not fall; after three attempts, with planings of the trap, which worked perfectly when he was *not* on it, they desisted, and his sentence was commuted to life imprisonment. Now if this story is true, and if there is no ground for supposing the hangman to have *both* communicated with Lee *and* hocused the mechanism, then it would appear to me reasonable to have feared that this was a divine attestation of his innocence, and to have let him free.

But, one may say, perhaps one can *do* something otherwise permissible, 'because one dare not do otherwise' in a case where there is no sign that the man is presumptuous and he does what is either from God or is presumptuous; but can one *believe* something for such a reason: namely that the man who says it is from God or presumptuous, and there is no sign that he is presumptuous? Surely one wants positive reason to believe, and not merely absence of positive reason to disbelieve?

This, it seems to me, is correct, and goes with the thesis that in some sense there cannot be a prophet with a new doctrine.

4*

Hume on Miracles

Hume's Chapter or, as it is often called, Essay on miracles has the fame of a little masterpiece among those of the general public who will have heard of it, or may even have read it, and don't dislike its conclusions; while among those who do dislike its conclusions it gets the adjective 'notorious'. It ostensibly sets out to give the 'wise and learned' an argument which will forever arm them against any defence of religion, any argument purporting to establish a religion which appeals to miracles, and, equally, to prophecies the fulfilment of which Hume considers to be also a sort of miracle. But if we restrict the title 'wise and learned' to people who've looked into Hume's arguments strictly, or as philosophers at least, we find that those who like his outlook often appear to be much embarrassed—Antony Flew, for example, in his chapter on the subject in *Hume's Philosophy of Belief*,** and, as I understand from A E Taylor, T H Huxley; while a man who appears to be merely dispassionate, C D Broad, simply makes mincemeat of the argument, as unreasonable in itself and as in any case inconsistent with Hume's philosophic position. Indeed it seems, from the judgment of such 'wise and learned' men, to have been a correct instinct which makes of this chapter of Hume's *Enquiry* a separable Essay.

Selby-Bigge remarks that its insertion in the *Enquiry* is 'due doubtless ... to other considerations than to a simple desire to illustrate or draw philosophical corollaries from the philosophical principles laid down in the original work';[1] and elsewhere he shows what he

* From an undated and unpublished manuscript.

** Antony Flew, *Hume's Philosophy of Belief: A Study of his first Enquiry* (London: Routledge & Kegan Paul, 1961).

[1] David Hume, *Enquiries Concerning Human Understanding and Concerning the Principle of Morals*, reprinted from the posthumous edition of 1777 and edited with introduction, comparative table of contents, and analytical index by L A Selby-Bigge, third edition with text revised and notes by P H Nidditch (Oxford: Clarendon Press 1975), p.xix. [Hereafter: *Enquiries*]

thinks the motive was: Hume wanted to 'create a murmur among the zealots'.[2] In this he succeeded; and succeeded also, if it's permissible to guess at part causes in the history of opinions, in being influential. For certainly appeal to miracles and prophecy by way of argument for the truth of Christianity has completely gone out of fashion since Hume's time. Not that Hume would be more than a contributor to this effect; another rather different one also belonging to the eighteenth century will have been Lessing, with his 'On the proof of spirit and of power' — *sc.* the proof of spirit and of power by the performance of miracles, as opposed to its proof by a report of their performance.* And no doubt many other influences stemming from that century especially have played their part. But it seems likely that Hume has had some share in producing the temper of the present time.

A strong reason for the fame of the Essay, I should judge, is the literary skill, which is greater in the *Enquiry* than in the *Treatise*. Literary skill is independent of soundness in argument or truthfulness in reporting. One of the most agreeable passages in Hume's chapter, for example, is that in which he reports an account by Cardinal de Retz of an alleged miracle in Saragossa:

> There is also a memorable story related by Cardinal de Retz, which may well deserve our consideration. When that intriguing politician fled into Spain, to avoid the persecution of his enemies, he passed through Saragossa, the capital of Aragon, where he was shewn, in the cathedral, a man, who had served seven years as a doorkeeper, and was well known to everybody in town, that had ever paid his devotions at that church. He had been seen, for so long a time, wanting a leg; but recovered that limb by the rubbing of holy oil upon the stump; and the cardinal assures us that he saw him with two legs. This miracle was vouched by all the canons of the church; and the whole company in town were appealed to for a confirmation of the fact; whom the cardinal found, by their zealous devotion, to be thorough believers of the miracle. Here the relater was also cotemporary to the supposed prodigy, of an incredulous and libertine character, as well as of great genius; the miracle of so *singular* a nature as could scarcely admit of a counterfeit, and the witnesses very numerous, and all of them, in a manner, spectators of the fact, to which they gave

* See the previous paper on 'Prophecy and Miracles' in this volume.

---

[2] *Enquiries*, p.xii.

> their testimony. And what adds mightily to the force of the evidence, and may double our surprise on this occasion, is, that the cardinal himself, who relates the story, seems not to give any credit to it, and consequently cannot be suspected of any concurrence in the holy fraud.

But if one looks up the passage one has to conclude that Hume was probably relying on his memory to report it, and his memory cooked it up a bit in the interests of his argument.* E.g. you would think from Hume's passage that de Retz had questioned the townspeople, whereas all he reports is what the Dean and cantors (elevated by Hume into the greater dignity of canons) told him. The comic effect, from the point of view of pious credulity, of a story of being cured by lamp oil, is taken away by making it 'holy oil'; the Cardinal's own caution in committing himself as to whether the people, whom he saw at a day's journey away covering the roads on the way to Saragossa, really were going there to celebrate this miracle—which suggests that he wasn't sure it was not a leg pull on him—is transmuted into his having found that the whole company in town, by their zealous devotion, were thorough believers in the miracle.

Again, in reporting on the evidence—if one is to be willing to entertain evidence at all—for the miracles at the tomb of the Jansenist saint, Paris, Hume is able to indulge his malicious wit at its most brilliant:

* See *Mémoires du Cardinal de Retz contenant ce qui s'est passé de remarquable en France pendant les premiers années du regne de Louis XIV*. Nouvelle edition exactement revue et corrigée. Tome troisième. (Geneva: Fabry & Barillot, 1777), pp.483-484:

> L'on my montra un homme qui servoit à allumer les lampes qui y font en nombre prodigieux, & l'on me dit qu'on l'y avoit vu sept ans à la porte de cette église avec une seule jambe. Je l'y vis avec deux. Le doyen avec tous les chanoines m'assurerent que toute la ville l'avoit vu comme eux, & que si je voulois encore attendre deux jours, je parlerois à plus de vingt mille hommes, meme du dehors, qui l'avoient vu comme ceux de la ville. Il avoit recouvré la jambe, à ce qu'il disoit, en se frottant de l'huile de ces lampes. On célebre tous les ans la fête de ce prétendu miracle avec un concours incroyable de peuple, & il est vrai qu'encore à une journée de Saragosse, je trouvai les grands chemins couverts de gens de toute sorte de qualités qui y couroient.

A marginal note in the manuscript of her paper records that Anscombe had consulted an earlier edition of 1718 of the *Mémoires* (volume 5) published in Amsterdam, the text of which may have warranted her saying that de Retz referred to cantors rather than canons.

> There is another book in three volumes (called *Recueil des Miracles de l'Abbé Paris*) giving an account of many of these miracles, and accompanied with prefatory discourses, which are very well written. There runs, however, through the whole of these a ridiculous comparison between the miracles of our Saviour and those of the Abbé; wherein it is asserted, that the evidence for the latter is equal to that for the former: As if the testimony of men could ever be put in the balance with that of God himself, who conducted the pen of the inspired writers. If these writers, indeed, were to be considered merely as human testimony, the French author is very moderate in his comparison; since he might, with some appearance of reason, pretend, that the Jansenist miracles much surpass the other in evidence and authority.[3]

'What', he says in the main body of his argument, 'have we to oppose to such a cloud of witnesses, but the absolute impossibility or miraculous nature of the events, which they relate?'[4] Well, Hume has suppressed what—namely the lack of sobriety on the part of those who went in for the cult of those miracles—which was also a cult of going into wild convulsions and similar things. Indeed of his three stories, the only one of which he gives a really pretty fair account is the Tacitus one—which is, upon the whole, rather convincing than otherwise.

The accusations against Hume's arguments by his critics, which seem sound enough, can be listed quite briefly:

1. Hume dodges about between different definitions of a miracle as (i) anything contrary to the uniform course of experience[5], or (ii) a transgression of a law of nature by a particular volition of the Deity or by the interposition of some invisible agent.[6]

2. The first definition is question begging, as may be seen from his remark: 'it is a miracle, that a dead man should come to life; because that has never been observed in any age or country.'[7]

3. Indeed Hume carries the first definition to an extreme point of absurdity: 'There must therefore be a uniform experience against every miraculous event, otherwise the event would not merit that

---

[3] *Enquiries*: Additional Note to p.125, l.4, at p. 344.

[4] *Enquiries*, p. 125.

[5] *Enquiries*, pp. 114–15.

[6] *Enquiries*, p. 115.

[7] *Enquiries*, p. 115.

appellation.'[8] This is self-defeating, as the alleged miraculous event, having possibly happened, would be enough to call its miraculous character in question—since if it *had* happened there would *not* be uniform experience against it; and hence its miraculous character could not be adduced as an argument against it having happened.

4. Hume's aim is to procure (what has indeed been procured) that the miraculous character of an event shall be *sufficient* reason to reject the story of its having occurred without investigation of any evidence. This is a strange termination of an argument which starts with the thesis that a wise man proportions his belief to the evidence.

5. Hume misdescribes the role of testimony in human knowledge. 'The reason', he says, 'why we place any credit in witnesses and historians, is not derived from any *connexion*, which we perceive *a priori*, between testimony and reality, but because we are accustomed to find a conformity between them. But when the fact attested is such a one as has seldom fallen under our observation, here is a contest of two opposite experiences.'[9] Well, I have not merely not often, but never, experienced an earthquake; yet there is no conflict, no principle of experience which in this case gives me a 'degree of assurance against the fact' that witnesses to earthquakes endeavour to establish.

6. On the point of consistency with his own philosophy, there could hardly be a defence. Hume is so clear that no amount of uniformity of experience can possibly be a rational ground, or evidence, let alone proof, that the like must happen in a similar case, that it really looks as if his tongue were in his cheek when he says that the occurrence of a miracle is disproved just by the fact of its being a violation of the laws of nature; that it is ruled out as an impossible event. In the very next chapter but one he repeats his constant position that, reasoning a priori, we must grant that anything may produce anything. 'The falling of a pebble may, for aught we know, extinguish the sun.'[10] And yet in *this* chapter we get him saying 'The raising of a house or ship into the air is a visible miracle. [He wasn't thinking of cataclysms!] The raising of a feather, when the wind wants ever so little of a force requisite for that purpose, is as real a miracle, though not so sensible with regard to us.'[11] In short, for purposes of this

---

[8] *Enquiries*, p. 115.

[9] *Enquiries*, p. 113.

[10] *Enquiries*, p. 164, in Section XII 'On the Academical or Sceptical Philosophy'.

[11] *Enquiries*, p. 115, footnote 1.

chapter he is adopting the mechanistic determinism—the picture of nature bound fast in fate by inviolable laws—which belonged not to Hume's conceptions but to those of his century—the effect of Newtonian science (?). His own view is

> *That there is nothing in any object, consider'd in itself, which can afford us a reason for drawing a conclusion beyond it;* and *That even after the observation of a frequent or constant conjunction of objects, we have no reason to draw any inference concerning any object beyond those of which we have had experience;* I say, let men be once fully convinc'd of these two principles, and this will throw them so loose from all common systems, that they will make no difficulty of receiving any, which may appear the most extraordinary.[12]

7. On Hume's own account of belief, belief in miracles is actually a thing that can't happen.

> All belief of matter of fact or real existence is derived merely from some object, present to the memory or senses, and a customary conjunction between that and some other object. Or in other words; having found, in many instances, that any two kinds of objects—flame and heat, snow and cold—have always been conjoined together; if flame or snow be presented anew to the senses, the mind is carried by custom to expect heat or cold, and to *believe* that such a quality does exist, and will discover itself upon a nearer approach. This belief is the necessary result of placing the mind in such circumstances. It is an operation of the soul, when we are so situated, as unavoidable as to feel the passion of love, when we receive benefits; or hatred, when we meet with injuries. All these operations are a species of natural instincts, which no reasoning or process of the thought and understanding is able either to produce or to prevent.[13]

This he knows how to turn to his own advantage—it gives more inwardness and point to the mockery at the end of the chapter on miracles:

> So that, upon the whole, we may conclude, that the *Christian Religion* not only was at first attended with miracles, but even at this day cannot be believed by any reasonable person without one. Mere reason is insufficient to convince us of its veracity: And whoever is moved by *Faith* to assent to it, is conscious of a continued miracle in his own person, which subverts all the principles

[12] David Hume, *A Treatise of Human Nature*, edited by L A Selby-Bigge (Oxford: Clarendon Press, 1888), p.139.

[13] *Enquiries*, pp.46-47.

> of his understanding, and gives him a determination to believe what is most contrary to custom and experience.

Broad may say, like someone criticising a student's essay, that Hume doesn't in this essay maintain his otherwise 'extremely high standards'; he mistook what Hume was at. The essay is brilliant propaganda. For the question of consistency is not very important; but the argument for Hume's account of causality, that this just is the unavoidable way we do think, is as silly if addressed to believers in miracles as the proof of God from universal consent addressed to atheists. But Hume turns the difficulty he is really in to most successful account.

These are the principal objections urged against Hume' Essay. But there is something further, I think, to be said about the argument, which will throw light on the persuasive skills with which it is constructed.

The principle which Hume sets up for rejecting all testimony as to miracles is this: 'Suppose ... that the fact, which the testimony endeavours to establish, partakes of the extraordinary and the marvellous; in that case, the evidence, resulting from the testimony, admits of a diminution, greater or less, in proportion as the fact is more or less unusual.'[14] In pursuance of this principle he draws the conclusion, from the uniformity of experience against miracles and their consequent impossibility, that one ought to reject all testimony in favour of a miracle, that no testimony is sufficient to establish a miracle, unless the testimony be of such a kind that its falsehood would be more miraculous than the fact which it endeavours to establish. The conclusion, which is to the taste of many people, it must be admitted, is nevertheless ostensibly a development of a thesis *not* relating to miracles but only to what is 'extraordinary and marvellous', i.e. what is out of the way, like earthquakes (to people in this part of the world), fireballs, going as stiff as a board under hypnosis so that you can receive repeated heavy blows without pain or harm, or lie across a gap with only your head and heels supported and be sat on by three hefty men as if you were a bench.

It is easily checked by probability theory what the true state of the case is. If, relative to our background information, the probability of an earthquake in Spain on a given day is less than the probability of a mendacious journalistic report the next day that there had been an earthquake in Spain, then the probability of the earthquake's having

[14] *Enquiries*, p.113.

happened, even when we read the report in today's newspapers, is still less than ½. This much we can concede to Hume; it both accords with probability theory and is intuitively acceptable. (It used, Keynes tells us, to be disputed whether the improbability of an event did not make the report of it *more* probable.[15]) On the other hand, the odds in favour of there having been a Spanish earthquake yesterday *are* increased even in this case by the appearance of a newspaper report today unless the journalists are such awful liars that they are just as likely to report a non-existent earthquake as one that did happen. This condition could scarcely be fulfilled, for it is a near certainty that they would report an earthquake that did happen, and nothing like a certainty that they would invent an earthquake in Spain rather than some other lie.[16]

Thus Hume's argument that the more improbable the event the less weight has testimony to it is sound enough. But we did not need that argument to show that if an event is of a kind to have no finite probability at all – i.e. if it is an impossible event – then testimony to it has no weight at all, does not add to the probability one whit, so that there is no need to look into the evidence that it has occurred. That is clear from the impossibility, without recourse to the thesis that the more improbable the event, and the more probable lying or deceiving testimony to it, the less weight has any testimony to it. The way the argument is developed gives one the impression that testimony cannot add to probability at all where lying or deceived testimony is more probable than the event. To be sure, Hume does not *say* this, whence then the impression? It arises, surely, because he has used the point about the diminishing weight of testimony as the first step in an argument which *begins* by saying 'A wise man proportions his belief to the evidence' and *ends* by saying a wise man need not look at *this* sort of evidence at all. Only if testimony here could not add to the probability at all could this be a reasonable course of argument. Of course he has put in that it can't add to the probability because the event is impossible – but then the earlier argument is not needed, has no serious role. And it sounds as if the earlier argument – the argument that the non-occurrence of the event plus testi-

[15] John Maynard Keynes, *A Treatise on Probability* (London: Macmillan Co, 1921), p.183. [What Keynes actually says is '... Laplace in his *Essai philosophique* (pp.98-102) ... argues that a witness is less to be believed when he asserts an extraordinary fact, declaring the opposite view (taken by Diderot in the article on 'Certitude' in the *Encylopédie*) to be inconceivable before 'le simple bon sens'.']

[16] For the formula, see Keynes, *loc.cit.*,

mony is more probable than its occurrence plus testimony *if* false testimony to it is more probable than it is—were being invoked or echoed in the conclusion, that the falsehood of the testimony has got to be more *improbable* than the miracle, i.e. has got to be a greater miracle, if the testimony is to be worth considering. For that the testimony is otherwise not worth considering would follow by the *a priori* argument that its falsehood had got to be a greater miracle than the event—and so more improbable. Here a finite probability is being conceded, at least rhetorically, as you can't have a greater improbability than an impossibility! An argument of such a kind, to show that no testimony can have any weight, must be fallacious if the finite probability is conceded; for the ratio of the probability that the event will be reported *if* it has occurred (near certainty for some events of an extraordinary nature, if publicly occurring) to the probability that, if has *not* occurred, that particular lie should be invented, may be high. It is in this ratio that the consequent odds (odds after testimony) exceed the antecedent odds in favour of the event.

5*

Paganism, Superstition and Philosophy

After some uninteresting speculations about the origins of the Jewish people, Tacitus writes of them as follows:[1]

> Most authors agree that when there was a disfiguring disease in Egypt, King Bocchoris consulted the oracle of Jupiter Ammon to find a remedy and was told to cleanse his kingdom and expel that race of men as hateful to the gods. The people were collected and dumped in the desert; they were sunk in weeping, but one, Moses, advised them to expect no help from gods or men, as they were deserted by both, but with a guide in the sky should trust him, by whose first help they had got rid of the miseries they were then suffering. They agreed and went forward in ignorance and randomly. Nothing troubled them so much as lack of water and they collapsed all over the plain near dead, when a herd of wild asses went from their pasture to a shadowy rock in a grove. Moses followed them and, going by there being grass, found a good supply of water; this relieved them. After six days they founded a city and temple in a place from which they drove out the farmers.[2]

* The Gildersleve Lecture delivered at Barnard College, February 1984. First published in *The Thoreau Quarterly* 17 (1985), pp. 20–31.

[1] *Histories*, Book V.

[2] Plurimi auctores consentiunt, orta per Aegyptum tabe quae corpora foedaret, regem Bocchorim adito Hammonis oraculo remedium petentem purgare regnum et id genus hominum ut invisum deis alias in terras avehere iussum. Sic conquisitum collectumque volgus, postquam vastis locis relictum sit, ceteris per lacrimas torpentibus, Moysen unum exsulum monuisse ne quam deorum hominumve opem exspectarent utrisque deserti, sed sibimet, duce caelesti, crederent, primo cuius auxilio presentes miserias pepulissent. Adsensere atque omnium ignari fortuitum iter incipiunt. Sed nihil aeque quam inopia aquae fatigabat. Iamque haud procul exitio totis campis procubuerant, cum grex asinorum agrestium e pastu in rupem nemore opacam concessit. Secutus Moyses coniectura herbidi soli largas aquarum venas aperit. Id levamen; et continuum sex dierum iter emensi, septimo pulsis cultoribus obtinuere terras in quis urbs et templum dicata.

Moses, wanting to establish the people for himself for the future, gave them religious rites which were new and contrary to the rest of mankind. Everything sacred to us is profane to them; by contrast they allow what we see as incest. They consecrated the image of a donkey in their inmost shrine, that being the animal that had saved them from wandering and thirst. They kill the ram, as if to insult Jupiter Ammon. They also sacrifice the ox, because the Egyptians worship Apis. They abstain from pork because of the disease they had once got from swine which are liable to it. They bear witness to their former long hunger by many fasts, and have unleavened bread to recall their snatching at grain. They are supposed to rest on every seventh day because that ended their struggles, and, tempted by idleness, they give up every seventh year to inactivity.[3]

These practices, however introduced, have antiquity in their favour. Their other customs are sinister, validated by their filthiness. For all the worst of mankind, despising their own ancestral religious ways, came and brought their tributes and presents and so the Jews' wealth increased. Among themselves they are firmly faithful, ready with compassion, but everyone else they hate as enemies. They eat and sleep away from everyone else, and don't associate with alien women though they are extremely lustful; among themselves nothing is illicit. They instituted circumcision of the genitals so as to be recognised by their difference. Their converts do it too, and the first thing they learn is to despise the gods, to shuck off their fatherland, to count parents, children and brethren cheap. However care is taken for the increase of the people. For it is a crime to kill their kind, and they think the souls of those who die in battle or torture are eternal. Hence their love of propagation and contempt for death. They follow the Egyptians in burying bodies rather than burning them, and take the same

---

[3] Moyses quo sibi in posterum gentem firmaret, novos ritus contrariosque ceteris mortalibus indidit. Profana illic omnia quae apud nos sacra; rursum concessa apud illos quae nobis incesta. Effigiem animalis quo monstrante errorem sitimque depulerant, penetrali sacravere, caeso ariete velut in contumeliam Hammonis. Bos quoque immolatur, quoniam Aegyptii Apin colunt. Sue abstinent memoria cladis quod ipsos scabies quondam turpaverat, cui id animal obnoxium. Longam olim famem crebris adhuc ieiuniis fatentur; et raptarum frugum argumentum panis Iudaicus nullo fermento detinetur. Septimo die otium placuisse ferunt, quia is finem laborum tulerit; dein blandiente inertia septimum quoque annum ignaviae datum.

> care about it, with the same belief about the infernal regions; but they differ about the heavenly.[4]
>
> The Egyptians venerate several animals, and multiform effigies; the Jews by their mind alone think of only one divinity; they count profane whoever make images of gods out of mortal materials in the likeness of men: that one is supreme and eternal, neither representable nor perishable. Therefore no images are set up in their cities, let alone in their temples. That flattery is not paid to kings, nor honour to the Caesars. Because their priests used to chant with flutes and cymbals and wore garlands of ivy, and a golden vine was found in the temple, some have thought they worshipped Father Liber, the conqueror of the East; but their customs are not consonant with this at all. Liber established festive and jolly rites, but the custom of the Jews is absurd and sordid.[5]

Historians! Take it to heart that a great historian wrote so. His account has a few vestiges of truth in it. Mostly it is absurd. Where it is a reflection of what happened, it is a distorted one. So, whatever your field or your period, take it to heart—as I take it to heart when I read in Alan Turing mention of the fact (a non-fact) that Muslims believe that women 'have no souls'.

Tacitus is a talented and sophisticated writer of history. He is about to tell of the war of Titus, and, as he calls it, the death of a famous city—Jerusalem. His account of the Jews is absurd. But it is a

---

[4] Hi ritus, quoquo modo inducti, antiquitate defenduntur. Cetera instituta sinistra foeda pravitate valuere. Nam pessimus quisque spretis religionibus patriis tributa et stipes illuc congerebant; unde auctae Iudaeorum res, et quia apud ipsos fides obstinata, misericordia in promptu, sed adversus omnes alios hostile odium. Separati epulis, discreti cubilibus, proiectissima ad libidinem gens, alienarum concubit abstinent; inter se nihil inlicitum. Circumcidere genitalia instituerunt, ut diversitate noscantur. Transgressi in morem eorum idem usurpant, nec quidquam prius inbuuntur quam contemnere deos, exuere patriam, parentes liberos fratres vilia habere. Augendae tamen multitudini consulitur. Nam et necare quemquam ex agnatis nefas, animosque praelio aut suppliciis peremptorum eternos putant. Hinc generandi amor et moriendi contemptus. Corpora condere quam cremare, e more Aegyptio; eademque cura et de infernis persuasio, caelestium contra.

[5] Aegyptii pleraque animalia effigiesque compositas venerantur; Iudaei mente sola unumque numen intellegunt: profanos qui deum imagines mortalibus materiis in species hominum effingant; summum illud et aeternum neque imitabile neque interiturum. Igitur nulla simulacra urbibus suis, nedum templis sistunt. Non regibus haec adulatio, non Ceasaribus honor. Sed quia sacerdotes eorum tibia tympanisque concinebant, hedera vinciebantur, vitisque aurea templo reperta, Liberum patrem coli, domitorem Orientis quidam arbitrati sunt, nequaquam congruentibus institutis. Quippe Liber festos laetosque ritus posuit, Iudeorum mos absurdus sordidusque.

true account of something else. He was a thoroughly civilised pagan. Unknowingly, he gives us a true picture of paganism's hatred of the true religion.

What is paganism? It is having various gods, often quite a lot. It can acknowledge all the gods of others—but not the god of this one people. Sometimes it acts or reacts with the thought that various things might be gods. Two natives of Papua New Guinea were crossing the island forty years ago in difficulty and hunger. They saw a little crocodile in a grove and thought of catching and eating it. The one who lived to tell the tale refused to do this, in case the crocodile was a god.

Tacitus' paganism was not such that he would have told such a story of himself. It was the paganism of a great part of the civilised world. I once heard a farmer in England speaking contemptuously of a thievish gypsy family which had settled down in a village near him. 'Instead of doing the same as everyone else they act so and so' he said. The same note is struck by Tacitus: Moses invented novel rites, contrary to what everyone else does. The explanation?—that he wanted to fixate that people on him for the future. They are an absurd and disgusting people, allowing what the Romans counted as impious and incestuous (this last may have reference to a man's being supposed to raise up seed for his dead brother)—and counting as profane things others held as sacred. All the worst people, who despise their own traditions, run off to join them and increase their wealth. (The Jews annoyed by receiving runaway slaves from other nations.) They cut themselves off from everyone in bed and at board, but are frightfully lustful and allow just anything in their group or with their own. They despise the gods, won't have statues - though, by the way, they have one of a donkey in their inmost shrine. They go in for a purely mental conception of just one divinity —*numen*—which can't be represented in a picture, is eternal, and won't perish—instead of having gods' images in the likeness of men or of more composite beings, like the Egyptians. *Their* customs can't have anything to do with cheerful and festive ceremonies, their customs are gloomy, ludicrous and sordid—like circumcision, for example, which they do in order to be *recognisably* different.

This account of how objectionable a people the Jews were turns strongly on the unlikeness of their ways to everyone else's. The idea that it is of importance to be and to do roughly like everyone else, especially in matters concerning the gods, we find also in Socrates' *Apology*. Socrates asks his accuser Meletus why one of the charges against him is that he doesn't believe in the gods of the city but in new deities of his own. The latter indeed Meletus does not seem to maintain, and no other accuser makes an appearance in the *Apology*. 'Do you say' asks Socrates, 'that I believe in no gods?' 'Yes'. 'You surprise me' says Socrates. 'Are you suggesting that I don't believe the sun and the moons are gods, like everyone else?' Meletus says yes, Socrates thinks the sun is a stone and the moon a mass of earth, and Socrates mocks and upbraids him for confusing him, Socrates, with Anaxagoras: Socrates wants it to be understood that he *is* 'like everyone else' in this matter, he doesn't think like Anaxagoras, he does believe the sun and moon are gods.*

In paganism, different tribes, nations and cities may have different gods, sometimes a bit different in spite of basically belonging to the same culture, and though cross-identification is often possible; sometimes different by a quite big difference, as the Egyptian gods were unlike the Greek and Roman ones. What then is the complaint against the Jews? Clearly, that they do not worship the gods. They positively despise the gods. Their singularity is so great that it has to be put into their history that Moses persuaded them to abandon hope of any help from the gods, by whom they were manifestly deserted, and so on purpose to insult Jupiter Ammon they sacrificed rams—for he was represented as a ram; and likewise they sacrificed oxen because the Egyptians worshipped an ox; and they taught their converts loathing and contempt for all the gods. To the elder Pliny they were known as a people distinguished by their insults to divinities; *gens contumelia numinum insignis*.

None of this part of the account is a misrepresentation. The prophet Ezekiel calls the gods of the Gentiles shit or turds, though it is usually translated more prettily as 'filth'. Elsewhere we read the sentence 'Of the abominations of the Gentiles we sacrifice to the Lord our God'. The point is that they called the gods of the Gentiles 'abominations'. These included rams and oxen, for example, which were sometimes worshipped by the Gentiles. So they were saying: what the Gentiles worship we sacrifice to God.

Tacitus' Latin does make it sound as if he was a bit impressed by the idea of 'that supreme and eternal, neither representable nor perishable': *summum illud et aeternum neque imitabile neque interiturum*; that single divinity, grasped only by the mind: *unum numen, mente sola intellegunt*. But if he was at all impressed, it was only faintly. This

* Plato, *Apology* 26c-e.

is still part of being wilfully unlike everyone else: just one incomprehensible divinity, an object of thought alone, no images, no decorations, none of the customary honours to Kings or Caesar even. No festive splendidness, no jollity.

This 'not like everyone else' comprises in 'like everyone else' the whole world where many gods were worshipped with many handsome rituals. One nation doesn't have to have the same gods as another; you may think your tribe's gods are better than the next tribe's, and so feel superior to those neighbours. Still, other people's deities are gods. It might be 'unRoman' to introduce the cult of Bacchus or Mithras. The objection was a sort of respectable conservatism. But it would soon pass away. You wouldn't think that the gods of other nations were not gods; at the least, they had their gods and you had yours. The Romans objected, we are told, to Druidism as involving a frightful enormity, a '*dira immanitas*', because of their practice of human sacrifice, which the Romans only engaged in on rare and desperate occasions. Some Roman author comments sarcastically that the Egyptians worship figures composite of man and beast which would appal us as monstrosities if born of women. No doubt some worships of other nations, also parts of the Roman empire, did not spread into Rome. But upon the whole this marks paganism: it is assimilative. It will at least acknowledge divinities of other nations, and will quite likely swallow them up, take them on board.

Why, then, was it a charge against Socrates that he invented new deities? Well, it was only part of the accusations against him. They included not believing in the old ones. The nation or city must keep its old deities, even if new ones are added. The 'new deity' charge doesn't seem to have been important, or to have been meant at all by Meletus, the only accuser who personally appears in the *Apology*.

Socrates, as I have reminded us, insisted that he was just like everyone else in acknowledging the gods. Tacitus shows us that the ancient Jews earned the hatred of the pagans precisely by not being like everyone else: by not acknowledging but rather spurning and despising the gods and the worship of other nations. The hatred of them was not racist, it was religious.

In our day, paganism, as I have defined it, does still exist. It exists somewhat on the retreat between the encroachments of Islam and of Christianity, in Africa. Kwame Nkrumah of Ghana was reported to have poured libations to their old gods. Pouring libations is not familiar to us, even in a shadowy form, but is anciently found as a sacrificial action in the cultus of the divinities. In India full-fledged paganism is ancient, rampant and pervasive; the sacredness of the cow for example is written into their constitution. I will make two observations about the religion, which is Hinduism. One, that I know it is various: though there are hardly any temples of Brahma the Creator, perhaps he has his worshippers. There are also pious Hindus who are described as monotheistical by sympathetic outsiders. But this monotheism goes, *not* with hostility and disfavour towards that worship of many gods and their divinised images which is the major characteristic of Hinduism, but with a tolerance of such religion of the simple, who are not elevated in mind or instructed enough to have passed beyond it. Nor, from my reading, have I the impression that the high minded Brahminical pundit will not have images of gods in his house, made sometimes for the occasion of a festivity out of some soluble material and hosed away when the festivity is over. I have observed the rather human-faced head (trunk and all) of the elephant-headed god Ganesha in the form of a ceramic hanging on the wall of a bank in Bombay: not itself of course a divinity, but only a picture of one, a pious object. Someone is advised that it is quite good to have a favourite deity and to concentrate her devotion on that deity, but is warned against failing to acknowledge the other deities. And a tale is recorded of someone with an exclusive devotion to Shiva, who was warned by Shiva appearing to him that he should also make gifts and pay honours to the other gods. He neglected this in spite of repeated warnings, and then Shiva appeared to him, one half recognisable as Shiva, and the other half as Vishnu, but he placed his offering only on the Shiva-like side. At this Shiva gave up; though whether that just means that he never more appeared to his votary, I do not know. Jesus the Hindus would readily count as an avatar, one among many.

The many deities are occasionally spoken of as all aspects or significations of the one, the invisible. As some speak, it is that which is really one's inmost self, (though it is intense labour to realise this): 'I am in every religion, as a thread through a string of pearls' – this I have seen as a quotation from *Bagavadgita*, though I have not tracked it down here.

Here I come to my second observation. Considering the large amount of spiritual literature connected with Hinduism, and recalling that the ancient Egyptians had their Book of the Dead, and evidently much that is lost; and remembering the laments for the loss of spiritual religion in the Hermes Trismegistos (a lament because of

Egypt's conversion to Christianity, evidently a sort of atheism) I am surprised at the lack of anything comparable in Greek or Roman paganism: Aristotle, remarking that Platonic forms are nothing but such objects as we have here below, being merely imperishable versions of them, adds contemptuously that this is like the way that the gods are just immortal human beings.

He, Aristotle, had a different conception of deity, much like that of Anaxagoras. Anaxagoras himself was convicted of impiety in Athens for what he said about the moon, which unlike Socrates he did not regard as a god. When sentenced he said to the jurors, 'Sirs, you and I were all condemned to death a long time ago'. He left Athens before he could be executed. Aristotle in turn left the city at the threat of prosecution on the same charge of impiety. Anaxagoras went on to Lampsacus, and when he was dying they asked what to do in his memory. 'Make a school holiday for the children' he said, and so it was done. They also erected an altar to *nous kai aletheia*, mind and truth, because they had gathered that these were his gods (or that this was his god).

Now for my question: was reflection on the divine *only* done by philosophers? Or should we see Homer and Hesiod as the holy books of the Greeks? Or is there a lost literature connected with the Mysteries? Have we perhaps a somewhat false picture of Greek and Roman paganism? When St. Paul addressed the Athenians he remarked on having seen an altar's dedication to an unknown god – '*agnosto theo*'. It would be surprising if he didn't understand such a dedication: receiving a benefit, someone could not think of any particular god to attribute it to – so lest he be apparently ungrateful, he dedicated an altar to the unknown god who had done him this kindness. St. Paul said he would tell them who this unknown god was. Here, I use the example to infer that devotion and thanksgiving of a quite personal nature must have been part of the religion. We never hear anything about that, or hardly. But Socrates' last words were about the cock he owed to Aesculapius.

Tacitus calls the new Christian religion 'superstition', and one would expect that the Romans would tend to reckon the ancient Hebrew religion such too; but I have no quotation that comes to mind, except the saying '*Credat Judaeus Apella*', equivalent to the English 'Tell that to the Marines', and evidently expressing contempt for Jewish credulity. Paganism is practice rather than belief, and the absurdity of the pagan legends would therefore seldom be of significance against paganism for pagans. But the Jews were marked by belief and so they were thought of as credulous. In one application 'superstition' is a term of abuse for a religion deemed false by the speaker, and calling this religion 'superstition' would be an expression of condemnation as false, in a culture where the acceptable religions were not regarded as true, but simply as the normal human practices. So the term 'superstition' would naturally be applicable only to a religion which was strongly marked by beliefs and also was exclusive, separating its adherents from the rest of mankind.

Christians at a much later date called Islam superstition and paganism superstition and rabbinical (i.e. post-Christian) Judaism superstition. Protestants called Catholic Christianity superstition, and also Russian Orthodoxy, if they travelled in Russia and observed what it was like. Catholics did not return the compliment to Protestants, speaking rather of the many Protestant heresies, and similarly for the other many and various heresies that sprang up in the history of the Christian Church. To those who think they have no religion at all, in the U.S.A. for example, it is a frequent fixed opinion that everything they identify as religion is *eo ipso* superstition. Thus, this old usage survives to a certain degree. On the other hand there is something else which very many people of different religions would agree in calling 'superstition': things like the use of charms, reading tea leaves, the I Ching, thinking it unlucky to have a rowan tree in your garden, thinking that if you break a looking-glass you must throw salt over your shoulder to avert bad luck, thinking certain numbers are unlucky, or the sight of a black cat lucky. About such things people will sometimes say: 'I'm afraid I *am* superstitious', and here it is tempting to make Wittgenstein's remark: 'Don't be proud of *seeming* a fool, you may be one'.

There are sometimes bridges between the two uses of the word 'superstition': fortune-telling may be associated with someone's practising as a witch (i.e. a medium) and that with the religion called 'spiritualism'. Medals and relics probably strike Protestants as like magic charms and so might be pointed at to justify calling the Catholic religion 'superstition'. The Hindu idea that if you sacrifice a hundred perfect stallions in a perfect way on a hundred successive days you will guarantee living for 1,000 years seems to be superstitious in both senses. I once asked Wittgenstein what he understood by 'superstition'. He said that he imagined he meant the same as I did. I thought it was not in the 'false-religion' sense that he was thinking of it, but the other one; he wasn't offering a definition, but would call the same things superstition as I would. That he did not intend it in the 'false-religion' sense (in which neither am I accustomed to use the word) looks likely from his hostility to the 'science has shown us that this is a mistake' attitude about such things as poison oracles and other magical practices. Speaking of such matters I once asked him whether, if he had a friend, an African whose plan or possibility after being in England for a bit, was to go back home and take a training and then practise as a witch doctor, whether he, Wittgenstein, would want to stop him from doing this. We walked in silence for a space and then he said: 'I would, but I don't know why'. We talked of it no more. I incline to think that a vestige of the true religion spoke in him then; for that religion, whether in its ancient Hebrew or its Christian phase, has always said 'No' to such things.

And now I come to philosophy; more particularly to a certain current in philosophy which has a strong historical connection with Wittgenstein. Wittgenstein himself wrote something in one of his many notebooks denying that – or raising the question whether – it would matter for the Christian religion whether Christ did any of the things recorded of him, or indeed existed at all. He reproved a Jain friend for speaking somewhat contemptuously of the Jain beliefs about the journeyings of the soul after death. He said on other occasions that if someone came to him with religious doubts he would probably raise doubts about the doubts.

Now I can't speak for Wittgenstein, I only report one or two things here from his tongue or pen. But there is an attitude or fairly characteristic strain of thought in some of his followers which seems like a partial reflection of some of what I have quoted, though as I will formulate it I don't mostly claim that anyone has definitely spoken so.

1. There is no such thing as a religion's being true. This is feebly indicated by saying: 'this (religious) proposition (whatever it may be) isn't like a proposition of natural science'.

2. Religious belief is better compared to somebody's being in love than to his believing anything true or false.

3. Someone who has been taught to pray finds out that you have to be completely honest for your utterance to count as prayer. He finds it out by being confronted with a personal problem.

4. So far as *realisation* and *understanding* are concerned, what is in question is an attitude which one man may have and another lack – an attitude towards punishment, for example. *One* regards punishment as a regrettable affliction which he wishes he could have avoided in spite of having done what earned it; another

regards it *as* punishment, which means he takes up a quite different attitude to what he has to suffer, and thinks that he *ought* to suffer it.

5. There is in some cases a running of one's head against the walls of language — a *misuse* of words as far as concerns any sense that can be put on them. (Here I am using Wittgenstein's own words.) 'Nothing that anyone does can harm me' is given as an example of such thought — because in some inexpressible way nothing that might happen to me at anyone's hands would *count* as harm. Why? There isn't a reason. Or again: 'God will not suffer you to be tempted beyond your strength'.* That sounds as if you could be confident, that, though there were things that would break you, God won't allow them to happen. And so I would take it, but I would be called wrong: for — I would be told — it isn't a negative prediction that things of a certain effect won't happen. As that, it might be false. But if you mean it religiously you possess it in a way that is immune to the idea of refuting examples. Now suppose you said 'My bank account can never be overdrawn'. We'd want to know why you think that. Has some Arab oil sheik given orders that your account is to be replenished whenever an overdraft threatens? No, nothing like that. Have you some insane conviction about your bank account? No - but (on the model of 'Nothing can harm me', or 'I won't be tempted beyond my strength') you have given expression to something that 'runs up against the limits of language'. About a bank account, that sounds and is ludicrous; Wittgenstein's own example[6] was about feeling oneself to be absolutely safe.

I hope I have said enough to indicate the sort of thinking I am talking about. Now it seems to me that it is very closely connected with a conclusion that in any sense in which a religion can be 'true', which is a pretty odd sense, *any* religion is or can be true. It all depends *who* has it and *how* he has it. He may be shallow, even though enthusiastic and argumentative; and then he is missing the boat all the time. He contrasts totally with someone else, who has depth — in character, in attitudes, in his meditations and reflections and reactions to other people and to what happens — and this man has not missed the boat. To alter the analogy a little, he is on some boat of the kind in question. As for the shape and fitment of the boat, they can be of any kind, if we are speaking in generalities.

* 1 *Corinthians* 10.13.

[6] In his 'Lecture on Ethics', published in *The Philosophical Review* 74 (1965), p. 3–12.

The view that I have drawn out as such a conclusion is in one way a very common one. In this way it does not aspire to any heights, or pretend to any depth. 'All religions are the same really: they are a lot of different paths to the same end', or 'a lot of different ways of having to do with God', or with what is spiritual. One hears or reads this rather often; more often as journalism than anything else. Upon the whole I judge it thoughtless. It makes me want to interject: '*nice* religions, you mean, don't you?' But it is not much good making such an exclamation because so little thought has been expressed.

The philosophic form which I have described does by contrast have a fair amount of thought in it. My purpose has been to point to it as an expression of what I showed as the heart of actual historical and present paganism: namely having and respecting the various worships of many gods and hating the exclusiveness of the true religion. That exclusiveness branded the ancient Jews as atheists, enemies of the gods. For our philosophic pagans there is no such thing as the true religion or the true god; the many religions can perhaps be like many pearls on a string. That one string which each religion may be hung on, is something rich and significant in the depths of the self. All peoples have gods and it is contemptible to be scornful of them for this: what matters is whether there is this depth (of religion) in a man's heart.

But the question is: Why? Why should it matter?

6*

On the Hatred of God

Long since you destroyed my yoke and broke my chains and said: I will not serve.

— *Words from the prophecy of Jeremiah.*

The great philosopher Spinoza denied that God could be hated by men. He relied on false arguments. For he thinks that the idea of God that exists in the human mind is always perfect and adequate. Certainly if we were to mount to an insight into the divine nature itself, we would necessarily love God as the supreme good and source of all goodness, but at present we see through a glass darkly, as the Apostle says, and we only know God by his works in this world. Of these his effects, some are intrinsically lovable and delightful, nor can God be hated on account of them; but to human nature corrupted by sin the divine law repressing vices seems intolerable, and much more the punishments which are to be inflicted on us for our offences. On account of such effects, as is said by the Angelic Doctor, God is hated by some, inasmuch as he is apprehended by them as forbidder of sins and inflicter of punishments.

From such hatred of God some have fallen into open atheism: they do not want God to exist, hence they do not acknowledge God. For nearly two hundred years now philosophers have been entangling themselves in involved arguments that they may believe there cannot be one supreme and infinite divinity: in fact on this account they reject the worship of God as being unworthy of a free spirit; they despise the worshippers of God and mock them as slaves. Yet others publicly profess to love God, but do not any the less hate the true God: as in former times rebels who wished for revolution began by attacking not the king but the king's ministers, so these men praise God, but pour abuse on the saints and prophets. These false wor-

* A translation of a Latin sermon delivered before the University of Oxford and published in *Theology* 79 (1976), pp. 131–2.

shippers of God are easily known by the following sign: they condemn the fear of God; further, they do not know the divine law compelling virtue; they think the divine love towards men consists in men's leading a pleasant life and having the fleshly desires of their hearts satisfied, that virtue is 'to believe in man'; that such a faith is supremely manifested in the life of Christ. Where then is the severity and mercy of God (of which the Apostle speaks)? Severity is held to be a myth; mercy they do not understand; for they think that punishments cannot be justly inflicted, if they can be remitted without injustice. About such there are words from the mouth of the Lord in the prophecy of Ezekiel: 'You are become to them like a musical song, which is sung with a sweet and pleasant sound'. But soon there comes: 'When what was predicted shall have happened (for behold, it is coming) then they will know that there was a prophet among them.'

7*

On Attachment to Things and Obedience to God

Christianity is thoroughly conditioned by original sin. For that reason secular Christians—that is, Christians who reside in the world, having property, pursuing the possibility of a happy life, perhaps marrying—are a pretty suspect sort of Christians. Suppose someone—some religious confectioner—portrays the excellence and innocence of these things in an attempt to maintain that the secular Christian is not after all a second-class Christian in his form of life: no, he is absolutely grade A1 as far as that goes. That is to say: apart from his personal faults—which need not come into consideration because monks and nuns have those too. Such a writer, who portrays the excellence of marriage and of life in the world in this interest, shows he has forgotten all about original sin.

The confusion manifested here is frightful. It is true that we have nothing to do, absolutely nothing, but to keep the commandments in faith and in hope. There is not a lower sort of life, which is keeping the commandments, and a higher sort of life which is going three better than the commandments, a life in which you do not just keep the commandments but do better, you observe the counsels of poverty, chastity and obedience. No: but the truth is that those who do not observe the counsels are less likely to keep the commandments

* Text of an unpublished manuscript which Elizabeth Anscombe sent to Mrs Rosemarie Dolan (wife of the late Professor John Dolan) in December 1965. John and Rosemarie Dolan were close friends of hers. John Dolan sent me [LG] a transcript of the manuscript in July 2005, shortly before his death. It is not clear for whom this paper was originally written, but it is evident from a covering letter that the motive for sending it to Rosemarie Dolan was a desire that she should understand something of what the author considered important in her own thinking.

because they are less likely to be detached from the goods of the world.

Spiritual evil is: to be attached only conditionally, or not at all, to God. This is so for men and for angels. This likeness is why men are said to have a spiritual nature, which otherwise seems not to be so because we are plainly a sort of animal and not a sort of spirit.

Spiritual evil being only conditional attachment to God, detachment from his own will is necessary for the good of a creature with a spiritual nature. For unconditional attachment to God would mean that attachment to any other object was conditional, so attachment to any other object would not be firm; it would be a sort of detachment. But detachment of a will from everything except God would be detachment from itself, because attachment to God is only by obedience. The object of the will would be to obey God because God is highest, and so it would not have a substantive object of its own but would deny itself all objects it might try to possess at least by willing its possession of them to be strictly conditional.

Without detachment from everything but God we will not (as we do not) keep the commandments. Detachment is this: one would renounce a thing, whatever it was, if the choice were between having it and remaining obedient.

Now suppose that there is no *actual* renunciation for the sake of detachment. Then we can form the following fantasy: it is possible that all we secular Christians who have chosen the good of the world can truly say 'I would renounce everything to remain obedient to God'. Not every hypothetical has to be actualised in order to be true. It isn't in doubt whether I would empty my bank account if that would save my child's life. It does not have to *come about* that I do so, in order for me to become a lover of my child's life more than of my bank account. And so … !

But when it comes to detachment from the world, then because of original sin the hypothetical 'If it were necessary I would', without *actual* renunciation, becomes not merely doubtful but certainly false.

That is why secular Christians, who have chosen a form of life that is the opposite of renunciation, are a suspect sort of Christians. And drivel about the infinite self-sacrifice of the mother of a Catholic family is what it looks and tastes like: religious confectionery, whose promotion is proper to a salesman. It is not that detachment is impossible for those who are living in the world and for the married. It is only that the conditions are so inimical that it is unlikely. The actual preference of obedience to God above what one would choose for oneself seems an indispensable condition of it. But do not deceive people. Do not suggest that they are exercising such a preference just because they respond to ordinary demands for self discipline. Any reasonable human being recognizes these demands on him in the ordinary course of life spent in the pursuit of the prospect of happiness for himself and those that he cares about. It does not take divine grace to respond to such demands and the response does not show that one is detached according to the demand that our Lord made.

8*

Twenty Opinions Common among Modern Anglo-American Philosophers

Analytical philosophy is more characterised by styles of argument and investigation than by doctrinal content. It is thus possible for people of widely different beliefs to be practitioners of this sort of philosophy. It ought not to surprise anyone that a seriously believing Catholic Christian should also be an analytical philosopher.

However, there are a number of opinions which are inimical to Christianity which are very often found implicitly or explicitly among analytical philosophers. A seriously believing Christian ought not, in my opinion, to hold any of them. Some analytic philosophers who have no Christian or theistic belief do not hold any of them or hold very few of them. But it is so frequent for at least some set of them to be found in the mind of an analytic philosopher, that it is worthwhile to give as complete a list of them as I can. This may be useful as suggesting warnings to some who have not always realized that certain views are inimical to the Christian religion. It may also be helpful to have these opinions collected together so that they can be surveyed together.

1. A dead man—a human corpse—is a man, not an ex-man.

2. A human being comes to be a person through the development of the characteristics which make something into a person. A human

* Text of a paper delivered at a conference in Rome in April 1986 and published in *Persona, Verità e Morale. Atti del Congresso Internazionale di Teologia Morale (Roma, 7–12 Aprile 1986)* (Rome: Città Nuova Editrice, 1987), pp. 49–50.

being in decay may also cease to be a person without ceasing to be a human being. In short: being a person is something that gets added to a human being who develops properly, and that may disappear in old age or imbecility.

3. We aren't (mere) members of a biological species, but *selves*. The nature of 'the self' is an important philosophical topic.

4. There is no such thing as a natural kind with an essence which is human nature. This opinion is an effect partly of the philosophy of John Locke and partly of confused thoughts about evolution and a theory of natural selection which is accepted as explaining evolution.

5. Ethics is formally independent of the facts of human life and, for example, human physiology.

6. Ethics is 'autonomous' and is to be derived, if from anything, from rationality. Ethical considerations will be the same for any rational being.

7. Imaginary cases, which are not physical possibilities for human beings, are of value in considering moral obligation. Thus it may be imagined that a woman gives birth to a puppy or that 'people-seeds' float about in the air and may settle and grow on our carpets; this will have a bearing on the rightness of abortion.

8. There are no absolute moral prohibitions which are always in force.

9. The study of virtues and vices is not part of ethics.

10. Calling something a virtue or vice is only indicating approval or disapproval of the behaviour that exemplifies it. The behaviour is a fact, the approval or disapproval is evaluation. Evaluation or 'value judgements' are not as such true or false.

11. It is a mistake to think that 'ought' has properly a personal subject, as in 'X ought to visit Y'. It properly governs whole statements, as in 'It ought to be the case that X is visiting Y'.

12. If there is practical reasoning of a moral kind, it must always end in a statement of the necessity of doing such-and-such.

13. It is necessary, if we are moral agents, always to act for the best consequences.

14. There is never any morally significant distinction between act and omission as such. This is shown by producing an example where that difference does not make any difference to the badness of an action.

15. Causation = necessitation, and is universal: so determinism is true.

16. Either there is no such thing as freedom of the human will, or it is compatible with determinism.

17. Past and future are symmetrical. There is no sense in which the past is determined and the future is not determined.

18. A theist believes that God must create the best of all possible worlds.

19. God, if there is any God, is mutable, subject to passions, sometimes disappointed, must be supposed to make the best decisions he can on the basis of the evidence on which he forms his opinions.

20. The laws of nature, if only they can be found out, afford complete explanations of everything that happens.

In saying these opinions are inimical to the Christian religion I am not implying that they can only be judged false on that ground. Each of them is a philosophical error and can be argued to be such on purely philosophical grounds.

9*

The Immortality of the Soul

It seems clear that the immortality of the soul has something to do with its spirituality, so I shall begin by trying to discover what spirituality is. I cannot at present accept the idea that spirituality is soulishness itself, or the character of being a rational soul, for the only well developed argument I know to this position seems unconvincing to me. I mean the argument that thought and understanding are immaterial, since no act of a bodily organ is thinking or understanding, as e.g. an act of a bodily organ is seeing; hence thought and understanding are the acts of an immaterial part, and immateriality is spirituality. Certainly thought and understanding are immaterial – if that means that they are not material, both in the sense that they have no organ, and in the sense that to call something a thought is not to characterise it as a physical event. For example, it would certainly be a case of thinking if I were to take a piece of paper and a pencil and write down a calculation, as I might do now for the sake of illustration, and a purely physical description of this procedure could be given. But that description would not characterise it as thinking or calculating: it would not characterise what I write as a sum. I should argue that this was not because the description omitted to mention certain non-physical occurrences that went on at the same time. Such non-physical occurrences (which might be there) as certain feelings and images, would not of themselves be a sufficient addition to the list of happenings to make them a case of thinking; and if you say 'No, it is not those, but the thinking itself that has been left out of the description', I reply that it has indeed been left out, but not in the sense that it is an additional element existing side by side

* Text of an undated and unpublished typescript of a paper given to the Philosophical Enquiry Group that met at the Dominican Conference Centre at Spode House, Staffordshire. (See Preface.) Probably dating from the late 1950s.

with those others. One way of showing this would be this: the thought is evidently all-important; it is the thought that I mean to convey to you, and do convey to you, if I show you the calculation; but I only show you the bit of paper, perhaps uttering some sounds as I do so; if the thought were an additional secret element, I could not convey it at all, and further it could not matter whether I conveyed it or not. The concept 'thought' is one which everybody has, and of which it is extraordinarily difficult to give an account. I cannot give an account of it, I know; all that I so far understand is that it is not material, in the sense that I have outlined. But that is not to say that it is an act of an immaterial, or spiritual, substance; a parallel set of considerations lead me to judge it a crude mistake to suppose that the number 2 is a material thing, and this I might conceivably express by saying that the number 2 is immaterial, but I should only mean by this the denial that is was material. In that case I should be little tempted to advance from calling it immaterial to calling it a spiritual thing. In the case of the soul, the inclination to make that advance, from non-materiality to spirituality, exists because the soul is spoken of as if it were a substance or part of a substance as the hand is part of a man. If I am told 'not as the hand is part of a man, because that is a material part, whereas the soul is an *immaterial* part' I can only say that I do not understand; of course it is clear to me that it is not a material part, but then I do not understand what it means to call it a *part* at all, at least in a sense that would justify the thought that it could exist separately.

The foregoing is a rough and short indication of the kind of difficulties I feel in arguing from the nature of thought and understanding as such, to the spirituality of the soul. I do not in fact mean that I do not understand if someone speaks of the immaterial or spiritual part, or the thinking part, of a man; I do understand and use such expressions myself. But I understand and use them, either with no particular implications about separability (his thinking part is quite atrophied; spiritual disease; concern with the immaterial part; etc., etc.) or as a formulation, not a justification of certain beliefs.

I may reasonably be asked: when I say that the nature of thought and understanding do not show me the spirituality of the soul, *what* am I saying that they do not show me? I have seemed to imply that spirituality is a nature in virtue of which it is possible that the soul should exist separate from the body—i.e. non-material substantiality. One reason why it is possible to take spirituality to mean this is that presumably it is the nature of *spirits*; now a spirit is a person without a body, i.e. an immaterial person, i.e. an immaterial substance. Therefore if the soul partakes of the nature of spirits, it is an immaterial substance, or at least exists in the manner of one when it is separate. It might seem, then, that if I think that the nature of thought does not show the spirituality of the soul, I believe either that something else shows its immaterial substantiality, or that nothing shows its spirituality. This is not my meaning. I believe that something does show the spirituality of the soul, but that nothing shows its immaterial substantiality: in fact, that the latter conception—the conception of an *immaterial substance* at all—is a delusive one.

Substance is a classification, but whether of things or of concepts is difficult to determine. If you ask what falls into the class of substances an answer is 'eg. men, horses, cabbages, gold, sugar, soap'. That is, you mention things, not concepts or words, so substance might seem to be a classification of things. On the other hand if you were to ask in virtue of what properties these things were substances, as you might ask in virtue of what properties apples and peaches are *fruits*, it would become clear that the two cases were different in kind. One does not establish that these things are substances by noting their properties; the description of their properties is already of the form: description of the properties of substances. I am not saying that it cannot be an empirical question whether such-and-such is a substance; it can for, say, the sky, or rainbows. But these are exceptions. It is not a *well established hypothesis* that gold is a substance, or that (in a manner of speaking less familiar in modern English, but I expect familiar enough here) a man is a substance. It relates to the existence of a special restricted sense for the question 'what?', the answer to which is of great practical importance and of great interest to us. The sense is that in which I ask 'what?' when pointing to an unfamiliar tree or plant or rock or parcel of stuff in a jar. The question 'what?' may be asked in such a way that the questioner has no clear conception of the form the answer may take, and it may then receive as answer the name of a substantial kind; or it may expect such an answer and not get it because there is no such answer to give; or it may be definite in quite another way than that of asking for the name of a substance; still there is this special restricted sense, and substances are those things that are named in answer to this restricted sense of 'what?'. The question relates to a certain sort of knowledge that people have, and which is important. It follows that the term 'substance', which serves a very useful purpose here, is out of place where that kind of knowledge is not and cannot be in question. To put it very briefly, a natural object of human knowledge is the τί ἐστι (*quod quid est*) of material things: or rather, τί ἐστι itself expresses the *form* of one of the most important parts of our natural knowledge. But I do not wish to say: and therefore the τί ἐστι (*quod quid est*) of immaterial things is beyond our ken, for although that sounds modest, it in fact unconsciously prejudges the matter. It is as if I were to say: it is only the square roots of *numbers* that *we* are able to calculate; the square roots of metals are not for us; perhaps the angels know them.

This is why I call 'immaterial substance' a delusive conception. The idea of substance, and the ramifications of properties of substance (in an indefinitely wide sense), as constituting reality itself, is so very strongly rooted in us that if I simply said that, I should be taken by most people with any familiarity with the term, whether they thought they agreed with me or not, to be *denying the existence* of spirits. I hope it is clear that I am not. But the reasons why the rejection of an idea of immaterial substance sounds like an expression of disbelief in spirits are worth considering.

It is not simply that the surface grammar of language gives us substantive words for spirits; for it gives us substantive words in hundreds of cases where we are not under any temptation to speak of substances. I suppose for example that no one has ever felt the least inclination to think that the alphabet was a substance. But here, and in most of the cases where no such inclination is likely, the direction of an answer to the question 'what?' is roughly clear; it is clear that it lies in a description of the procedures in connexion with which we speak of the alphabet and not in that of a description of a *nature*. An exception to this generalization is *number*; no one thinks of numbers as *substances*, but they have been thought of as *objects*, by Frege, for example; now if one were to say 'If objects, are they substances or accidents?' the question would appear inappropriate.

The reasons for the special temptation in regard to spirits are, I suggest, (a) that as spirits are persons without bodies it is natural to apply to them many of the conceptions that we use in connexion with persons, and hence also the *logical* conceptions, and hence that of substance; (b) the ambiguity and extreme indefiniteness of the question 'what?' and the notion of 'something'. It is clear that you can ask 'what?' about anything, and that you may be extremely vague about what sort of answer you expect; the answer you are in fact given may help to determine the sense of the question in your mind. E.g. someone who asks what dreaming is may have no idea whether he wants a physiological or psychological answer; and also he might conceivably have an idea that as 'to dream' is—i.e. seems to work like—a word signifying an operation of a psychical subject, a proper answer would take the form of an account of such an operation; though he has only the vaguest notion of what such an account would be like. I suggest that there is an analogy in this to the conception of a spirit as an immaterial substance. Now to answer 'nothing', to the question 'what?', is to claim that the term about which 'what is it?' is being asked is false or delusive; and if you reject as false and delusive some preconception as to a possible form of answer then just because that preconception existed it sounds as if you were saying that the term itself was a mistaken, delusive one. Compare Plato: 'The soul is something, isn't it?' It could not be replied: 'no'; for that would mean that anyone who said anything about souls was talking nonsense, which is evidently false; but when one has said the 'yes' that is forced by this consideration one has really said very little. In just the same way one would have to say 'yes' to 'numbers are something', 'the alphabet is something' and a host of other things. Thus if someone says to me 'You must at any rate hold that spirits are something' I reply 'Certainly, but that is not to say as much as you, perhaps, imagine if you think of it as determining that a certain philosophical position must be maintained'. (It is of course to say a good deal, if my interlocutor does not believe in spirits and says, 'You really believe that there are such things?')

To say that we have no more business to formulate the idea of a τί ἐστι than that of a square-root, for a spirit, *sounds* like saying: there is not anything that a spirit is; and if so, a spirit is nothing. But this is because of the slip from 'what it is' when this corresponds to that important range of knowledge that we exemplify every time that we knowledgeably use the names of substances to a 'what it is' corresponding to some other part of knowledge. (There are indefinitely many parts. Consider how, and in how many senses we know 'what it is' of e.g. a procession, or an emotion, or a coefficient of expansion; and how curious it is that this one formula covers so many different kinds of knowledge.)

These are the reasons why I reject the very conception 'immaterial substance' without meaning by that that I disbelieve in spirits. They are reasons for saying 'Stop it' to someone who is beginning to construct a certain sort of intellectual scheme. The relevance to the immortality of the soul is simply that a whole way of considering it is in this way closed to me.

I put it forward that the spirituality of the human soul is its capacity to get a conception of the eternal, and to be concerned with the eternal as an objective, and perhaps also as something that can be leant on and feared. I do not say 'God' because the thing is clear independently of people's believing in God; it is clear for example in the existence of such an idea as Nirvana. What shows this capacity is the religions, and ethics, and in some way (which I will not go into) art; but they do not show it as circuses show the acrobatic possibilities of the human body, but rather as the existence of arithmetical studies shows the arithmetical capacities of the human mind. I mean that you can see what an acrobat can do without exercising a similar capacity yourself, but you cannot see what someone who does arithmetic can do without the exercise of arithmetical ability. If you were determined to describe arithmetical activity without exercising any arithmetical capacity in doing so, every step would appear arbitrary in the sense of pointless, though not arbitrary in the sense that the steps would appear not chosen but compulsive (as we speak of neurotic compulsions). Similarly if religious and moral life is described irreligiously and unethically everything appears pointless and compulsive. There is a middle course which is sometimes taken with regard to religion and sometimes too with regard to ethics, namely that of reacting to them as to poetic qualifications—e.g. of being affected by them as by a purge as Aristotle describes it in the *Politics** —which may come more or less close to seeming to acknowledge the spirituality of the soul. The reason for this I take to be that poetry is itself inspired. But the inappropriateness appears as soon as it is made explicit; there is so evident a contrast between the relations: poet and enjoyer of the product of a poet; and: believer, or agent, and poetically affected observer. When the contrast is seen it appears that someone who reacts to religiousness or ethics as poetic qualifications is like someone who thought he was watching a play when some real action was going on. If he realises this, shame may prevent him from writing off what he has been observing, as, say, all superstitious stupidity; but it is easy to fall back upon being what in German is called *pathetisch* about it—a word difficult to translate, but in this context the nearest equivalent is perhaps 'sentimental'.

* See, for instance, *Politics* 1342a4-16 on the effects of music.

I have mentioned this because there is a good deal of what looks like a vague acknowledgement of *something* that might go by the title 'spirituality of the soul' which is not accompanied by any acknowledgement of the eternal. Besides this, there is something else which can sometimes be noticed, not in conjunction with being poetically affected by e.g. the idea of God in other people or in writings; but in conjunction with a vague dumb reaction of respect towards it—namely a dislike of blasphemy against something deep and serious in human beings. This latter reaction might be the beginning of an acknowledgement of spirituality.

(To avoid misunderstanding I ought perhaps to say that I don't regard the possibility [or actuality] of great heroism [say in exploring, or in making scientific discoveries], or of self-sacrifice for the natural good of other people, as marks of spirituality; nor yet again any capacity to do or bear a great deal, however remarkable or noble this may be.)

I have said that spirituality does not seem to me to be demonstrated by capacity to think, reason, and understand as such. A corollary to this would be that it does not seem impossible for there to be rational—i.e. language-using—beings, who were *not* spiritual. Such beings would not be able to understand the locutions of natural religion. In thinking of God, for example, the word 'makes' is used in a way that is reminiscent of a cook making a dish or a sculptor a statue, and yet in a new sense, which is shown by our saying 'God made the world *out of nothing*'; as 'I did the sum *in my head*' is like 'I did the sum' and yet introduces a new sense of 'doing the sum'. If God had been supposed to make the world out of something, like a cook making a dish of ingredients, the common suggestion that we should look for traces of such an event, in order to prove that there is a God, would be reasonable. The argument might be: the ingredients could not have got into the state of being a world without someone's doing the mixing (cf. Plato's *Philebus*) and then it could reasonably be asked how we know that certain ingredients got into the state of being a world. But as soon as 'out of nothing' is introduced we are using 'makes' in a new way, which paralyses critical questions based on the implications of the former way: but the fact that it is a new way is not itself a criticism; it would not be possible to erect a principle of never using words in a new way without paralysing language. Imagine that someone said 'I touched him with no part of me''. As things are, in our language, that is equivalent to saying 'I did not touch him'. So far as I know no one has ever suggested that in a parallel way 'God made the world out of nothing' is equivalent to 'God did not make the world'. People who heard it like that would have the right to say that they could make nothing at all of the teaching that God made the world out of nothing; because it evidently could only mean that God did not make the world, but then he was constantly spoken of as the maker of the world. Why should it not be that some people could never get the hang of *certain* new locutions, although nothing requisite to getting the hang of them seemed to be lacking? Meaning-blindness about certain new locutions (transposed expressions) might be characteristic of certain races. For that reason I cannot determine that rational beings must be capable of grasping the idea of God. Nevertheless such meaning-blindness as I am imagining does not occur as far as I know. (It has nothing to do with the *professions* of non-comprehension that one sometimes hears.)

Now let me imagine someone who, e.g., believed in God, and believed in the soul's spirituality, but disbelieved in immortality entirely. Perhaps there are many possibilities, but what I imagine for him is this: following Schopenhauer,* he says: 'The fear of death is the fear of losing the present (the fear that there will be a present without me); but that is just as if people were afraid of slipping down the sides of the planet; the top is wherever they are, so they can't fall off the top. So the present is where I am, and there can be no such thing as losing it'. Therefore—he goes on—even if I *did* live on for ever, that would not correspond to the spirituality of the soul; and if you say there is something about this endless life that does so correspond, then I reply that if that something can supervene upon an endless life, it can equally well supervene upon a terminating life. Why should heaven or hell—eternity—be compared to a very, very—an endlessly—long time, rather than to a moment? And why should not the moment which corresponds to eternity occur in *this* life? It is only childish minds which have to be threatened with a hell of endless temporal duration, because if you threatened them with hell in a moment they would, by childish misunderstanding, say: 'At least it will soon be over'

I am inclined to reply to this by asking: 'Could anyone say 'I have lived through that moment'?' If so, then the position seems senseless.

* See Arthur Schopenhauer, *The World as Will and Idea*, translated by R B Haldane and J Kemp, Volume 1 (London: Trübner & Co, 1883), especially pp. 361ff.

But if not—either because the moment is supposed to be the moment of death, or because even though the person is not physically dead, he has no more life that means anything—the simplest picture is of some sort of madness—then I do not see that there is any answer outside the authority of revealed religion. Except for one thing: it is difficult to believe that the consequences of the interior life are so exclusively interior. The interior life that is less than heavenly or hellish has outward expression; no outward sign but what would be the expression of hellish interior life, if it were the expression of anything eternal, can be imagined in this life, in which there is no manifestation of glory coming from human beings except in products of art (but these are not the expressions of glorious interior life). Then the hellish moment is perhaps credible but not the heavenly. The only things to be the manifestation of the moment corresponding to eternity would be the circumstances of this life, and these, if they are the outward sign of such a moment at all, *can* only be those of the hellish moment. This is no proof of immortality, but a proof that if there is not immortality, there is no good eternity. This seems to fit in with St. Paul: 'If Christ did not rise, then the dead do not rise; you are still in your sins, and those who have fallen asleep in Christ have perished'.*

In these surroundings, I can take for granted belief in the resurrection, unless anyone is doubtful whether to remain a Catholic or has simply hardly had his attention directed to this part of the creed. What I cannot take for granted, but should maintain myself, is the following: there is no reason whatever for believing in a temporal immortality of the soul apart from the resurrection; above all, there is no 'natural immortality of the soul' that can be demonstrated by philosophy. (I am not sure how far philosophy is competent to attack a belief in the temporal immortality of the soul, without the body, if some *religion* teaches it.) I take the Christian doctrine of immortality to be the doctrine of an unending human life, happy or unhappy, after the resurrection, and not the doctrine of an immortal sort of substance, the soul, to which is appended the doctrine of the resurrection because a disembodied soul is not a complete man; though I know that in apologetics the matter is often presented like that.

But it is also Christian doctrine that the soul is judged at death and then suffers or is in glory till the resurrection. Must one not have a theory of how it can exist? I reply to this that no one can be obliged to

* 1 *Corinthians* 15.16–18.

have any theories at all; but one may feel irresistibly impelled to try to have a theory. I have an inclination to say that the good which philosophy could do here would be to cure one of this irresistible impulse. A pious person, not attacked by it, might say: 'Don't try to find out; we shan't be able to find out, and perhaps are not meant to know; at least we certainly don't need to know'. I am not that person; when I hear it suggested that something which is not clearly a divine mystery—like the Trinity, the Incarnation, the Eucharist—is beyond our ken, I feel an itch of irritation, as if I had been fobbed off; the thing has been put in the wrong light. I should like to say: I can't be 'not meant to know' something I could not know, but only something I could know. So it is not in *that* spirit that I say the good of philosophy will be to cure us of the impulse to try and have a theory of the existence of the separated soul.

First, I want to argue that though our religion teaches us the existence of the souls of the dead between death and the resurrection, it does not do so in a way that justifies us in saying: so you see the soul *has it in it* to exist apart from the body, so that it *might* exist forever apart from the body. My only reasons for saying this are Scriptural; the passage from St. Paul just cited, and what is said of Judas Maccabaeus; that he 'thought well and godly about the resurrection', considering that it would have been vain to pray for the dead, if it were not for the resurrection.* If this is so, we should be on our guard against any thinking that would make the existence of the separated soul an absolute possibility. We should not be tempted to say things like: 'If the soul can exist at all without the body, then it could exist forever without the body'; or 'The resurrection, which comes later, cannot be a condition of the possibility of the existence of the separated soul, which comes earlier'.

There will be the resurrection, and *we* pray for the dead, and to the saints, *meanwhile*. The time of this 'meanwhile' is a matter of years and seasons and clocks. It is because the resurrection will be a sensible event like an earthquake that *temporal* immortality of the soul (i.e. of human life) is a doctrine with any substance to it. But what does it mean to say that one thing is *at the same time* as others if there is no mediating system? For some reason we are apt, in our imaginations, to be vehemently convinced that we know what this expression 'at the same time' means, regardless of any mediating system, but however strongly imagination impresses us, our conviction signifies no

* 2 *Maccabees* 12.44–45

more than that we have a mental picture of two events occurring at the same time and say that we mean by 'at the same time' in some other quite different case just what was meant in this one. Now in the case of the dead there is just this mediating system in *our* praying for and to them. It is not a system of assigning a history to them.

It may be asked: 'Are you saying that to say the dead exist between death and the resurrection is to say that people pray for and to them?' The answer is, certainly not, but to pray for and to them is to *say* that they exist and I know no other saying that they exist which has any content but that of an *idle* picture or of a superstitious fear or conventional reverence (for we can forget the idle picture).

Imagine a modern man, so very modern that he no longer has the idea that he can judge a savage's religion of placating spirits to be a delusion, on grounds of 'science', common sense, Western enlightenment, and so on. He says 'I do not do this; but I cannot call it mistaken'. Now he is confronted by three spectacles: a savage fearful of malicious spirits, carrying little bags of hair and nail parings about, appealing to witches to break spells and so on; a representative of some old civilization (I am vaguely thinking of China, but know too little about it, so I would rather make it fictitious) leading a dignified life in which the ritual honouring of ancestors plays a conspicuous part, and who speaks and acts like someone who regards the spirits of his ancestors as in constant attendance on his house, involving them in his regular activities (mealtimes and so on) and also in critical matters, very piously; and lastly, a Christian who, he knows, keeps on praying for dead people he has known and to the saints he has a devotion for. He says of none of these that he is wrong, nor yet that he disbelieves their presuppositions about the existence of those spirits, but only that he does not do any of these things.

Ought he to be able to judge that one or other of these three is wrong? Say the savage at least, for fearing harmless things? But if the harm the savage fears is not just a particular result, but some unspecified harm from that action, this may make him not so easy to refute in practice, especially if a few accidents happen. I am inclined to think that it is only if that man I imagined brings in the thought of God that he will be able to call any of these things lies: only if, e.g. he can say such a thing as: one should not trust or fear any spirit because God is the master of everything. If he says this, he can discriminate between the Christians, who fear or placate no spirits, and except when they grow superstitious seek nothing from spirits but intercession,[1] on the one hand, and the ancestor worshippers and again the superstitious savages, on the other.

For reasons too complex and various for me to describe, to someone trained in a certain sort of modern philosophy the question 'Are there, or could there be, spirits?' lacks mindhold (like a precipice lacking foothold). Instead the question 'What should be thought of someone who speaks of spirits?' looks tractable. So let me imagine one case, though I suppose it is rarely to be met with. But suppose someone had the idea that a devil—or devils—were out to plague him; to hide what he looks for, to make him miss trains; even to peer at him from discoloured patches on walls or the patterns of lace and shadow in window curtains. Must he be either mentally ill or making some blunder of judgment? Obviously he may be; but the question is settled by what else goes with his trouble; we may be able to judge it as plain silliness or painful neurosis. But that judgment must be based not just on his having that idea, but on a general impression and a good knowledge of him. Neurosis is one pattern, or set of patterns, silliness another. It may be that there is nothing to criticise in him and nothing suggesting treatment. Then a Catholic would, if he were concerned, pray for him and might be able to encourage him to pray, possibly recommending him to accept the plague as a thorn in the flesh (not to try to overcome it, but to 'stand in the rain'). I suppose that a certain sort of rationalist would say flatly that the man was certainly the victim of delusive ideas. But what is the delusion? To this the 'rationalist' will reply: 'If not delusion, then truth, and I say that this kind of thing cannot be true; there is nothing there'. I reject this dichotomy: 'If not delusion, then truth' because the meaning of my saying 'truth' in this case is that *I* say 'the devil is plaguing him', and while I might be drawn in to his trouble in such a way as to say that, I need not be; I may say only 'he needs help and I can try to give him help' or perhaps 'he needs help but I am a long way from being able to give him any'. But to the talk of 'if not delusion, then truth', I might want to say 'Shut up!' Not that judging that it was not delusion would necessarily result in, so to speak, bowing to the man's idea. It might be possible to say 'Don't! Don't think these thoughts!' But that again might be wrong and it might be right to say instead 'Think also of this whenever those thoughts come to you'.

I will try to explain now what this digression was for. I replaced the question 'Are there spirits?' by 'What should be thought of some-

---

[1] Nor do they believe, except when they grow superstitious, that the spirits so much as hear or intercede for them *nisi in Verbo*.

one who speaks of spirits?' and by constructing a particular case aimed at receiving the answer: 'he might have to be taken seriously', where giving medical treatment is *not* taking seriously. (It may be worth saying that in constructing this case I am not trying to delineate anything essential to having the idea of spirits.) Now what has been achieved? Someone may concede this, and say: 'but that does not enable me to speak of spirits'. Of course it does not; but what of that? And if he says: 'What is more, I am sure I never shall, at least, not if I am in my right mind', the only answer is: you do not know what may not happen. It is like finding nothing in an author; if one is clear that one understands him, and judges that there is nothing in him, that is all right; but if one *merely* finds nothing in him (without being able to see what is supposed to be in him) then one cannot say 'Never, in my right mind, will I admire him'.

A spirit is a person without a body. (I am not counting God, here, among spirits, because it appears to me that the idea of God could exist without the idea of a spirit. Imagine people who believe in God, but have no conception of spirits at all; that is, they agree that God, who is beyond everything, is not a body, but they have no word 'Xs' one of which God is, and of which there may be other examples, which bodies are not. They might reject any such suggestion as wrong, as trying to put God into a class of beings. So the fact that people truly believe in God, and that God is spirit, is neither here nor there for settling the question whether they have the idea of *a spirit*. I will not try to determine whether, if they do not, they are incapable of the idea that *God created man in his own image*. Nor do I know whether that doctrine is supposed to be purely one of faith or to be known by reason, or even whether this question has ever been canvassed.)

Taking spirits, then, as a class of beings, spirits are persons without bodies, and we are not counting God among them. Now the idea of a person without a body is fantastic from certain familiar points of view. 'A person without a body – that is like a cat or cabbage or table without a body'. In fact, if one were asked to make something of these conceptions, one would probably say: 'You mean as if a cat or cabbage or table had a *spirit*'. That sounds more nonsensical – i.e. less of an idea one could do anything with in one's imagination – for cabbages than for cats and for tables than for cabbages. The reason is that cabbages and tables have no *dealings* with us, though we can more easily imagine a cabbage having dealings with us than a table. A table would have to have movement as a whole from within, which it has not, before we could credit it with spirit. If a spirit is something that has dealings with us then a table has no spirit; but if it were something that we dealt with, then it could have one. I mean that people might lay a spiritual table with spiritual knives and forks. But I never heard of such an activity or anything like it; whereas people do address or honour or fear or placate persons without bodies. From a certain point of view this seems as insane as laying a spiritual table sounds (i.e. going through the motions, when there is no table or knives or forks; and for this to be an activity with a certain special kind of importance in human life). Now suppose someone were to reply to those holding that point of view: How do you know it is not right to be insane in some such way? It would be insane to put your right foot over the edge of a precipice and tread as if there were ground there. But suppose that people who did that succeeded in walking?—until, indeed, they went over, *because*, as the rest of us say, they persisted in putting their right feet there; but we all fall over the precipice somehow in any event? The 'insanity' is then no argument, and in fact it turns out only to have meant not relying on sensible things, physical probabilities, and purely conventional procedures.

Some sort of 'insanity' which has a family resemblance to that of taking account of spirits, of placating fairies, for example, is characteristic of any effective belief in the eternal. (A non-effective belief either borders on sentimentality or is expressed only in purely conventional procedures.) The resemblance consists in the fact that both involve acting as if something unseen were there, to be respected in some way. A great difference lies in whether it is only temporal things that are sought or avoided. This means that the contrast between superstition and religion is especially evident when the unseen thing to be respected is simply an end sought (so long as the observances involved do not seem too trifling and insignificant). This may explain why some forms of eastern religion strike some people as particularly 'high'.

Here we come to the most essential feature of a non-superstitious and non-fabulous belief in spirits, which explains why it should have any connections with religion. It is that spirits are good or evil; not mixtures of good and bad, or oscillating between them like a human being. Without this qualification they are only fantasy, or suitable topics for psychical researchers; a name for more or less uninteresting phenomena. That they are good or bad—indeed mostly bad, dangerous things—is a common idea among people who believe in them. 'An evil spirit' is not so much like 'a wicked man' as 'a white man'; i.e. a man must be of a definite colour and his colour cannot be altered. It is this that confines spirituality to personality and makes spirituality into a significant concept rather than a composite fantasy like a centaur or a talking jug; we are back in the sphere of such fantasy the moment shilly-shally or a mixed character is ascribed to a spirit. Hence if spirits are supposed to play a part in human lives, it is a part that essentially concerns good and evil; so that even in a degenerate, superstitious development it is proper for a spirit to play nasty tricks rather that to be harnessable like a force of nature.

I suggest that the reason for speaking of the spirituality of the soul—that is, for using the adjective of 'spirit'—is not a quasi-physical common property, but that human beings are in for a final orientation towards or away from the good. Now this could be believed on Schopenhauerian lines (I mean as suggested by the remarks in the quotation given above) in some such way as I indicated before, without any belief in immortality; spirituality, so explained, does not indicate immortality. But an immortal existence is as it were the body to this as its soul. To sum up: (1) without this an immortal existence, concretely expressed as the life of the resurrection, as in orthodox Christianity, would have no significance; (2) temporal immortality of the soul without the body is empty of content; (3) spirituality, consummated without immortality, is like a *meaning* without a *vehicle*. To say that is not to show that the idea of it is delusive. It is only from revelation that we can believe in anything else—namely in the resurrection.

10*

On Transubstantiation

I

It is easiest to tell what transubstantiation is by saying this: little children should be taught about it as early as possible. Not of course using the word 'transubstantiation', because it is not a little child's word. But the thing can be taught, and it is best taught at mass at the consecration, the one part where a small child should be got to fix its attention on what is going on. I mean a child that is beginning to speak, one that understands enough language to be told and to tell you things that have happened and to follow a simple story. Such a child can be taught then by whispering to it such things as: 'Look! Look what the priest is doing ... He is saying Jesus' words that change the bread into Jesus' body. Now he's lifting it up. Look! Now bow your head and say "My Lord and my God"' and then 'Look, now he's taken hold of the cup. He's saying the words that change the wine into Jesus' blood. Look up at the cup. Now bow our head and say "We believe, we adore your precious blood, O Christ of God"'.[1] This need not be disturbing to the surrounding people.

If the person who takes a young child to mass always does this (not otherwise troubling it), the child thereby learns a great deal. Afterwards, or sometimes then (if for example it asks), it can be told what the words are which the priest says and how Jesus said them at the Last Supper. How he was offering himself up to the Father, the body that was going to be crucified and the blood that was going to be shed. So he showed that on the next day, when he was crucified, his death was an offering, a sacrifice. You can tell an older child how from the beginning priests have offered sacrifices to God (and to other, false, gods too) bringing animals, the best that the people had,

* Pamphlet published by the Catholic Truth Society (London, 1974). Reprinted with the permission of the Catholic Truth Society

[1] The cry of the Ethiopians at the consecration of the chalice.

and offering them on altars: that this was how gods were worshipped, for sacrifice is the principal sign that something is being worshipped as a god. Jesus was a priest offering himself and what he did at the Last Supper showed that that was what was happening the next day on the cross. You can tell the child how he told the Apostles to do what he did at the Last Supper, and made them priests; and that that is why his words when used by a priest have the same power that they did when he said them at the Last Supper.

The worship that we learn to give at the consecration carries with it implicitly the belief in the divinity and the resurrection of the Lord. And if we do believe in his divinity and in his resurrection then we must worship what is now there on the altar.

Thus by this sort of instruction the little child learns a great deal of the faith. And it learns in the best possible way: as part of an action; as concerning something going on before it; as actually unifying and connecting beliefs, which is clearer and more vivifying than being taught only later, in a classroom perhaps, that we have all these beliefs.

One might not even think of mentioning our Lord's resurrection explicitly in this connection. But it is there implicitly—for it is no part of the Catholic consciousness, no part of our way of speaking of or to our Lord, to think he only comes to be, as it were intermittently, upon our altars. No, we speak of the risen man as always a living man in heaven and say that the bread and wine are changed into him. And because he is alive and not dead, his flesh is not separated from his blood, and anyone who receives any of either, receives the whole of him. So, in learning this, children learn afresh that he is alive.

I have spoken of teaching little children, both because it is important in itself, and because it is the clearest way of bringing out what 'transubstantiation' means. The word was devised (first in Greek and then in Latin by translation) to insist precisely on this: that there is a change of what is there, totally into something else. A conversion of one physical reality into another *which already exists*. So it is not a coming to be of a new substance out of the stuff of an old one, as when we have a chemical change of the matter in a retort from being one kind of substance into another. Nor is it like digestion in which what you eat turns into you. For these are both changes of matter, which can assume a variety of forms. When one says 'transubstantiation' one is saying exactly what one teaches the child, in teaching it that Christ's words, by the divine power given to the priest who uses them in his place, have changed the bread so that it isn't there any more (nor the stuff of which it was made) but instead there is the body of Christ. The little child can grasp this and it is implicit in the act of worship that follows the teaching. I knew a child, close upon three years old and only then beginning to talk, but taught as I have described, who was in the free space at the back of the church when the mother went to communion. 'Is he in you?' the child asked when the mother came back. 'Yes', she said, and to her amazement the child prostrated itself before her. I can testify to this, for I saw it happen. I once told the story to one of those theologians who unhappily (as it seems) strive to alter and to water down our faith, and he deplored it: he wished to say, and hoped the Vatican Council would say, something that would show the child's idea to be wrong. I guessed that the poor wretch was losing the faith and indeed so, sadly, did it turn out.

'But the thing is impossible, contradictory: it cannot be believed! It has to be only a figure of speech!' Well, indeed it cannot really be understood how it is possible. But if it is claimed it is impossible, then a definite contradiction must be pointed to, and if you believe in it, you will believe that each claim to disprove it as contradictory can be answered. For example, someone says: how can a man who is, say, six foot tall be wholly in this small space? Well, indeed not by the coincidence of his dimensions with the hole in space defined by the dimensions of the remaining appearance of bread: let us call this the 'dimensive' way of being in a place. 'But that is the only way for a body to be in a place!' How do you know? We believe that something is true of *That* which is there, which contradicts its being there dimensively. And certainly the division and separation from one another of all these places where That is, does not mean division and separation of *it* from itself. So considered dimensively, a thousand such diverse places can be compared to a thousand pieces of mirror each of which reflects one whole body, itself much bigger that any of them and itself not dimensively displaced. But when we consider *That* which the bread has become, the place where we are looking has become (though not dimensively) the place where *it* is: a place in heaven.

It would be wrong to think, however, that the thing can be understood, sorted out, expounded as a possibility with nothing mysterious about it. That is, that it can be understood in such a way as is perhaps demanded by those who attack it on the ground of the obvious difficulties. It was perhaps a fault of the old exposition in terms of a distinction between the substance of a thing (supposed to be unascertainable) and its accidents, that this exposition was sometimes offered as if it were supposed to make everything intelligible. Greater learning would indeed remove that impression. For in the philosophy of scholastic Aristotelianism in which those distinctions were drawn, transubstantiation is as difficult, as 'impossible', as it seems to any ordinary reflection. And it is right that it should be so. When we call something a mystery, we mean that we cannot iron out the difficulties about understanding it and demonstrate once for all that it is perfectly possible. Nevertheless we do not believe that contradictions and absurdities can be true, or that anything logically demonstrable from things known can be false. And so we believe that there are answers to supposed proofs of absurdity, whether or not we are clever enough to find them.

II

Why do we do this—why do we celebrate the Eucharist? Because the Lord told us to. That is reason enough. But we can reflect that it is his way of being present with us in his physical[2] reality until the end of this age; until he comes again to be dimensively and visibly present on earth. We can also reflect on the mysterious fact that he wanted to nourish us with himself.

This to my mind is the greatest mystery of all about the Eucharistic sacrifice, a greater mystery than transubstantiation itself, though it must be an essential part of the significance of transubstantiation. To try to get some understanding of this, let us first ask ourselves what our Lord was doing at the Last Supper. If you ask an orthodox Jew to say grace at your table, he will take a piece of bread in his hands, will pray and break the bread and distribute a piece to each person present. So our Lord was then saying grace—and on a special occasion. He was celebrating the Passover; this supper was the first, highly ceremonial meal of the days during which Jews celebrate the passage of the angel of the Lord over Egypt when they were about to escape from their Egyptian slavery. Then they had to sacrifice a lamb, in groups large enough to eat it up, they were to smear their

---

[2] Theologians have not been accustomed to say that our Lord is 'physically' present in the Eucharist. I think this is because to them 'physically' means 'naturally', as the word comes from the Greek for *nature*—and of course our Lord is not present in a natural manner! But to a modern man to deny that he is physically present is to deny the doctrine of the Catholic Church—for meanings of words change. Pope Paul VI tells us in the Encyclical *Mysterium Fidei* that 'Christ is present whole and entire, bodily present, in his physical reality'.

doorposts with its blood; the angel of the Lord passed over their houses, destroying the first-born children of all other houses. The Jews ate their sacrifice, being commanded on this occasion to eat all up and leave nothing behind; they stood ready to go on their journey, ready to leave Egypt. This meal in preparation for the journey out of bondage has ever since been memorialised in the supper—the Seder as present-day Jews call it—which was celebrated by our Lord with his disciples. But to the grace our Lord adds the words 'This is my body' and after the rest of the celebration, he takes the cup of wine and says it is 'my blood which will be shed for you'. We have seen how this showed that his coming death was a sacrifice of which he was the priest. (For his death was voluntary; no one could take his life from him if he would not give it up.) His actions showed that for us he himself replaced the Passover lamb, which was originally both a sacrifice and the meal in preparation for the journey of escape from slavery, and also provided the sign of difference between the escaping Jews and those who would have detained them.

There are two sorts of sacrifice, the holocaust, or 'wholeburning' in which the whole of the sacrificed victim is destroyed in the sacrifice, and the kind in which the people eat what is sacrificed.

Christ made of himself the second kind; his first command in his grace-saying was to eat; it subsequently emerges that he is making a sacrificial offering and that he is superseding the paschal lamb, assuming its place. Catholics believe that we cannot eat and drink what he commanded without having the same bread and the same cup to eat and drink of; and *that* we can only do by reproducing his own offering. This, then, is why we identify the offering of the Last Supper with the sacrifice on the cross and with every mass.

So his flesh and blood are given us for food, and this is surely a great mystery. It is clearly a symbol: we are not physically nourished by Christ's flesh and blood as the Jews were by the paschal lamb.

We Christians are so much accustomed to the idea of holy communion that we tend not to notice how mysterious an idea it is. There is the now old dispute between Catholics and Protestants whether we eat what only symbolises, or really is, the flesh of the saviour when we eat the bread consecrated in the Eucharist; drink his blood only symbolically or really. Because of this dispute, it appeared as if only the Catholic belief were extravagant—the Protestants having the perfectly reasonable procedure of *symbolically* eating Christ's flesh and drinking his blood! The staggering strangeness of doing such a thing even only symbolically slipped out of notice in the disputes about transubstantiation. But let us realize it now.

For why should anyone want to eat someone's flesh or drink his blood? 'I will drink your blood' might be a vow made against an enemy. Indeed in Old Testament language eating a man's flesh and drinking his blood is an idea expressive of just such deadly enmity. Or savage peoples have wanted to eat the flesh of a brave enemy to acquire his virtue. Someone puzzled at the Christian Eucharist, whether celebrated under Catholic or Protestant conceptions, might wonder if that was the idea; but he would be far off the mark. Are Christians then like savage tribes, which on special occasions may eat the animals that are tabu at other times? No, that is not it.

It is surely clear that the reason why Christians have this sacrifice is obedience to the injunction of the Saviour. He told his disciples to do this as *his* reminder (*sc.* to the Father), and said that what they ate and drank was his body and blood. And they might claim not to understand the matter, not to know any more about it than that he told them to do it and said it was a means to eternal life. I mean: it is not necessarily as it were a natural or intelligible gesture for them to make. To see this, imagine that there were a ceremony called 'kissing the feet of the Saviour' or 'binding oneself to him'. These would be intelligible gestures, one would understand the thought of which they were the expression. But *eating* him?

Certainly this eating and drinking are themselves symbolic. I mean that, whether this is itself a literal or is a purely symbolic eating of his flesh and drinking his blood, *that* is in turn symbolical of something else. So if we only symbolically (and not really) eat his flesh, our action is the symbol of a symbol. If we literally eat his flesh our action is a direct symbol. The reason why the action is in any case strange and arcane is this: it is not a natural or easily intelligible symbol. How, and what, it symbolises—that is deeply mysterious.

In modern times some theologians have tried to explain transubstantiation as trans-signification. The 'substance' of some things is the meaning they have in human life. This is certainly true of some things, like money, and they have wished to say it is true of bread and wine: these aren't chemical substances, but mean human food and drink. Well, as to the first point (that they aren't single substances) that's true enough; but the bread and wine that are fit to use at the Eucharist are defined by the natural kinds they are made from, by wheat and grape. For the rest, what is said may be very true—but the odd thing, which apparently is not noticed, is that what gets trans-signified in the Eucharist is not the bread and wine, but the body and blood of the Lord, which are trans-signified into food and drink. And that is the mystery.

When Jesus said, 'I am the bread that came down from heaven', his words were a metaphor for the same thing. The metaphor is that of saying 'I myself will be the nourishment of the life of which I speak'. The saying is dark, like his saying 'I *am* the way', 'I *am* the truth' and 'I *am* the life' or again 'I *am* the door'. Not 'My way is the way' or 'I show you the truth', but 'I am the way and the truth'. Similarly not 'I have nourishment for you' but 'I am the bread'. The commanded action of eating his flesh creates the very same metaphor as the words—whether we take the description of the action literally or symbolically. For, even if the words 'I am the bread (i.e. the food) that came down from heaven' are to be taken literally, still that which they say, and which on *that* understanding is literally so, symbolises something *else*.

The clearest of his metaphors is that of the vine. We can say *un*-metaphorically what that says—that the life he speaks of is his own; as the life of the branches is that of the vine. So this is the teaching that disciples are not merely disciples (taught) but are to share in the divine life, the divine nature itself. But here again understanding stops. Except that if it is so, we get an inkling why he does not merely say that he shows the way, the truth, a life, and can supply what is needed for that life (as the teacher can give studies that will nourish the pupil), but that he *is* the way, is the truth, is the life. But no one can know what it means for us to live with the life of God himself. That is why I say that what is symbolised by that symbol, the eating of that flesh and drinking of that blood (whether that is done literally or in turn only in symbol) is deeply mysterious. No wonder the early Christians were accused of some weird orgy in their Eucharist, and answered only with denials that any abomination took place.

'He gives us his body', so Augustine wrote, 'to make us into his body.' This brings out how the sacrament symbolises and effects the unity of the people who join together to celebrate the Eucharist and to receive communion. The 'mystical body of Christ' which we call the church, is a *body* in figure or metaphor. The unity of mankind is already spoken of in the metaphor by which we are considered to be born all 'members of Adam'. Calling this one body, as if all men constituted one big man, is of course a figure or metaphor; the unity of life that is pointed to in the metaphor is itself no metaphor, for we are all, all the races of men, of one stock and one blood. Now by baptism we are said to be grafted into the body of a new Adam, and here again we have the metaphor of being the members—which means the limbs and other bodily parts—of the body of one man. Once again, *the unity of the life that is pointed to* in the figure of speech is *no* metaphor. Of this life Christ called himself the food. It is the food of the divine life which is promised and started in us: the viaticum of our perpetual flight from Egypt which is the bondage of sin; the sacrificial offering by which we were reconciled; the sign of our unity with one another in him. It is the mystery of the faith which is the same for the simple and the learned. For they believe the same, and what is grasped by the simple is not better understood by the learned: their service is to clear away the rubbish which the human reason so often throws in the way to create obstacles.

11*

Authority in Morals

To many, at least of those who study philosophy, there are difficulties about any notion of authority in morals. There are, of course, various forms of authority. There is the right to declare to someone else what is true—in this case what is right and what is wrong, and to demand that he accept what one says and act accordingly. There is the authority of superior knowledge—in this case, it would be the authority, i.e. the outstanding credibility, of an expert on right and wrong, virtue and vice. There is again the authority of someone exercising his prophetical office, who teaches *qua* one set up by God to teach; in this case, declaring what is right and wrong, virtuous or vicious.

Now the first of these, however distasteful it may be, is a sort of authority that can hardly be denied to exist by the most recalcitrant modern philosopher. For it is exercised by people in bringing up children; and if there is such a thing as authority of a commanding kind at all, or if there is such a thing as a right, this authority and this right can hardly be denied, since it is quite necessary, if children are to be brought up, that their bringers-up act as if they were exercising such an authority; and since what is a necessity can hardly fail to be a right, so anyone who has to bring children up must have this right.

This authority, however, is not accompanied by any guarantee that someone exercising it will be right in what he teaches. When he is wrong, then, what is the position as regards his authority? To say he still has the right to demand that he be believed is absurd; for there can be no right to be believed when what one says is not right, and no right to demand what one does not have a right to obtain. It would commonly be said that such a person—a parent, say, with erroneous convictions about right and wrong—has a right to be

* Paper read at an Anglo-French symposium at the Abbey of Notre-Dame du Bec in Normandy in April 1961 and published in John M Todd (ed.), *Problems of Authority* (London: Darton, Longman & Todd, 1962), pp. 179–88.

obeyed as far as external actions were concerned, so long as what he demanded was not wrong, or very burdensome and unreasonable. However, I am not interested in that, but only in the character of his authority in declaring what is right or wrong and requiring that his children accept what he says. Authority seems a relatively clear notion when it means the right to be obeyed, even if you are wrong in giving the order, as it does when authority over actions is what we are considering. But it is much more difficult to explain authority to teach, such as a parent exercises in bringing up his children. If this is an authority that he only has when he is right, then, it may be asked, how is it authority at all? The child only has to think him wrong, in order to have to reject his authority: this is to say, for the child to think him wrong must lead to the child's rejecting his authority, if the child is logical. But then how can it be a reproach to the child that it did not believe what he said, and so dishonoured its father's authority? And if it cannot, in what sense is there authority here?

Or does authority to teach, such as a parent has—and which he must have inasmuch as he positively has a duty to teach—after all *not* carry with it a right to be believed? But does it not carry a right to demand belief? A right, for example, to order a child to stop being silly?

Nevertheless there is a difference between saying: You did not do as I told you, and that is bad, because it was I, whom you ought to obey, who told you, and: You did not believe what I said, and that is bad, because it was I, whom you ought to believe, who told you.

The difference lies in this: that the one with authority over what you do, can decide, within limits, what you shall do; his decision is what makes it right for you to do what he says—if the reproach against you, when you disobey him, is only that of disobedience. But someone with authority over what you think is not at liberty, within limits, to decide what you shall think among the range of possible thoughts on a given matter; what makes it right for you to think what you think, given that it is your business to form a judgement at all, is simply that it is true, and no decision can make something a true thing for you to think, as the decision of someone in authority can make something a good thing for you to do.

This comes out in the fact that one tells the person under one's authority to do thus and so, but, more often, not to believe this and that, so much as: that this and that is true. The demand that a child accept what one says is based on the claim to know what he does not and to have the job of telling him. 'Why ought I to do that?'—'Because I say so'; if 'Why ought I to believe that?' is answered by 'Because I say so', that can only be because my saying so is good evidence that the thing is true, and in general it would not be so answered.

Thus, while it is possible to beg or counsel someone to believe something while admitting that one does not believe it oneself, it is not possible authoritatively to order someone to believe something while admitting that one does not believe it oneself. (There are plenty of situations in which one may intelligibly order someone to believe or not to believe something; I will not elaborate them.)

This is connected with the fact that to teach authoritatively is primarily to declare the things one is teaching, demanding attention and mastery of what one says from one's pupil. Now 'such-and-such is the case, but I do not believe it' is notoriously a contradiction, even though of a rather curious sort.

So far, our problems have been concerned with the authority of a fallible teacher, whatever he is teaching, not especially with the teaching of morals. But morals I suppose are what is most universally taught by fallible teachers informally at least, by praising and blaming other people, by reining the child in or giving him free rein in various ways (encouragement, reward, etc. and their opposites).

It looks both necessary and impossible that there should be teaching authority on the part of fallible people. A professional teacher, however, presumably has authority to teach; and this does not seem so difficult. Naturally he cannot justifiably claim his teaching commission in support of his teaching when what he teaches is untrue. So he too has a commission only to teach what is true. But the child who will not learn what the teacher teaches—is he not guilty of rejection of authority? And to learn is necessarily to accept, i.e. to believe, a good deal of what one is taught. If a child were liable not to believe his teacher, how could it happen that he selected only those things to disbelieve that were in fact untrue? So he needs to be liable to believe his teacher. If he is, he will learn at any rate some truth; by its aid he will eventually be able to reject what he is taught that is false so far as it is important that he should: or so it is to be hoped.

The right that a fallible teacher has, in that he has authority, then, is the right that those he has to teach should be generally prepared to believe their teachers. At all frequent disbelief when what he says is true will be, then, an injury done to the authority of a teacher—as well as having about it whatever badness one attaches to being wrong without excuse.

The great assumption lying behind this is that no one who is taught at all can fail to be taught a great deal that is true and that to a great extent *verum index sui et falsi*.

We sometimes imagine someone with a terribly bad upbringing, who is taught all sorts of misbehaviour as right, and taught to despise much that is good, and we think: what about such a person? But people of the most horrible principles know quite well how to cry out against injustice and lying and treachery, say, when their enemies are guilty of them. So they in fact know quite a lot.

There need not be some common kernel of morals that everyone learns who learns anything. The moral law is a range; some people have one part of the range, some another.

But is there something essentially less teachable about morals than, say, chemistry or history or mathematics—or, again, religious dogma? This view might be maintained in connection with that *autonomy of the will* about which Kant wrote. To take one's morality from somewhere else—that, it might be held, would make it not morality at all; if one takes it from someone else, that turns it into a bastard sort of morality, marked by heteronomy.

Now it was wrong, in the list of teachable things with which to contrast morality, to put mathematics alongside the others. 'Be ye doers of the word and not hearers only'* I once saw as the motto of a chapter in a big text book of higher mathematics, and it was right; one does not learn mathematics by learning that mathematical propositions are truths, but by working out their proofs. Similarly it might be held that one's morality *must* be something one has formulated for oneself, seeing the rightness and wrongness of each of the things one judges to be right or wrong; so that if ever anyone else taught one, he was the occasion of one's formulating for oneself what he taught, rather than the source of information.

There is tied up with this view the idea that one's own personal conscience is necessarily the supreme arbiter in matters of right and wrong. And here we are often not clear whether the necessity is a logical necessity, or a necessity under pain of doing ill: whether, in entertaining the idea of not going by one's conscience, one is supposed to be guilty of a linguistic absurdity or a reprehensible departure from the right way.

There is a confusion here. Let conscience be one's judgment of right and wrong, i.e. of good and evil in conduct, of what is virtuous and what vicious to do. Then to say that one's own conscience is nec-

* *James* 1.22.

essarily supreme arbiter in such matters is to say that necessarily what one judges right and wrong, one judges right and wrong.

One could similarly say that one cannot think anything to be true without thinking it. But that does not tend to show that one cannot think a thing on the strength of what someone else says, judging that that is much more likely than what one could have been inclined to think if left to oneself.

The confusion can perhaps be best cleared up if we consider the parallel case of memory. I can make no judgment about the past without some reliance on my own memory. But only a fool thinks that his own memory is the last word, so far as he is concerned, about what happened. A man may have reason to judge that other men's memory is more reliable than his; and will in any case be well advised to check his own memory against theirs. He may also have reason to believe that some public record is more reliable than his own memory. Of course he would not have any basis for such judgments if he did not already rely on his own memory to some extent; but it would not be reasonable to argue from this that his own memory must after all be for him the last word about what has happened in the past.

Similarly, in practical matters, a man must put some reliance on his own conscience: that is to say, on those judgments of right and wrong which he makes for himself. I call it a judgment that he makes for himself when he judges on a ground that he can see for himself; he does not merely judge 'that is wrong', he judges 'that is wrong because...' and then follows some further account of the action, which he can judge and which he also judges to make the action wrong. To rely exclusively on one's own conscience (one's 'unaided' conscience) is to refuse to judge anything in practical matters unless in this sense one is able to judge for oneself. Now in this sense of 'one's own conscience' only a foolish person thinks that his own conscience is the last word, so far as he is concerned, about what to do. For just as any reasonable man knows that his memory may sometimes deceive him, any reasonable man knows that what one has conscientiously decided on one may later conscientiously regret. A man may have reason to judge that another man's moral counsel is more reliable than his own unaided conscience; he will in any case be well advised to take counsel with others; he may, moreover, have reason to believe that some public source of moral teaching is more reliable than his own unaided judgment. Of course he would not have any basis for such judgments if he did not already rely on his own moral judgments to some extent; but it would be sophistical to argue from this that his own conscience must after all be for him the last word about what he ought to do. This sophism, though, aided by confusion with the sense in which it is indeed impossible to take anything but one's conscience as arbiter of right and wrong, has led people to embrace Kant's thesis on the autonomy of the will and to attack, either as illogical or as reprehensible, those who, say, consult the divine law and accept its judgments, though themselves unable to see why, say, something forbidden by that law is wrong.

A strong sense of duty may attach to the deliveries of one's conscience – whether they are the deliveries of the 'unaided' conscience or are one's ultimate decision. Some people think that this sense of duty is to be unquestioningly obeyed and that such obedience is a moral vindication. But it is not reasonable to hold that one can so easily get away with having thought good what was bad and bad what was good, and acted accordingly – by having had a sense of duty in connection with what one did. It would have an adverse effect on the seriousness of one's concern to avoid sinning, if one was guaranteed against it by following one's sense of duty – no matter what road it lead one on. I do not mean that it would necessarily make one worry less; in some circumstances it might make one worry more; for only an endlessly conscientious style in one's behaviour, only endless bellyaching, could reassure one that one was exercising the sense of duty. Nevertheless that isn't seriousness.

To return to the comparison with mathematics. That suggested that as one cannot just take mathematical information but must think for oneself, so one cannot just take moral information but must think it for oneself; this would be reason to think that one could not be taught morality except in the sense that one can be taught mathematics.

Now there is something right about the comparison. But it is rightly made, not as I made it, by speaking of formulating one's morality for oneself, but as the mathematical textbook made it, by quoting the text from St James: 'Be doers of the word and not hearers only'.

You have to do the mathematics; and the teacher can get you to do it: that is what teaching mathematics is. Similarly teaching morals will be, not getting the pupil to think something, not giving him a statement to believe, but getting him to act; this can be done by someone who brings up children. One does not learn mathematics, I said, by learning that certain propositions – mathematical ones – are true, but by working out their proofs. Similarly one does not learn morality by learning that certain propositions—ethical ones—are true, but by learning what to do or abstain from in particular situations and getting by practice to do certain things, and abstain from others.

However, the reckoning what to do or abstain from in particular circumstances will constantly include a reference, implicit or explicit, to generalities. So much so, that this seems to be an important part of what makes morality. Because of it human conduct is not left to be distinguished from the behaviour of other animals by the fact that in it calculation is used by which to ascertain the means to perfectly particular ends. The human wants things like health and happiness and science and fair repute and virtue and prosperity, he does not simply want, e.g., that such-and-such a thing should be in such-and-such a place at such-and-such a time. Such generalities or principles are: to do good and avoid doing harm; not to do what will get you disrepute; not to do what will make you poorer; not to take other people's property. And the questions arise, which of such principles are true and which false, which quite general and which to be modified in suitable circumstances; whether indeed they can be called true and false, right and wrong, and why; what should be the application of this or that one, in describable particular situations. Even if the purpose of such a theory is, as Aristotle says, not knowledge but practice, the considerations are theoretical in the sense that they are capable of being argued in the study. A human being can be brought up without any such study-theory, but the study-theory of some of the people who have gone in for that kind of thing is liable in the long run to exert an influence on the practical principles of the general run of people. If parents teach their children to be reflective, they may themselves teach them a certain amount of moral theory, and if there is such a thing as a public teaching, it is likely to be in great part theoretical, i.e. general, leaving individuals and their advisers to make applications.

Now there is indeed a sense in which only the individual can make his own decisions as to what to do, even if his decision is to abide by someone else's orders or advice. For it is he who acts and therefore makes the final application of whatever is said to him.

It may be said, concerning his judgments in the field of theoretical morals, that in the same way it is he who thinks what he thinks, and so too only he can make his own decisions as to what to think. No doubt; but here there is such a thing as believing what he is told without reflection, consideration or interpretation; doing what one is told is an interpretation and so with doing, however obedient one is, one can hardly escape being one's own pilot. I have said that a man would be foolish who would not take advice; but there comes a point where he must act and that is the end of listening to advice. But with believing it is otherwise; a man may decline to be his own pilot for certain of his beliefs and altogether rely on authority, without doing anything on his own account to digest and assimilate the beliefs. This would be possible in moral matters only to the extent that his beliefs were idle, without consequences, i.e. if they concerned matters that he never had to deal with.

Now some dogmatic beliefs are revealed and could not be known otherwise. The question arises whether this could be essential to some moral beliefs. That is to say, whether there are any that are *per se* revealed.

There are two different ways in which a moral belief may be *per accidens* revealed. One way is when someone relies on an authority for something that a man could have thought out for himself. He does not know, let us suppose, whether it is all right at all to beat a child for its misbehaviour. So he asks a modern educationist, supposing him to know, and gets the answer: no; or, if he has different predilections, he consults the Bible and gets the answer: yes. He forms his opinion accordingly. Note that if he is to *act* on it, and the opinion he has adopted is the positive one, he has got to be his own pilot in deciding when and where. But at present we are speaking only of belief, which may perhaps never come to practice. Here, then, is one way in which a moral belief may rely *per accidens* on authority, whether on the authority of an expert (someone supposed to be wise in the field, though of course not supposed to be infallible) or on that of someone with a prophetical office.

Another way is this: some of the facts, of what is the case, will help to determine moral truth—i.e. some of the truth about what is the case will help to determine the truth about what kinds of thing ought and ought not to be done. Now some such truths about what is the case are revealed; original sin for example. There are also revealed some conditional promises, to disregard which is to despise the goodness of God. Both of these things lead us to infer the rightness of an asceticism which would otherwise have been morbid or founded on a false view of life. Here then is something one could not have worked out for oneself: the furthest one could have got would be to see the advisability of weighting the scales a certain amount against the pleasures and enjoyments of life, as they can be seen to have a practical tendency to corrupt people, i.e. to soften them, make them greedy and pervert and coarsen their judgement. But this would not justify anything severely ascetical.

Here there is room for accepting authority also on the moral conclusions to be drawn from the facts; but *this* acceptance – the acceptance of *consequences* as following – is similar to the acceptance in the first type of *per accidens* revelation of moral truth, just as the grounds on which the authority itself tells you moral truth may be either *per se* revealed truth as to facts, or facts discoverable by reason's unaided investigation.

What there does not seem to be room for is moral truths which are *per se* revealed. Given the facts about original sin and the promise of the possibility of a man's joining his sufferings to those of Christ, the goodness of severely ascetical practices, so long as they do not damage the body or its faculties, is obvious; there is no such thing as a revelation that such-and-such is good or bad not for any reason, not because of any facts, not because of any hopes or prospects, but simply: such-and-such is good to do, this is to be believed, and could not be known or inferred from anything else. How can one instruct an archer to aim at an unseen target? There would be no room for that knowledge by connaturality which is characteristic of the understanding of a virtuous person, in such a case; no room, therefore, for understanding application of what one believed to be right or wrong.

Mr Michael Dummett, reasoning on the topic of cause and effect, came to the conclusion that, but for the goodness of God in revealing it to us, it could not have been known that it would be wrong to engage in certain practices whose object it was to procure that such-and-such should *have* been the case; we might have discovered that something always turned out to have been the case if we subsequently recited some formula, and so recite the formula in order to secure that the past was as we wanted it to have been. Now this is a case in point. If it is not unreasonable, if it is not foolish and superstitious to do this, then there could be nothing wrong with it and there is no room for the exercise of the goodness of God simply in forbidding it. To do it would only be *malum quia prohibitum*.

12*

On Being in Good Faith

It is a widespread belief, implicit among many non-Catholics and explicit among many Catholics, that a man is personally guiltless in doing what is in accord with his conscience. Think of such phrases as 'he acted according to his lights', 'they sincerely believe that they ought to do as they do', whose purpose is to exonerate. Catholics taught by the English Catechism** learn that it is impossible to sin mortally without full knowledge and full consent, and that it is right to act according to one's conscience, and a sin to act against it, even though what one's conscience requires of one is wrong; and, in general, that good faith exonerates. Many also familiarly use a distinction between 'material' and 'formal' sinfulness; a thing is 'formally' sinful (i.e. doing it is really a sin on the part of the agent) only when the agent believes that it is sinful or wrong.

We may note here, what has been noted before, that on this view sufficient thoughtlessness is a safeguard against committing mortal sin. Further, on this view it is difficult to see how it must be mortal sin to give up belief in Christ and the Catholic Church. For at least some cases of infidelity are occasioned by it strongly appearing to a man that Christian belief is untrue or unreasonable. And if when he is in this frame of mind he abandons faith, how can he be said fully to

* Text of an undated and unpublished typescript of a paper given to the Philosophical Enquiry Group that met at the Dominican Conference Centre at Spode House in Staffordshire (see Preface), dating probably from the late 1950s or early 1960s.

** Anscombe was mistaken in claiming that *A Catechism of Christian Doctrine* (first published by the Catholic Truth Society, London, in 1889) taught that it was impossible to sin mortally without full knowledge and full consent. Review of all printings of the *Catechism* back to 1929 provided no evidence of such a teaching in it. However, similar teaching is certainly in *A Catechism of Christian Doctrine Prepared and Enjoined by Order of the Third Plenary Council of Baltimore* (originally published in 1885): 'To make a sin mortal three things are necessary: a grievous matter, sufficient reflection, and full consent of the will.' (page 11 in the 1937 edition) know that he is rejecting the truth revealed by God? In general, on that view, it is difficult to see how it is possible to commit grave sin with the intellect. Consider a rash and uncharitable judgement which led one to slander someone gravely. One does not—usually at least—say to oneself 'Now I will judge rashly' or 'I am determined, rash as it is, to judge that so-and-so'—one simply judges rashly. What does 'in good faith' mean? If it means that one has not got one's tongue in one's cheek, is not consciously lying or hypocritical, then good faith is not enough to exonerate. If it is enough to exonerate, then the slander uttered under the influence of a rash and passionate conviction is not a statement made in good faith. It is the same with the notion of sincerity. If I am sincere so long as I believe what I say, then sincerity does not exonerate me from the charge of calumny. Thus good faith or sincerity are either not much good as a defence, or not so easily assured as we might think at first. Or else we must take the line that it is not possible to sin gravely with one's power of judgement. But if so, then abandonment of faith need not be a grave sin.

'He ought to have realised...', 'He ought to have thought of...', 'He had no business to suppose that...', 'He ought to have found out...', are phrases that bear witness to the fact that a man's beliefs do not suffice to justify him so long as he acts accordingly. Someone realises he has sold petrol by mistake for paraffin, and thinks: 'They'll be sure to notice it is petrol', and does nothing about it. 'He had no business to think that' would be the usual reaction. If he said it to someone else the question as to his sincerity would sound like a question whether he really thought it or was consciously saying something he did not think. If he said it to himself, we can still ask 'Did he really think it?' But in this use, the question 'If he thought it, all the same did he sincerely think it?' seems not to arise, for sincerity is being treated as a matter of thinking what you say; so 'sincerely think' contains a redundancy. But if we can ask 'Did he sincerely think it?' this suggests there is such a thing as insincerely thinking it—but insincerely thinking something will still be thinking it. Here then the question as to sincerity is not 'Does he think the same as he says?' but 'Granted he thinks that, is it a sincere thought?' That though he thought it, it was not a sincere thought, could mean a variety of things. It need not mean that some hesitancy or feeling of difficulty accompanied the thought. For it depends on the content of the thought whether a feeling of difficulty would be counted as showing that the man did not sincerely think it. In the paraffin-petrol case we should indeed say that the man who, with an uneasy feeling, thought 'They'll notice it' was insincere precisely in suppressing the knowledge that made his thought doubtful. But notice that what counts here is that his thought would really be a most dubious one to have. In another kind of case, the uneasy feeling would not prove the insincerity of the thought, e.g. a man believes in the assurance of a friend that there are no steps to fall down in a dark passage, but has uneasy feelings as he walks the passage. That is to say, although at first sight the question as to the sincerity of a thought is a question purely about the inner state of the thinker, i.e. about something formally independent of external circumstances, on reflection we find, at least sometimes, that the circumstances and subject-matter would have to be considered. It may be said: in the petrol-paraffin case, only an idiot could sincerely think ... and so in other cases the question as to sincerity will be a question as to the inner state, not to be judged in the light of circumstances and subject-matter. But what sort of statement is it, that only an idiot could sincerely think ...? If sincerity is as it were an interior colour of one's thoughts, then how can it be said that only an idiot could sincerely think ...? Is this proved by induction? If the question can ever be judged in the light of circumstances and subject-matter, that shows that sincerity is not as it were a secret colour of one's thoughts.

It is the purity of one's intentions in thinking these thoughts. By the purity of intention I mean not the ultimate purpose but the immediate purpose in thinking. The thought is thought, or there is an inclination to think it, because it appears to be the relevant truth on the matter in hand; as opposed to its appearing to be the relevant truth on the matter in hand because it is a convenient or otherwise tempting thought, i.e. because there is an inclination to think it.

When it is said that full knowledge and consent are necessary conditions of mortal sin, the statement is ambiguous. I believe that it is sometimes—even often—take to mean that unless the agent fully understands that what he does is wrong, then what he does is not mortal sin. But the statement need not mean this; it may well mean only that the agent must have full knowledge that what he is doing is such-and-such, when such-and-such is in fact gravely wrong, in order to commit mortal sin. For example, if I do not know, in giving my child, say, a drink, that it is a deadly poison, then I am not guilty of murder in so causing his death. But if I do know it, and give the drink fully intending that it shall kill him, then on one construction of the condition 'full knowledge and full consent', I commit mortal sin, and the fact that I perhaps believe it right to kill him is no impairment of the conditions for mortal sin. Now this, I should think, is the meaning of the doctrine: for it has obvious connections with the ethical tradition of Aristotelianism, according to which ignorance of circumstances can prevent an act from being voluntary—and only what is voluntary can be sin. But ignorance of principle is not a cause of involuntariness, but of scoundrelism, according to Aristotle and those who have followed him. This, then, will be the meaning of the condition 'full knowledge': given that to do X is gravely wrong, then a man is guilty of wrongdoing in doing what is in fact doing X, only if he knows that he is doing X. He may be doing what is in fact doing X without knowing it. To take a classical example, he may shoot his father by mistake for a stag. Then what he materially does is to shoot his father, but this was not his formal object—his formal object was to shoot a stag, and so he is not guilty of the sin of parricide. The distinction between material and formal is so made, in this case, by St. Thomas; and possibly we have here the historical origin of the expression 'material and formal sin'; but we must notice that as he uses the distinction of material and formal, there is no room for these as adjectives of sin. What the man actually does (what happens with him as agent) is the material action; what he supposes himself to be doing is the formal action, and it is the rightness of what he—reasonably—supposes himself to be doing that determines his innocence; not the rightness that he supposes to attach to what he does or thinks he does. If, then, in teaching that full knowledge is necessary before a person can commit mortal sin, we give the impression that a person can only commit mortal sin if he conceives himself to be committing mortal sin, i.e., that if he does not believe himself to be doing wrong, he cannot be committing mortal sin, then it seems that we are teaching something different from any meaning of the formula 'without full knowledge, it is not possible to commit mortal sin' in which it can be reconciled with traditional teaching.

It is clear that, for any deed X, you cannot have intentionally done X unless you know you are doing X, except in a psychoanalytical sense in which there can be unconscious intentions, but I leave that aside, since unconscious intentions are not e.g. suitable matter for confession. If, then, you are to be charged with a certain intentional act, it is an adequate defence that you did not know you were doing that. And in many cases, this is an adequate defence against a charge of having done X guiltily. This, then, is the truth in the condition of 'full knowledge' for mortal sin: where the mortal sin is a specific act in a kind of case which requires intention on the part of the accused, then the act of mortal sin was not committed by an agent who did not have full knowledge. We can often say that an action was *either* intentional *or* involuntary.

I do not think that the condition ought to be more generously stated than that. For the limits of the voluntary are far wider than the limits of the intentional; but sin essentially requires, not intention but voluntariness. A man may be not guilty of murder of malice-prepense—i.e. of having intended the death of someone he did kill and had no right to seek to kill—but yet guilty of homicide, in circumstances where, if he did not know what he was doing, he ought to have known it. If he drives a car at 90mph through a city street and kills one or two people in doing so, perhaps it did not occur to him that this was likely to happen. So he did not intend their deaths; but he ought to have realised what was likely, and his not realising it does not excuse him. And it seems ludicrous to suggest that unjustified homicide, in circumstances where a man could have realised if he had thought, is not a mortal sin, is not gravely wrong. I am not supposing him mad or drunk, but only thoughtless; and the case is not an imaginary one.—You may say: he committed with full knowledge the mortal sin of driving at breakneck speed through a city street. But the reason why it is a sin to do this is that it is dangerous. There could be little objection to it otherwise.—Perhaps we should say: a man who does this does know the danger even if he does not think of it. Then there can be knowledge without realisation. 'I did not think of that' or 'I did not think of it like that' do not disprove knowledge. At least the condition 'knowledge and consent', if it is really quite generally requisite, does not mean that the matter must present itself to the man as such-and-such—the condition which holds in the narrower sense, in which e.g. a man cannot be accused of deliberate murder unless he conceived himself to be engaged in killing someone.

In the sense in which there can be knowledge without realisation, then I know what I am doing in forming a rash judgement. But I do not conceive it as forming a rash judgement; and is it not a misuse of words to say I know what I am doing in such a case? Rashness, carelessness, omission to think or to act, negligence: it is not reasonable to say that these are never morally sinful, but the sense in which, so far as they are guilty, they are accompanied by knowledge is an extended sense of 'knowledge'. Perhaps the car-driver knew what he did not think of; hence here we might easily say 'You knew perfectly well'; in other cases we say rather 'You would have known if you had thought'.

Abelard was condemned for the opinion that those who crucified Our Lord were not guilty of mortal sin because by Our Lord's own testimony they did not know what they were doing.

The question arises: 'You would have known, if you had thought *when*?' The answer need not be: at the moment of action, when you acted ignorantly. In the time between the arise of the situation and the action you have to take in it, you may easily be in a state of invincible ignorance—i.e., you may be in a state of ignorance that cannot be overcome in that space of time. It might then be argued that you are always in this sense in a state of invincible ignorance at the time of action, if you are in a state of ignorance at all—at least in cases where to act and to abstain from acting are equally critical or you think they are; e.g., you think you ought to perform an abortion in certain circumstances and they arise; or anything else that you think you ought to do, when in fact you ought not to do it.

Here I have changed the ignorance from ignorance of circumstances to ignorance of law. If we revert to ignorance of circumstances, we shall see that the argument is preposterous, for it would exonerate you if you thought (rightly) that you ought to do such-and-such in certain circumstances, and thought (rashly and wrongly) that those circumstances held; the action being such as is wrong in the circumstances that actually held; e.g. you think (rightly) that you ought to dismiss an employee who is selling information where it will do harm, before certain information becomes available to him; and you judge (rashly and wrongly) that this employee is selling information where it will do harm. You had plenty of time in which to make a reasonable investigation, but you formed your judgement without reasonable investigation; now, at the time when you ought to dismiss him if your judgement is right, it would take time which you have not got, to undo your rash judgement. This sort of invincible ignorance would hardly exonerate you.

Thus the answer to our question: 'You would have known, if you had thought *when*?' is: if you had thought when you ought to have thought.

St. Thomas has an article in the *Summa theologiae*: Whether a will that departs from an erroneous conscience is bad?[1] e.g. if a man thinks he ought to fornicate, but chooses not to, is his will bad? St. Thomas's answer to this question, which as he says is the question

[1] 1a 2ae, q.19, a.5.

whether an erroneous conscience binds, is that it does bind: such a will is bad. The reason is that for the will to be bad, it is enough if what a man does is done *qua* bad, i.e., under the conception of evil; so that if he thinks he commits some kind of wrongdoing in doing a certain thing, then formally he does commit it. This point of doctrine is well known and fits in well with the position I sketched at the beginning.

St. Thomas' next article is less well known, and does not fit in with that position at all. For in it he raises the question whether a will that accords with an erroneous conscience is good[2]; and this, as he says, is the same as the question whether an erroneous conscience excuses. His answer is that such a will is bad unless the error, or ignorance, is the kind of ignorance that makes an act involuntary. Further he appears to think that the only kind of ignorance that does make an act involuntary is ignorance, without any negligence, as to some circumstance of a man's action. E.g., to commit adultery one must have intercourse with someone else's spouse; if a man did this knowingly, believing that one ought to, then his will is bad, because the prohibition of adultery is part of the law of God, which a man is obliged to know. But if he thought the woman was his wife—as might happen through his ignorance of, say, a previous valid marriage on her part—then his ignorance, as causing his action to be involuntary, would excuse him. We may note that to make the matter quite clear we could say: the ignorance makes his action involuntary *under the description* 'intercourse with someone else's wife'. However he would be unwilling to say that the appropriate ignorance made the action involuntary under the description 'infringing the law of God', or 'a wicked action', and his reason is clearly that such ignorance is blameworthy, because anyone ought to know that it is against the law, or is wicked, to commit adultery. He appears to adopt the general principle that ignorance of the law does not excuse. Now later theologians, most notably St. Alphonsus, have successfully taught that not all ignorance of the law (i.e. natural law) is blameworthy;* the question whether it is is not, as far as I know, discussed by St. Thomas. St. Alphonsus certainly followed St. Thomas in holding that ignorance of the wrongness of adultery—and even fornica-

* Saint Alphonsus Maria Liguori, *Theologia Moralis, Tomus Primus* editio nova, cura et studio P.Leonardi Gaudé (Romae Ex Typographia Vaticana, 1905): Liber Primus, Tractatus Secundus: De Legibus, Caput IV, Dubium 1: An ignorantia excusat, pp. 147ff.

[2] 1a 2ae, q.19, a.6.

tion—could not but be blameworthy; what was not necessarily blameworthy in his view was ignorance of recondite parts of the law of nature; decisions about right and wrong involving remote and unobvious conclusions from the main outlines of the law—the 'main outlines' being perhaps such as are adumbrated in the ten commandments. St. Thomas at any rate distinguishes between the ten commandments (apart from the ceremonial character of the particular specification of the law demanding that time be set aside for divine things, i.e. the law concerning the sabbaths) and other matters of morals, on the score that the ten commandments are what is most obvious and primary of such laws as come after principles like 'Do good and avoid evil': i.e. as we should say, as have particular content.

For it is surely nothing special about moral laws as opposed to matters of fact that brings about the condemnation of ignorance of them, even if some people have thought so. To see that a type of practice (like St. Monica's cakes) has the malice of superstition or idolatry about it, for example, may need knowledge and judgment above the ordinary; to know concerning negroes or Tierra del Fuegians in dealing with them that they are humans needs no such thing. The one is a matter of law, the other of fact: but it is the matter of fact that a man should be reproached with not realising, and not the matter of law. As is often remarked, recognition of a situation or a proceeding here and now as falling under such-and-such a description is essential to the application in practice of any general law; thus if there is no such thing as an obligation to judge situations right, there can be no such thing as an obligation to act thus and so in such-and-such a situation, but every obligation must be, as many are, conditional on the agent's realisation. This may seem to be so, since if for example someone does not realise the situation because he is drugged or unconscious, we do not think he has any obligations in it: indeed, whatever his body did we should hardly ascribe to him, but should deny him the character of a moral agent altogether. However this does not show that a man must realise the situation in order to have obligations in it but only that he must be able to take care, and by taking care to realise the situation.

Suppose, however, that someone leaves a baby on a doorstep in the winter. If I take care—i.e., if being in the house I look outside the door—I shall realise the situation and so become obliged to rescue the baby from the cold. Further, I am able to take care. In the view I have suggested, does this mean that I am obliged to rescue the baby, and am guilty if I do not take the care that would result in my realising that it was there? This would be an absurdity; this is precisely the sort of situation in which my obligation is conditional on my realising the situation. When then am I to blame for not taking care? Clearly it is wrong to say: when I can take care and don't. The answer must be something like: when it is my job to take care in the kind of way that would in fact lead to realisation.

Yet even that is not enough. Suppose I ought to look out of that door periodically to look at a thermometer there. Then it is my job to take care in a way that would lead to discovery of the baby; yet if I neglect my job, my guilt in respect to the baby's getting frozen, if I have any, is not at all the same as any guilt in respect of ill following upon the gap in the record of thermometer readings. It looks as if (a) one ought to be alert to one's immediate surroundings insofar as it is not reasonable to take it for granted that they don't need attention; (b) one ought to be alert to facts and true consideration concerning what one is doing.

There is a story of a schoolboy who said that pins saved millions of lives every year by not getting swallowed. Someone who tries to explain what is absurd about this may say that a negation cannot be called a cause of anything. However, do not cooks spoil potatoes by not putting salt in the water? and do not signalmen cause accidents by not giving signals?

There are, then, two different ways in which one thing is said to come of another. Firstly, directly, when the other acts, so as to produce it—e.g., something gets hot by being heated by some other hot thing. Second, indirectly, from the mere fact that the other thing does *not* act. For example, we say a ship sank because of the pilot, if he stopped navigating it. All the same, what follows on a failure to act is not always assigned to the agent—*qua* not acting—as a cause, but only when the agent can act and ought to do so. For example, we should hardly say, at least imputing responsibility, that the pilot lost the ship by failure to navigate, if he had died. But if the pilot committed suicide, the statement again becomes reasonable. Again, we should hardly say that a cook gave me a good night's rest by not putting Benzedrine in my dinner, even though it was perfectly in his power to do so, because in any case he ought not to have been putting Benzedrine into his dishes.

We must ask what 'can and ought' mean here. For example, it might be said that a rope saved someone's life by breaking at a critical moment; and perhaps this is so because in some sense the rope could have and ought to have held; could have, at least in the sense that we could not have told that it must break just then; and ought to have, because ropes are meant to hold. In this sense, however, the pilot who dies at the critical moment could after all be said to have lost the ship: in this sense only to a pilot who was not supposed to be navigating the ship or who was not able to navigate because his instruments had broken down, could the loss of the ship for lack of navigation *not* be ascribed. (Of course, here we are not speaking of moral responsibility.)

Now suppose that for the pilot of a ship we substitute the will of a man. To ascribe to the will and to call voluntary are the same. Then if the man could have and ought to have done such-and-such a voluntary action, the failure to do it will also be voluntary; even though the failure is not because he chose not to do it; but simply that it was a voluntary action that he did not do when he could have and ought to have done it. Only if some necessary condition of his doing it is lacking and the lack itself is not voluntary, will his failure be non-voluntary, like the failure of the pilot when the machinery was out of order. Now an essential condition of acting is that you have an idea of doing such-and-such, and an essential condition of acting with a further intention is that you have an idea of such-and-such as your objective. Suppose then that you do not have the idea of doing the thing that you otherwise could do and ought to do, or that you do not have the idea of the thing you ought to be aiming at, what will follow about your guilt or innocence in failing to do what you ought to do?

Let us consider the statement that you could have and ought to have had the idea of doing such-and-such and that your failure is therefore voluntary. There is at once a contrast between this and the statement concerning the exterior act, that a man could have and ought to have done such-and-such and so that his failure was voluntary. For there, there was available one possibility of showing that he could not have done the thing: namely that he did not have the idea of it. But even if it can sometimes be said that a man ought to have had a certain idea, here at any rate there is no such possibility. It cannot be necessary to have an idea of having an idea in order to have the latter idea. If then the voluntariness of anything necessarily involves having an idea of that act, then having an idea cannot be a voluntary thing. One can most easily see this when having the idea is having an explicit thought prior to acting. Then the command to act *thus* is obeyed by first thinking of such-and-such; e.g. – at least in my own case – the command to point North East, say, for I have to orientate myself by thinking of a certain place. But the command to think of such-and-such would not then have to be obeyed by first thinking of something else—or, if it were, the command to think of that something else would not have to be obeyed by first thinking of something else again.

Thus either thoughts are not voluntary or voluntariness does not necessarily involve a separate idea of the thing that is called voluntary. While, then, it may be argued: a man *can't* do what he doesn't think of, when the doing is some exterior action, it cannot similarly be argued: a man can't do what he doesn't think of, when the doing is itself some form of thinking. We must therefore either deny altogether that thoughts are voluntary or admit that if you could and ought to have had such-and-such an idea, this is not conditional on your having the idea of having the idea. 'You ought to have done such-and-such...' can be countered by 'But I didn't know'; 'You ought to have known such-and-such' or 'You ought to have thought of such-and-such' cannot in general be countered in the same way.

Let us return to the analogy of the pilot and the ship. I said that the loss of the ship was ascribable to the pilot if he could have and ought to have navigated the ship; but remember that in this analogy 'could have' relates not to the condition of the pilot but to the navigability of the ship. And similarly, 'could have known' relates not to the condition of the man, but to the knowability of the thing to someone in his position. By 'in his position' I mean, given what he already knows, supposing it is not already to be blameworthy in its limitations; for no one is subject to obligations until he already knows a lot; ordinarily, not until he has mastered a language. (I say 'ordinarily' because of deaf-mutes who don't master a language but are not 'idiotic'.)

'Invincible ignorance' is sometimes spoken of as if it were a psychological condition—not necessarily of mental defect or insanity. I am suggesting that it means 'ignorance that the man himself could not overcome'; as appears from the standard example, that the man who has never heard of Christ is invincibly ignorant of Christianity. Here the impossibility is not an impossibility because of the bent of his mind; he simply has not the information available to attend to.

It will be clear that everything turns on the question whether our thoughts are voluntary: a very difficult question. To say that every thought is voluntary would lead us to say e.g. that a temptation, when this comes in the form of a thought like 'I could pinch that', is voluntary. To deny that thoughts are voluntary at all, except in so far as persisted in, would however seem equally absurd, since thoughts are essential to intentional action, and on this view intentional action will be in large measure non-voluntary. What exactly should be said about this I do not know. The truth about it would surely throw a great deal of light on voluntariness.

13*

Morality

Anybody here who is forty-five to fifty, or more, is sure to remember the fuss that there was somewhere around 1950 about a speaker called Margaret Knight, who announced on the radio that it was possible to have morality without religion. There was an enormous amount of fuss about this; the newspapers treated it as if it were a big extraordinary event that had occurred, and some of us were quite mystified why they should do so. The only explanation that I myself could think of was that it was on the radio; because the opinion was surely not an unusual one. But it was possible that Lord Reith hadn't let that sort of thing be broadcast before.

In the discussions that followed, many of which I heard, there was not very much pointed out about the confusion that there is in this thought: whether it means that (apart from that part of morality which is associated with duties to God) there is a logical independence, and that a decent person can think out a true morality if he keeps his head and is able to think clearly, without appeal to religious revelation; that you don't have to believe in God to object to lying, for example. That's one thing it might have meant. Another thing it might have meant, and I think is the one I want to concentrate on, though nobody referred to it at the time, is: 'give up religion, let religion completely fade away, (even more than it had by that time—and it had a lot, by that time) and there'll still be morality'. I remember nobody at all asking: 'Well, of course, human beings have always had morality, but the question is *what* morality?'

The suggestion that you should ask 'what morality?' was not made in any discussion that I heard. It always seemed to be assumed that if you could have morality, it would be... well, morality! There's only one! I suppose that to some extent Catholics themselves took

* Talk given on 20 February 1982, and subsequently published in C. Marneau (ed.), *Pro Ecclesia et Pontifice* (1982), pp. 16–18

that position; I remember Frank Pakenham* rather taking that position when talking about his friendship with Margaret Knight, and what a good person she was, what a good line she was taking... I'm sure that *he* thought it would be the true morality as taught by the Catholic Church, or if not, that there would be very peripheral points of disagreement.

I remember getting into a discussion (just to remind you of how rapidly things slid in the decades since then) at a party in Oxford, about contraception, then already widely approved, and remarking that you would surely get it leading on to abortion – I mean to abortions being generally acceptable – and my colleagues, the Warnocks, philosophers, being absolutely outraged at this suggestion. It was a completely blackguardly suggestion, they said, that if you believed in contraception you would get on to believing in abortion, or that people would make a slide towards abortion. Well, of course the facts have now proved that I was right as to what would actually happen. That there isn't a logical connection may be true; indeed, I do have non-Catholic friends who heartily approve of contraception and bitterly disapprove of abortion (and I don't know if they bother themselves about what methods of contraception are abortifacient!). So that is a possible position, but it is not a psychologically likely position.

Nowadays, when the fact that something is connected with disapproval of abortion is cited – say in the *London Review of Books* – as a proof of what a zany thing it is, or what a completely contemptible thing it is, it may be difficult to remember how, as recently as 1950, one could be thought to be absolutely blackguardly for saying a thing like: 'It's a first step, it'll go on to abortion, it'll go on from there to infanticide and to various other forms of murder.' Now one might think that I'm now talking about a great slide downhill in what's publicly accepted since the Second World War. Not so; we'd already started a considerable slide downhill before that: with everybody approving of measures of massacre of civilian populations as a method of warfare. This was a big step which had already been taken, and there was relatively little objection to it. And Catholics, I fear (I'm sorry to say this; I'm now talking about un-reconstructed Catholics, old-fashioned Catholics, people who were brought up on that excellent thing, the Catechism, as promulgated by the Bishops of England and Wales) they, I fear, had had their own slide downhill

* Francis Aungier Pakenham, 7th Earl of Longford (1905–2001), who became a Catholic in 1940, was a politician, author and social reformer.

already in a doctrine which is to be found in that Catechism: that full knowledge and full consent are necessary for the commission of mortal sin.* This—and it is a very important doctrine—appears to be false as well as being ambiguous. One might think that it was true, but warn against the ambiguity, and say: 'Look, it's like the doctrine of *mens rea* in the law; the doctrine of *mens rea* doesn't say 'You've got to feel guilty in order to be guilty'; it says that you have to have a guilty mind, and that means that you had to know that you were putting poison in your husband's soup—that if you didn't know that you were putting poison in your husband's soup, genuinely didn't know, and couldn't have been expected to know, well then, you haven't got a *mens rea* about having poisoned your husband, even though you did'.

Now, one might hold, and at one time I assumed that this must be the correct interpretation, that the doctrine that you can't commit mortal sin without full knowledge and full consent does not mean that you can't commit mortal sin unless you are fully conscious that it is mortal sin, and mean to commit mortal sin as such. What it means is that you've got to know what you're doing. Not in the sense that 'what you're doing is mortal sin' but in the sense that 'what you're doing is putting poison in your husband's soup'. Now, that appeared to me, when I first thought about it as a young convert, on the whole an acceptable doctrine. I fear that the other form—that you have to mean it as mortal sin (which renders it awfully rare, I should think, to commit mortal sin)—is a form in which it has got through into people's minds. But even in the form in which it seemed understandable to me then, I came to think it was unacceptable. And the way in which it is unacceptable is pointed to in what I said just now: 'If you didn't know *and nobody could expect you to know*'.

It's not enough to be ignorant; you must be not too blameworthily ignorant in order to be free of guilt in respect of an action. And it's simply not true that all affected ignorance, all 'taking care not to know', all 'not bothering to find out' is merely venial. This, I think, is a very deadly doctrine: that you have to be absolutely clear about just what you're doing, in saying something to somebody, in giving something to somebody, in taking money from somebody, before it can be a grievous sin. It seems to me on reflection to be a grievously false doctrine; and though not so bad as the idea that you've got to think of it as mortal sin for it to be mortal sin, all the same tending in the same direction. It leads to the idea that 'I am justified if my con-

* But see footnote ** on p. 101 of the previous paper 'On Being in Good Faith'.

science doesn't reproach me' which is directly contrary to what St. Paul says in one of his letters to the Corinthians.* It is false; and so is the idea that somebody may be exonerated on the grounds that they are caring and conscientious people.

To quote Scripture: 'The tender mercies of the wicked are cruel'.** Remember that we have just been celebrating one of those 'Years' that are announced nowadays: the 'Year of the Disabled'. And one of the ways in which we celebrated it in this country was to have the green light given to people who want to kill babies that their parents don't want.*** We have landed up in the position of an alcoholic who has installed a thousand gallons of ethyl alcohol, assuring everybody—and himself—that he doesn't mean to drink it at all, but he must have it, just in case. We are, in short, surrounded by murder. The second great sin recorded in Scripture. The first was disobedience, the second murder.

The belief that murder is something absolutely prohibited, that those whose feet are swift to shed innocent blood are utterly condemned, used not to be a peculiarity of those who conformed to the Christian religion, Protestant or Catholic. It is rapidly becoming, and I hope it will really become, a mark of those who adhere to the Catholic religion, at least. But we are surrounded by murder. First, a million or so abortions; second, the sophisticated weaponry we have recently been told about for overcoming the sophisticated defences of the city of Moscow; and third, the policy of killing born babies. And I mention murder because the prohibition of it is one of the most grave of the divine prohibitions. Take away justice, said St. Augustine, and what are governments but Mafias?**** That is the situation we are in; and we ought to regard ourselves, as we do not, I fear, as separate.

* 1 *Corinthians* 4.4: 'True, my conscience does not reproach me at all, but that does not prove that I am acquitted; the Lord alone is my judge.'

** *Proverbs* 12.10.

*** The reference is to the acquittal at Leicester Crown Court on 5 November 1981 of the pediatrician Dr Leonard Arthur of the attempted murder of John Pearson, a baby born with Down's syndrome whose parents did not wish him to survive. Dr Arthur had accordingly ordered 'nursing care only' for the baby, an instruction which meant the administration of heavy doses of a sedative (DF 118), so that the child would rarely demand to be fed. He died a little more than 69 hours after birth. For an account of the case see Luke Gormally 'Note: Regina v Arthur' in Luke Gormally (ed) *Euthanasia, Clinical Practice and the Law* (London: The Linacre Centre, 1994), pp. 104–7.

**** 'Remota iustitia, quid sunt regna nisi magna latrocinia.'

14*

Sin

Part I: Two Definitions

A. What is sin? It is usually thought of as a character of action, but we must not forget that there are also sins of negligence and omission, not all of which are very naturally called actions. We may say that there are two definitions of sin:

1. They are behaviours against [right][1] reason.
2. They are behaviours against divine law.

B. Thinking of sins under the descriptions 'wrong-doing', and so having actions in mind, we get a problem: how is wrong-doing possible? In Plato's *Protagoras* we find Socrates saying: 'I am pretty sure that no one among the wise thinks that anyone goes wrong or willingly does base and evil deeds'** For this opinion of the wise, argument is needed, which Plato gives us elsewhere. He convinced Aristotle, and through him many others, that there is a problem: How can anyone voluntarily do what he thinks is bad?

Definition (2) belongs properly with belief in God as law-giver. God is the cause of all other things, so how can anything happen contrary to the divine will? Must it not be accomplished in everything, including the actions of creatures having reason and will?

C. It emerges from Plato's thought quoted above, and from his argument, that wrong-doing is something involving will. What is voluntariness? That sins, or wrongful behaviour, are essentially voluntary either leads to the Platonic view that they cannot happen, or, if that is

* From the text of an unpublished typescript corrected by the author. The four parts of this paper are the four McGivney Lectures that Professor Anscombe delivered in 1989 at the John Paul II Institute in Washington, D.C.
** *Protagoras* 345d-e.

[1] Why I have inserted 'right' [in square brackets] in A1 will become clear.

false, the statement shows the importance of understanding voluntariness.

D. In Catholic Christian tradition there is a distinction between mortal and venial sins. Are these different in kind? The criteria for a sin's being mortal that are most widely accepted stem from St. Alphonsus Liguori. These seem to make it very doubtful whether there can be any mortal sins of omission which are not deliberately chosen.

E. Any punishment of sin by God has become an unpopular belief in many circles, most of all in the form in which it includes belief in Hell.—But Thomas More told his daughter: If he should go to Hell for his sins, still he would be serving for the glorification of God's justice.

F. Fallen human nature and original sin. The impossibility of avoiding actual sins for those who have reached the age of reason and are heirs of original sin. How is redemption conceivable? What is it?

The definition of sin

Let is now begin with our A. It is because of there being sins of omission and negligence—which I want to discuss later—that I put the word 'behaviours' rather than 'actions' into the two definitions of sins. For even when it does not itself involve any particular action—any act of choice for example or deliberate avoidance of something required in carrying out a duty—negligence is certainly a behaviour. So is omission, on the understanding that omission to do something is not just any non-doing. Everyone knows this: the fact that I am not currently opening my door or rolling up a carpet does not straightaway mean that I am *omitting* to do so. It is only in some present-day discussions of moral philosophy that this seems to be forgotten, for in such discussions authors sometimes write as if one is 'omitting' to do just anything which one is not doing and which it is possible for one to be doing. This thought is wrong. I have said enough for the moment to explain my counting omissions as well as negligence as 'behaviours', along with what it is natural to call 'actions'.

The two definitions are equivalent as far as concerns what they cover. In saying this, I am making certain assumptions. First, that it is reasonable to speak of actions at any rate as sometimes being 'against reason'. And second, that reason dictates the worship of the one true deity.

In both assumptions I am at enmity with David Hume. He thought reason's chief role in action was to avoid mistakes (about what we would now call 'facts') in choosing means to our ends. It can also inform us of possible things we might make our ends. 'Reason is and ought only to be the slave of the passions'.[2] With this he threw down the gauntlet at Socrates, who was horrified at the idea of reason, thought, intellect, being dragged about like a slave in the service of the passions. Hume secures himself, first by claiming that reason is purely discovery either of circumstances, or of the relations of ideas; second by professing to regard any argument from 'is' to 'ought' as unjustified; and third by distinguishing between 'calm' and 'violent' passions. Benevolence, for example, and love of truth are 'calm passions' and it would seem that having an aim must also be a calm passion, if it is not of the more ordinary kind. Because of its nature reason cannot be supposed to dictate anything at all, so it cannot be supposed to dictate our aims. It can only tell of means which are likely to help secure one's ends. There is a good deal more to Hume's moral philosophy than these points, but they are enough to show how he does object to the idea of actions and choices being 'against reason' except in the limited way I have mentioned.

I will oppose him here by saying: Suppose we change his dictum to 'Reason is and ought to be the slave of the will'. It is not so different if we remember that in the relevant sense of 'will' he should, though he does not, count will as a 'passion'. We need not discuss his quite stupid account of volition as 'the impression we feel and are conscious of, when we knowingly give rise to any new motion of our body, or new perception of our mind'.[3] We need only remark that it is false and useless. Voluntariness, though it is not an accompanying impression, is in what he here calls 'knowingly giving rise to'.

'Tis not contrary to reason to prefer the destruction of the whole world to the scratching of my finger'.[4] This 'preference' is will, though he speaks there of a *passion's* 'choosing'.

It is important to notice that it is human, once capable of it, to have generic ends. By 'generic ends' I mean such things as being rich, getting knowledge of natural science, being physically healthy and

[2] *A Treatise of Human Nature*, Book II, Part III, Section III. [Selby-Bigge edition, p. 415.]

[3] *Ibid.* Book II, Part III, Section I. [Selby-Bigge edition, p. 399.]

[4] *Ibid.* Section III. [Selby-Bigge edition, p. 416.]

active, having a life of pleasures. This observation does not controvert Hume. He wins, if he does win his game, with his assertions about reason. 'Reason is the discovery of truth and falsehood. Truth or falsehood consist in agreement or disagreement either to the *real* relations of ideas, or to real existence and matter of fact'.[5] He merely dogmatically asserts this. Reason issues no orders. By itself it can never 'give rise to volition'.[6] Hume has only this dogma for an implicit denial that reason *can so much as frame* directives also prescribing ends... 'Invest, and as wisely as you can'. Why? 'To become well off. Make that your aim'. This is no 'discovery'. But could Hume deny that these are formulations by the *faculty* of reason? They do not have to be right, or effective, to be that. Nor am I saying anything about whether they are good. But they are formulations constructible by the power of reason, and Hume's account would deny that they can be such. Their role is to formulate directives (to adopt, and how pursue, a generic end) to the will of the person they are addressed to. They imply he has or will have money to spare. Whether he accepts these directives, as with many directives, is up to him.

Hume assumes, as is often assumed, that 'reason' means 'right' or 'correct' reason. But he could hardly allow that anything, true or false, that *he* would call 'reason' could as such be a directive to a will; let alone one where obedience or disobedience would allow us to infer virtue or vice in the man whose will was addressed.

An imperative for men, good if taken as a first principle by anyone willing to govern his life 'by reason' is: Aim at what human life is for attaining; i.e. this imperative is good if there is such a true end. That there is can well be argued. It is also clear that here 'reason' does mean *right* reason.

My second assumption was that 'reason' demands the worship of the one true deity. It is not clear that anyone who believes in God must think that God makes laws to obey. Aristotle, for example, believed in what he calls νουσ και θεος – mind and god. (This is a double expression for one thing.[7]) He said that none of the 'goods of nature' was worth choosing or getting if this impeded the worship and contemplation of God. But in the same passage[8] he says that God

---

[5] *Ibid.* Book III, Part I, Section I. [Selby-Bigge edition, p. 458.]

[6] *Ibid.* Book II, Part III, Section III. [Selby-Bigge edition, p. 414.]

[7] See *Metaphysics*, Book VII.

[8] *Eudemian Ethics*, Book VIII, 1249b, 15–17.

does not direct – give orders – like medical science, but is the end for which practical wisdom is directive, as health is of medical science. I know of nowhere where he speaks of God as issuing commands, making laws which we are to obey. Therefore, I cite him to show that one may hold that reason demands the worship and contemplation of God without holding that sins are behaviours contrary to divine law. I labour the point because the thesis that sins – wrongdoings and bad behaviours – are 'against reason' is one which people might associate with atheism. If they do so, then they would not agree that the two definitions cover the same things. For if sins are behaviours contrary to the permanent law promulgated by God in human hearts, then that law includes divine worship, and it might be thought that, whatever else the two definitions of sin coincide in, the second one covers more than the first, since it would include neglecting to contemplate and worship God. But that is not a matter in which the two definitions do not coincide, if reason's discoveries rightly include deity.

I spoke of what a will needs intelligence to present to it as possible generic ends (and such, I said, it is human to have). I did not mean to say that reason recommends or demands that one pursue a given end just because it is of this kind. It is obvious, though, that reason may very well *criticise* some of them. A life of harmless pleasures is not an end in which one is likely to succeed; or even to rejoice in so far as one does attain it. A life of physical health and physical activity prompts reason to ask 'With a view to what?' and also to remind one that such strength at least fails with age. It is reason that can employ the conceptions of an end's being fine, noble or intrinsically worthwhile. Of all the ends we can call 'generic' and hence describe in a way that contrasts their attainment with particular happenings, a life of much contemplation and worship of the divine is the one which can least become empty. Only by one's becoming hopelessly insane or an imbecile or mindless can it be rendered impossible, perhaps or even certainly, as may seem if one sinks into a catatonic state. But if such happens, the whole question of the relation of reason to will falls to the ground. Thus I can speak unconditionally of reason demanding the worship of God, itself a fruit of contemplation, which has no greater object. Of 'generic' ends, without distinguishing their values, I gave a few examples. I have now added to this that reason may contemptuously criticise some of them as of little worth, or, as Aristotle says in the *Eudemian Ethics*, actually bad if – or when – they prevent the contemplation and worship of God.

Many people are affected by a false philosophical opinion which is probably traceable to Hume as having started it—though there may be a seed of it in Spinoza. It would lead them to say 'You have used the words 'fine', 'noble', 'worthwhile' and 'bad': now these are *value* terms, pro or anti terms, and as such are rooted in attitudes of will and emotion'. This is a foolish thought: if you want to think that, you will have to think the same of 'Swimming is good for the muscles'; 'It is the object of medical science and art to promote health and not to kill' and similar things. The rejection of teleology is often a concession to mere intellectual fashion: it is practised by students of biology who are apparently unconscious of using teleological concepts very often. But they are not supposed to think that final causes are respectable to believe in, and the dogmatism against teleology has had some momentous consequences.

It is a curiosity that Aristotle's 'ergon' in the first book of the *Nicomachean Ethics* is regularly and in each application of it translated 'function'. He enquires how, say, the eye can have a function (here the translation is reasonable) and the man whose eye it is, not. Students regularly reject the idea of a human being *qua* human having a *function*. But Aristotle's argument is a good one: if the whole does not have something, or things, it does (the proper meaning of 'ergon'), how can some integral part of it have a function *in* it? We may or may not arrive at the notion of some end that humans are to reach if possible, but it is beyond dispute that there are things it is human to do, and especially that there are ways of conducting their lives (well or badly) that are specifically human.

Actions 'against reason' are actions against nature, i.e. against what we ought to do according to our nature.

Suppose we were born able to talk, to run about like foals, to handle things and move them purposefully. Suppose we didn't need sleep, but a sleep-like condition was a rare thing with consequences that were bad for us.

Suppose there were 'people seeds' blowing about all the time. Suppose anyone killed would come to life again after a month if kept suitably—but unless they did they became literally rooted in the ground like trees. Suppose everyone changed to the opposite sex at the age of about thirty. There would be different rules of behaviour; moral virtues and vices would involve different actions from what they involve in our lives as they are.

If our nature is a divine creation, the divine law would be different if the nature created was different, and it would command and forbid the things that would then be good and bad according to that nature's needs. These things reason could work out without belief in divine commandments.

I am not saying that the two definitions of sin mean the same, that the words have the same sense. There is one quite striking difference: if we explain 'sin' in terms of a divine law, we introduce a concept of disobedience into the meaning of the word. Concepts of obedience and disobedience do not enter into the explanation: 'Sins are behaviours which are against reason'.

So far as I can tell, we owe the conception of divine law, which we ought to obey, to the old covenant. (This we are accustomed to call the 'Old Testament'.) If God revealed to the ancient Jews how they should live, the question arises whether and how other peoples could know the content of these laws, which were not given to them. At least a part of them, which was important for the human race as such to know, was not revealed to it then on Sinai. It is a very natural answer, which has indeed been given, that when human beings by their own reason have been able to think things out, their realisation was itself a promulgation to them of the divine laws. I am not sure how important this belief is. It may be implied in St. Paul's letter to the Romans.[9]

The apparent impossibility of wrong-doing

Here I will translate Plato's argument. There are bits of it in more than one dialogue, but this, which is the clearest and fullest statement of it, comes in the *Meno*.*

Meno: What I call virtue is: wanting noble things, to be able to attain them.

Socrates: So you are saying that wanting what is noble is wanting what is good?

Meno: Quite.

Socrates: So there are people who want ignoble things, while others want good ones. Doesn't everyone seem to you to want what is good?

Meno: No.

Socrates: Some people want bad things?

* *Meno* 77b-78a.

[9] *Rom* 1.18ff.

Meno: Yes.

Socrates: Thinking the bad things are good, or recognising that they are bad, and wanting them all the same?

Meno: Both, I think.

Socrates: Does anyone seem to you, Meno, to recognise the badness of what is bad and still want it?

Meno: Absolutely.

Socrates: What do you mean by wanting…? Is it wanting… to become something of yours?

Meno: Of course it is.

Socrates: Thinking that the bad things are useful to anyone who gets them, or recognising that they harm him?

Meno: Some think one thing, some the other.

Socrates: And do the ones who recognise the badness of what is bad think the bad things useful?

Meno: I don't think so.

Socrates: So isn't it obvious that the ones who don't recognise the bad things don't want *them*, they want things that they think are good, but which are in fact bad? So it's obvious that people who are wrong, but who do think those things good, want *good* things. Isn't it?

Meno: Apparently *those* do.

Socrates: What about the ones who, as you say, want bad things, thinking that they harm whoever gets them? Do they know they'll be harmed by them?

Meno: They must.

Socrates: But don't they think people are miserable if they are harmed?

Meno: That must be so too.

Socrates: And aren't miserable people unlucky?

Meno: I think so.

Socrates: Does anyone want to be miserable and unlucky?

Meno: I don't think so Socrates.

Socrates: So, Meno, no one wants bad things, unless he wants to be like that. For what is being miserable, except wanting, and getting, bad things?

There is the argument that no one can possibly voluntarily go wrong; do disgraceful or bad things. It stands there in the face of the fact that people manifestly do do wrong, do do disgraceful things. It is an essential part of the argument that Meno's supposition is that some do and some do not want and choose to do the disgraceful things *as such*. Those who do not, do not really want anything bad, they want good things. (Here it is not noticed that not wanting to do something bad *as such* does not mean one does not want to do it.) However, those who do choose bad things as such all the same cannot realise that they are bad, because no one wants to be harmed. It is here that the argument is most clearly mistaken; for it assumes that a conscious doer of a bad action knows that, *qua* bad, it will harm him. This may seem to be an exposition of Plato's view that all sin is ignorance, i.e. error about what you are doing. But it is not here in fact such an exposition. For it is not part of Socrates' argument that a conscious evil-doer does *not* know that evil-doing will harm him—the argument explicitly relies on it, at the end, that he does know that. The argument is that he does not think a bad action is any good, because he does not think it is useful, i.e. will procure good for him. Meno indeed is made to *say* he doesn't think that people who recognise the badness of what is bad regard it as useful but he should not have said that. We are very likely to recognise something as bad, but think it useful, and choose to do it for the sake of the advantage that we hope to get out of it. The evil-doer does in fact probably not know that evil-doing will harm him, and if he did, perhaps he would not choose it. In that sense, *if* reason (properly in command) would be against bad actions, it is indeed dragged about like a slave and made to serve bad wishes, or hang-ups. But Socrates' argument is that since the would-be evil-doer wants not to be harmed, he *cannot* be wanting to do bad things he recognises as bad—so, after all, there is no such thing as voluntary bad action.

It is true that it is usually for the sake of something one thinks advantageous (and so in a sense good) that one consciously misbehaves, but that does not mean that one's will is just for the good and not for the misbehaviour, recognisably such, at all.

That reason (intellect, knowledge) should be 'dragged about like a slave' is the thesis that Socrates finds appalling, and it is this that Aristotle deals with in the *Nicomachean Ethics*. His comments are various, but his main conclusion is that an action does not depend only on general principles but also on the diagnosis of particular facts. Murder is wicked—such an act as is here and now proposed would be murder—therefore one abstains or refuses. This is a possible example of a 'practical syllogism'. (The conclusion is the actual abstention.) There is, however, another example—and here I actually draw on Aristotle's text*—in which the main general premise is:

Eating sweet things is forbidden

and the main particular one is:

This is sweet

upon which, treating it as a practical syllogism, one abstains. But another possibility lurks. There is a different main general premise possible:

Sweet things are delicious

and if this, together with the same other (particular) premise, wins, one eats the sweet thing in spite of knowing the prohibition.

So, Aristotle says, the thing that Socrates was looking for (or investigating) really does happen. But it is not the knowledge of the general premise that is 'dragged about like a slave', but rather the particular one 'This is sweet', which is common to the proper practical syllogism and to what we may call the 'pleasure syllogism'.

Someone who investigates like this has been captivated by what Socrates presents—or what Plato makes Socrates present—in the *Meno*, yet is unwilling to draw the conclusion that any wrong-doing is just ignorance and is not voluntary as wrong-doing; he sees it all as a problem. So have many philosophers done since Aristotle, and it is a standard theme in modern Anglo-American philosophy. How can one do what one thinks is wrong? This often nowadays is discussed in the light—or darkness—of analysing thinking something wrong in terms of one's behaviour. I have not seen discussion of the argument Plato actually puts into Socrates' mouth. But, fallacious though it is, it is interesting, in particular for its conclusion that wrong-doing which is voluntary *as such* is impossible.

It may help to give a short abstract of the end of Socrates' argument: Evil-doing harms the evil-doer.—No one wants to be harmed.—Why then does anyone do bad things? He cannot; unless

* *Nicomachean Ethics* 1137a32–b5

it is for the sake of the good things he thinks they are or will get for him.—Then he isn't *wanting* the bad, but what is good. So he is not someone with a bad will.—Why then does he do the bad things? Through mistaken belief that they are good, or will get good, for him.—So in any case, there cannot be voluntary bad actions.

Part II: Voluntariness and Sins of Omission

In speaking of Plato's argument that all wrongdoing—as we should call it—is ignorance, I tacitly approved the implication that the will is involved in good and bad human action. As far as bad action is concerned, this is supported by the universal doctrine that wrongdoing, or sin, must be voluntary. What excludes voluntariness excludes guilt. However, note that 'voluntary' is being used in a specially broad way when we say that. If someone does something under threat from another man, say of pain or death or eviction, we would say it was forced on him. 'I did it quite voluntarily' implies that I acted without such compulsion. But when we are using 'voluntary' to speak of human acts as having to be voluntary—this being part of what we mean by a 'human act' or 'human action'—we do not say that acts done under threat are not voluntary. An act is voluntary in the way we are speaking of here if it is in the power of the agent to do it or not—he can resist the threat, that is: he can refuse to do what he is being 'made' to do, if possible, by threat. This 'can' is first and foremost a matter of physical possibility. If you chain me to a post and your chain is effective, I cannot walk away from the post if I cannot break or escape the chain by my own physical powers. So my remaining chained up is not voluntary unless I have e.g. arranged it with you and you will unchain me if I ask you to. This conception of *not being able to* gets extended metaphorically to one of reason's being 'so vehemently bent upon an act of sensual appetite that it is turned away from consideration in the particular case of what it habitually knows in a general way'.[10]

To regard this as taking away the agent's freedom to apply his mind or not to apply it, is, however, a mistake—a mistake made by people who will say that the force of pleasure or desire or anger is a compulsion like being physically chained so that one does what one does *necessarily*. This suggestion is considered by Aristotle in the

[10] St Thomas Aquinas, *Quaestiones disputatae de Malo*, q.3, a.9 c.: '... ratio ligatur ex hoc quod intentio animae applicatur vehementer ad actum appetitus sensitivi; unde avertitur a considerando in particulari id quod habitualiter in universali cognoscit'.

Nicomachean Ethics, and is rejected by him.* It is also considered and rejected by St. Thomas in his *Quaestiones Disputatae de Malo*. But he goes on to say:

> If passion's chain on reason went so far that it was not in the power of the will to break such a chain—say if someone were driven mad by passion—then whatever he did he would not be counted guilty any more than any other insane person. Unless perhaps as far as concerned the starting point of the passion, which was voluntary, for he was able at first to prevent his passion from going so far; as a homicide committed through drunkenness is imputed to a man as guilt, because the beginning of his drunkenness was voluntary.[11]

We should note that the example offered by St. Thomas is one in which there is a—perhaps brief—insanity. It is not suggested that anything like that is true of a more ordinary case of a man's being led astray by passion.

> Applying one's mind to something or not applying it, is in the power of the will. Therefore, it is in the power of the will to exclude the chaining of the reason. So the act committed, which proceeds from such chaining, is voluntary; hence it is not exonerated even from mortal guilt.[12]

This is an instructive passage. It needs amplification by the article in the *Summa theologiae* where the question is whether the will can be subjected to violence. We are given a distinction between the immediate act of the will, which is *willing*, and an act 'commanded by the will', which involves the mediation of another power; examples are walking and talking.

* *Nicomachean Ethics* 1110a4–19.

[11] *De Malo*, q.3, a.10c.: 'Si ligatio rationis per passionem in tantum procederet, quod non esset in potestate voluntatis huiusmodi ligamen removere, puta si per aliquam animae passionem aliquis in insaniam verteretur, quidquid commiteret non imputaretur ei ad culpam, sicut nec alii insano, nisi forte quantum ad principium talis passionis quod fuit voluntarium, poterat enim voluntas a principio impedire ne passio in tantum procederet; sicut homicidium per ebrietatem commissum imputatur homini ad culpam, quia principium ebrietatis fuit voluntarium'. St Alphonsus quoting this passage in his *Theologia Moralis (De Peccatis)* omits the reference to being driven by passion.

[12] *De Malo*, q.3, a.10 c.: 'Applicare autem intentionem ad aliquid vel non applicare, in potestate voluntatis existit. Unde in potestate voluntatis est quod ligamen rationis excludat. Actus ergo commissus, qui ex tali ligamine procedit, est voluntarius, unde non excusatur a culpa etiam mortali'.

> The act peculiar to the will cannot be subject to violence because this act is nothing but a turning towards something, which proceeds from an interior starting point of knowing something. But what is forced or subject to violence comes from something external. Hence it is contrary to the concept of the act of will itself for it to be constrained or forced ... A man can be dragged violently; but for this to be from his will is contrary to the concept of violence.[13]

The doctrine of an act directly of the will, which is *willing*, is dubious. How many such acts of will have I performed in the last five minutes? By physical violence you can drag me, applying force to my body. You cannot apply force to my faculty of meaning to ... Even if under threat I consented to your dragging me, I am not meaning to move because my powers of meaning to do this or that are being themselves acted upon by your physical violence, as my body is.

I have put the verb 'to mean' here, where St. Thomas speaks of 'willing', of the 'act of the will itself'. The influence of physical violence, if there was any such influence on what I did mean to happen, would always have been indirect: you hit me several times, let us say, and then I consented to your dragging me. We can say that, without speaking of an *act* of meaning to ... on my part. Anyone who then simply saw me dragged would rightly say that my motion was not physiologically voluntary.

Hence St. Thomas' last sentence in the quoted passage is more correct, not involving any theory of the proper act of the will itself: 'A man can be dragged by violence, but that this is from the will is contrary to the concept of violence'. A movement's being 'from his will' here means the same as its being physiologically voluntary; it is of course not excluded by 'not from his will' for him to have arranged with some people in advance that they should drag him. If he had, then his being dragged would be voluntary, though not physiologically so, and the violence would be being exercised on his body, not on his will or intention.

---

[13] *Summa theologiae* 1a 2ae q.6, a.4 c.: 'Sed quantum ad ipsum proprium actum voluntatis, non potest ei violentia inferri. Et huius ratio est quia actus voluntatis nihil est aliud quam inclinatio quaedam procedens ab interiori principio cognoscente, sicut appetitus naturalis est quaedam inclinatio ab interiori principio et sine cognitione. Quod autem est coactum vel violentum est ab exteriori principio. Unde contra rationem ipsius actus voluntatis est quod sit coactus vel violentus ... potest homo per violentiam trahi, sed quod hoc sit ex eius voluntate repugnat rationi violentiae'.

That last suggestion, of violence being exercised on his will, is contrary to the concept of violence as it comes into discussion of counter-voluntary actions. (I use 'counter-voluntary' to translate St. Thomas' 'involuntarium'.) An action may be counter-voluntary either through violence or through ignorance. It is counter-voluntary through violence when for example winds or strong men carry you *where you do not want to go*—you contributing nothing to your passage. Thus Aristotle in Book III of the *Nicomachean Ethics*.* He also remarks that the counter-voluntary always involves pain (distress, or grief—however you translate the Greek λυπη).** Now suppose you are lying in a punt—a flat-bottomed boat—and you meant to stay there awhile, you do not want to be carried out into the middle of the river. But someone jestingly pushes your punt out with a pole. Is this not counter-voluntary for you? You did not want to be pushed out. But suppose when it happens you are pleased? No distress or grief here—yet you were carried by being pushed where you did not want to go. St. Thomas perceived the problem, and in his commentary on the *Nicomachean Ethics*, he says that being *pleased* is a contribution on your part. This saves the case from being one of counter-voluntary motion.***

Thus in that context *violence* would involve your motion's not being voluntary. But if you introduce any aspect which makes it voluntary, you make it no longer fall under the concept 'counter-voluntary through violence'. Hence I like St. Thomas's speaking of voluntariness as conflicting with the concept of violence better than his speaking of violence as conflicting with the concept of the act of the will itself.

That voluntariness always involves an 'act of the will' is in any case actually denied by Thomas. He asks whether voluntariness can be there without any act at all. He says that what is from the will is what is called voluntary. But this 'from something' has two applications.[14] In one way the 'from' is direct because something proceeds from something else which is active, as heating proceeds from what is hot. In the other way it is indirect, from the very fact of not acting,

* *Nicomachean Ethics* 1110a3.

** *Ibid.* 1110b19.

*** Sancti Thomae Aquinatis *In Decem Libros Ethicorum Aristotelis ad Nicomachum Expositio*, Lib.3, lect.1, 387.

---

[14] *Summa theologiae* 1a 2ae q.6, a.3 sed contra: 'Illud cuius domini sumus, dicitur esse voluntarium. Sed nos domini sumus eius quod est agere et non agere, velle et non velle. Ergo sicut agere et velle est voluntarium, ita et non agere et non velle'.

as one says that the sinking of a ship comes from the pilot inasmuch as he was not engaged in piloting it. But it has to be realised that what follows from lack of action does not always go back to an agent as cause from the mere fact of his not acting, but only when he can and ought to act. For if the pilot *could not* pilot the ship, or if the piloting of it were not committed to him, the sinking of the ship would not be imputed to him, though it occurred for lack of a pilot.[15]

> Because, therefore, the will, by willing and acting, can and sometimes ought to prevent not willing and not acting, such non-willing and not acting is imputed to it as if having existence from it. And in this way what is voluntary can be without any external action, as when one wills not to act; but sometimes also without any interior act, as when one does not will at all.[16]

Thus the teaching of St. Thomas. And it goes further yet. Enquiring whether ignorance is a sin, he says: 'Ignorance means privation of knowledge when, that is, someone is lacking knowledge of those things which he is naturally able to know'.[17] St. Thomas is here distinguishing between ignorance and nescience. Nescience is merely not knowing; ignorance is primarily not knowing what one needs to know in living: such very fundamental things as *any* human being can be born able to know – i.e. to grasp as he develops. If he does not know them and – as we would nowadays naturally say – this cannot be attributed to brain damage, then he is called ignorant, whether he has actual false views on them, or never thinks about them at all. Some of these anyone (we might say, any responsible human being) ought to know:

> they are things without the knowledge of which he cannot engage in such action as is due from him. Hence all ought to know things of faith and universal precepts of the law; particular people ought to know the things that concern their condition or their job ... It is obvious that anyone neglecting to have or do what he ought to have or do sins by a sin of omission. Hence, on

[15] *Summa theologiae* 1a 2ae q.6, a.3 c.: '...submersio navis dicitur esse a gubernatore inquantum desistit a gubernando ... solum tunc cum potest et debet agere...'.

[16] *Ibid.*: 'Quia igitur voluntas, volendo et agendo, potest impedire hoc quod est non velle et non agere, et aliquando debet; hoc quod est non velle et non agere imputatur ei, quasi ab ipsa existens. Et sic voluntarium potest esse absque actu: quandoque quidem, absque actu exteriori, cum actu interiori, sicut vult non agere; aliquando autem et absque actu interiori, sicut cum non vult'.

[17] *Summa theologiae* 1a 2ae q.76, a.2 c.: 'Ignorantia vero importat scientiae privationem: dum scilicet alicui deest scientia eorum quae aptus natus est scire'.

> account of negligence the ignorance of the things that one ought to know is sin. But it is not imputed to a man as negligence, if he does not know what he cannot know. And ignorance of these things is called invincible, because it cannot be overcome by *studium* [i.e. by effort and application]. Since such ignorance is not voluntary ... it is not sin.[18]

St. Thomas teaches also that ignorance may be voluntary.

> It is voluntary either directly as when someone purposely wills not to know something so as to sin more freely, or indirectly when someone, either because of work or because of other occupations, neglects to learn what would draw him away from sin. Such negligence makes the ignorance itself voluntary and sinful; so long as it is ignorance of things which one ought to know and can know.[19]

Notice that 'ought and can' is a key expression for St. Thomas: a failure to do something is voluntary if one both ought to do it and can do it; ignorance is voluntary if it is of something one ought to know and can know. No decision not to do or not to find out is needed though of course it too would make the inaction or lack of application of one's mind sinful. But without any such decision there is still a sin of ignorance. 'The cause of the ignorance is the non-application of one's mind to knowing and this itself, this non-application of one's mind to knowing what one ought to know, is a sin of omission'.[20]

Some, though not all, of these passages are quoted by St. Alphonsus in his *Theologia Moralis*, in the section of the *Tractatus de*

[18] *Summa theologiae* 1a 2ae q.76, a.2 c.: '...illa scilicet sine quorum scientia non potest debitum actum recte exercere. Unde omnes tenentur scire communiter ea quae sunt fidei, et universalia iuris praecepta; singuli autem, ea quae ad eorum statum vel officium spectant ... Manifestum est autem quod quicumque negligit habere vel facere id quod tenetur habere vel facere, peccat peccato omissionis. Unde, propter negligentiam, ignorantia eorum quae aliquis scire tenetur, est peccatum. Non autem imputatur homini ad negligentiam, si nesciat ea quae scire non potest. Unde horum ignorantia invincibilis dicitur; quia scilicet studio superari non potest. Et propter hoc, talis ignorantia, cum non sit voluntaria, ... non est peccatum'.

[19] *Summa theologiae* 1a 2ae q.76, a.3 c.: '...ipsa ignorantia est voluntaria: vel directe, sicut cum aliquis studiose vult nescire aliqua, ut liberius peccet, vel indirecte, sicut cum aliquis propter laborem, vel propter alias occupationes negligit addiscere id per quod a peccato retraheretur. Talis enim negligentia facit ignorantiam voluntariam et peccatum, dummodo sit eorum quae quis scire tenetur et potest'.

[20] *De Malo* q.3, a.7 c.: 'Causa ignorantiae est animum ad sciendum non applicare, et hoc ipsum quod est non applicare animum ad sciendum id quod quis debet scire, est peccatum omissionis'.

Peccatis called 'De Peccato in genere'. He is keen to say that he accepts everything of St. Thomas that he quotes. Nevertheless, we can see, first, that there is a respect in which even in this part of his book he disagrees with St. Thomas even though he quotes him saying that negligence (what is in question is neglecting to know) is nothing but not applying one's mind to knowing the things one ought to know: the consequent ignorance is voluntary because applying one's mind to something or not applying it is in the power of the will; the consequent ignorance is therefore guilty. St. Alphonsus has a special thought which is a key to his teaching: without *advertence* to the badness of an act there is no voluntariness about the badness, because it is not known; so long as the thought of this does not occur, there is no sufficient principle or starting point of deliberation about the badness, therefore no liberty, therefore no guilt. To sum up: where there isn't knowledge (*cognitio*) there is not freedom (*libertas*) and where there is not freedom there is not sin (*peccatum*). He therefore holds it impossible that God's punitively removing further light from a sinner should bring it about that errors should be 'imputable' to the sinner which he never recognises as guilt in any way at all, either expressly or confusedly.

> Subtractio illa ... non efficiet quod ei imputentur errores quos nullo modo, neque expresse neque in confuso, ut culpas agnoscit; quia ubi non est cognitio, non est libertas, et ubi non est libertas, non est peccatum.*

Alphonsus also quotes with some apparent approval a remarkable sentence from one Saint Beuve (a doctor at the Sorbonne): 'If there is advertence only to an act considered materially or physically, and not formally or morally, only that act as it is something physical, and not as something moral, is willed; and so not as something bad: and in this there will be no badness (*malitia*)'.** We have here a foretaste of some present day talk of 'pre-moral evil'.

Now Alphonsus *says* he accepts St. Thomas' characterisation of acts done in ignorance of their nature: if the ignorance is the cause of the action, the action is *involuntarium* (counter-voluntary) and there-

* St Alphonsus Maria Liguori, *Theologia Moralis, Tomus Secundus*, editio nova, cura et studio P. Leonardi Gaudé (Romae Ex Typographia Vaticana, 1907): lib.V, Tractatus de Peccatis, Caput 1, De Peccato in Genere, pp.705-746, at p. 712.

** 'Si advertatur tantum in actum materialiter sive physica consideratum, et non formaliter seu moraliter, erit tantum volitus actus iste, ut est quid physicum, et non ut est quid morale; ergo non ut malum; et in hoc non erit malitia.' *Ibid.* quoted at p. 711.

fore no sin; only if the ignorance is voluntary, so will the act be too. He professes agreement with St. Thomas that something can be called voluntary if its cause is voluntary, so he cites that standard example of the man who voluntarily gets drunk and then does something bad. Also, one might deliberately not learn something and then the ignorance is voluntary.

However, when he comes to state the difference between mortal and venial sin, one of his three conditions for a sin to be mortal is 'full advertence'. But we have seen St. Thomas speaking of one's reason being bound—tied up, as it were chained by a passion—and saying:

> It is in the power of the will to exclude the binding of reason. So the act committed, which proceeds from such binding, is voluntary; hence the agent is not exonerated even from mortal guilt.[21]

But such an agent, while beginning to have his reason chained, and to be dominated by the passion that is enslaving him, surely cannot commit the sin which he is tempted to with *'plena advertentia' to its malice.* I do not know if St. Alphonsus would grant that, and say that all sins committed in a state of beginning to be blinded by passion are after all venial. It is rather curious that though he quotes that passage from *De Malo*, he actually leaves out the further bit about the passion perhaps destroying the power of the will to break the chains which were binding the reason: where St. Thomas describes this condition as in effect one of insanity. St. Alphonsus' purpose in quoting the passage seems to be to show that Thomas has the idea of some things being voluntary in their causes and yet not guilty in this. I am not sure of this, but he certainly quotes the sentence 'it would not be imputed to [the man] as guilt' without the surrounding sentences comparing the chained-up state of reason to madness, which would explain why we would not think the man guilty. St. Thomas' conception of voluntariness in a cause of madly passionate action, as *perhaps not* proving guilt, seems to be shown by his saying 'perhaps' about voluntariness in the beginning of the passion being enough to prove guilt.

However this may be, it does appear that St. Thomas did not have 'full advertence' as a necessary condition of mortal sin. Furthermore, St. Alphonsus says he agrees with St. Thomas about the ways in which someone's action done in ignorance of what he ought to know

[21] *De Malo*, q.3, a.10 c.: 'Applicare autem intentionem ad aliquid vel non applicare, in potestate voluntatis existit. Unde in potestate voluntatis est quod ligamen rationis excludat. Actus ergo commissus, qui ex tali ligamine procedit, est voluntarius, unde non excusatur a culpa etiam mortali'.

may be voluntary. What then becomes of his saying 'No liberty without knowledge, no voluntariness without liberty'? That at any rate seems to be an argument against the voluntary character of bad things done in culpable ignorance, whether ignorance of circumstances or of their kind of badness.

He could avoid an appearance of awkwardness and inconsistency—for the inconsistency is the second feature I was going to mention—if he would hold that all sins of omission are venial unless they are deliberate, i.e. unless one *intends* to omit. I do not think he does think that; at any rate he does not protest at St. Thomas for indicating the contradictory of this view.

Why have I spent time considering this question? St. Thomas is a strikingly good philosopher; St. Alphonsus not. But there is no doubt that St. Alphonsus's doctrine about the conditions for mortal sin has been immensely influential, most especially pastorally. Hearing someone* offer a new definition of mortal sin in a Roman conference on moral philosophy, where for 'full advertence' he substituted 'adequate reflection', I protested: this cannot be a necessary condition for mortal sin, because inadequate reflection may itself be mortally sinful. I would say the same about lack of 'full advertence'.

St. Alphonsus thinks he can claim agreement with St. Thomas, because St. Thomas always speaks of 'can and ought'. Ignorance is voluntary if it is ignorance of what one can know and ought to know. If the power of control by reason is gone, that's a sort of madness, and whatever someone does in that state will not be imputed to him as guilt. Add to this last, as St. Alphonsus does, what he quotes from Suarez: 'When no such thought gets into the mind, by which the will may be aroused to ... look for knowledge ... it is not in the man's power to move himself towards it; and consequently such ignorance cannot be charged against him'. St. Thomas does indeed say that it is 'not to be imputed to a man as negligence if he does not know things he cannot know; hence such ignorance is called invincible, because no effort (*studium*) can overcome it'. Alphonsus says that Thomas is teaching the same thing as Suarez!—I give the Latin. Suarez:

* The reference is to Joseph Boyle, 'Objective and Subjective Sin: Reflections on Full Consent', in *Persona, Verita e Morale. Atti del Congresso Internazionale di Teologia Morale (Roma, 7-11aprile 1986)* (Roma: Città Nuova Editrice, 1987), pp. 453–59. Boyle defends his position in 'The Personal Responsibility Required for Mortal Sin' in Luke Gormally (ed) *Moral Truth and Moral Tradition. Essays in honour of Peter Geach and Elizabeth Anscombe* (Dublin: Four Courts Press, 1994), pp. 149–62.

'Quando nulla talis cogitatio in mentem subiit, qua possit voluntas excitare ad ... quaerendam scientiam ... non est in potestate hominis se ad illam movere; et consequenter non potest talis ignorantia homini imputari'.* St. Thomas: 'Non autem imputatur homini ad negligentiam, si nesciat ea quae scire non potest; unde horum ignorantia invincibilis dicitur, quia scilicet studio superari non potest'.[22]

Let us return to the thesis that voluntariness can occur without any act at all, interior or exterior. This I find proved by the fact that one has it in one's power *not* to do some things which one also has in one's power to do. Sometimes one may make a definite (datable) decision not to do something, and that is an action. But one may merely not do something without any such decision. Inaction, or action of a particular sort may have consequences, perhaps of a bad kind. When such occur, is one to blame? Or can they be laid at one's door? Here the answer is that if it was one's business to do what one failed to do, and could have done, then indeed the ill consequences can be 'imputed' to oneself. Not every bad consequence of non-action can be called the fault of the non-agent; here it is clearest to say: the non-agent can be charged with the ill that happened, if he ought to have acted, as well as being able to.

This 'could and ought to have' is thus a required condition for the truth of a charge against someone that he is guilty of the ill consequences of his not acting. By extension, we can apply it in our account of blameworthy ignorance. We may not believe someone who says 'it never occurred to me that driving at 90 m.p.h. through a town might well result in someone's death'; but even if we do, we would be right to think 'it ought to have occurred to him'. If one does not know what an adult human being needs to know in order to conduct his life rightly, or does not know what someone in one's occupation or with one's tasks needs to know, then if one could know these things, the ignorance is culpable. For the conduct of life, a lack of control by right reason is either blameworthy or only blameless because one is blamelessly in a gravely disordered state approximating to insanity. I would suppose, however, that this latter state, when blameworthy, can become blameless, if it lasts for an unnaturally long time. This last, however, is obviously a complicated matter.

* St Alphonus Maria Liguori, *op.cit.* quotation at p. 711.

[22] *Summa theologiae* 1a 2ae q.76, a.2 c.

Thus it is that the mere 'can and ought to know' makes failure to know into a sin of omission.

I will finally revert to the unfinished business of voluntariness. We have seen that St. Thomas refers to an 'act of the will itself', and I have cast doubt upon this notion. I am not quite confident in my criticism, precisely because he maintains that there can be voluntariness without an act—that is: without any external *or* internal act, and therefore without an 'act of the will itself'. If this is so it shows that voluntariness cannot ever consist in there being—as John Stuart Mill thought—an act of will precedent to another voluntary act. The act 'peculiar to the will', St. Thomas says, is 'nothing but a turning towards... [*inclinatio ad*...] which proceeds from an interior starting point of cognition [*cognitio*]'.* An example would presumably be that one cognizes something as an apple and is *therefore just about to* reach out for it. This 'therefore just about to' would give us a case of the 'proper act of will'. But it does not supply us with an analysis of what is meant by an act's being voluntary. At most it suggests an analysis of an act of will occurring at the very beginning of a voluntary action. What makes the action 'voluntary', however, is not something at, or just before, the beginning of reaching out for an apple: reaching out for an apple is itself voluntary and we would have to ask what makes a movement merit the description 'reaching out for an apple'. There may be a voluntary action without any such beginning. One might perform the positive voluntary act of voting a certain way, for example, by remaining silent and making no relevant movement; one knows that in the procedure taking place this is a vote of 'no'. It might be objected that there is a 'therefore about to' proceeding from that knowledge. But no: there need be no such thing: one simply votes (in that way) and that is all there is to one's actual then-and-there performance. There need be no distinct 'therefore about to' then and there in one's mind. Yet in the circumstances, there is the positive voluntary act of voting, which here consists in not doing something.—'But must one not *have* decided?' No: the voting itself may be the decision.

To a modern St. Thomas reads as if he thought there was a 'peculiar act of the will itself' and this is what I criticised. Conceivably he did not think this. But in view of his saying that no act, interior or exterior, is necessary for something to be voluntary, and of his account of what an 'act of the will' is ('nothing but a turning-towards

* *Summa theologiae* 1a 2ae q.6, a.4c.

which proceeds from cognition') we may doubt whether he believes in any such quasi-Cartesian thing as I was doubting.

Whether or not this is exegetically correct, it is at any rate true to the facts about voluntariness. We need to stress a point which I have implicitly mentioned, namely: in the cases where we can speak of a 'turning-towards' something, our identifying this as an act of will at all, and all the more identifying it as such-and-such an act of will, depends on the circumstances if it is not to be completely wrong.

Part III: God's Causality

The impossibility of sin appeared in two forms: one, presented by Plato, argued that no one wants to harm himself, and sin or wrong-doing harms its perpetrator. Therefore what appears to be wrong-doing is in fact error on the part of the doer: his will is for what is good, but he makes a mistake in deciding what is good. The argument depends essentially on something true: namely that wrong-doing, or sin, must be voluntary. If by calling something wrong-doing or sin you refer simply to something done, to the mere event, then that may be counter-voluntary in its character through the mistake of thinking that it was good to do *that*. But the will was good, because it was only a will for what was conceived as good, i.e. it was a will for that *qua* good.

I observed that this argument makes the mistake of assuming that the goodness of the will resides just in its fastening on to something thought good – as if that guaranteed that there was no such thing as voluntary wrong-doing because the doing of no matter what for a good end was characterised by the goodness of the will for a good end as such.

We might also object on more specific grounds; for example, we might query the thesis that no one wants to harm himself. 'You have taken from me what I love most', an English king said to God, and, 'Therefore, I will take from you what you most want from me'... meaning his soul. He had lost a city in Normandy. Now this king was given to great fits of passion and we – or at any rate I – do not know whether he persisted in the will he expressed. However, the story serves as an example. Using it, we may say: Vengeance on God appeared good to him and his will fastened on it. This would be a case of an 'apparent good' being something that simply seems good.

Such cases, however, are probably rare, and my main criticism of Plato's argument remains. It may be added to by the thought that error about what holds of your actual end – error on your part – may call in question whether your will *is* good. Suppose you aimed at being rich as an objective, conceiving it to secure the thoroughly worth-while possibility of easily doing whatever you may be inclined to. This extremely common judgement about being rich could be held against you, and the fact that you made it would not show that you were of good will because what you wanted was a good and you wanted it *qua* that good.

So much for Plato's argument. The other reason for thinking sin impossible was that it is contrary to God's will, and God's will cannot be frustrated. Everything that exists or happens comes from God; therefore, sin is impossible.

This seems not to be a convincing argument, as Plato's may, that no sin *does* occur. Since, once we have replied to Plato, we can resume our confident belief that there is such a thing as wilful wrong-doing, the argument presents a problem to solve: *how* is it possible? The impossibility argued for is accepted, at least with reference to pain and misfortune, by people who use the actuality of those things to argue that there can be no deity, or that if there is, deity is ill-willed, or relatively impotent. This is a famous argument, formulated long ago, and favoured by Anglo-American philosophers in support of atheism.

Philosophers of this tradition hardly ever enquire what is actual Christian belief. They usually assume, for example, that an omnipotent deity must create the best of all possible worlds, not knowing that the very idea of a world than which none could be better is rejectable (was rejected by Aquinas for example) as absurd. And they also suppose that evil or suffering, which an all-powerful god could prevent, such a god must prevent if he has not an evil will. The conclusion is simple: either no deity or one that is not all-powerful or not benevolent.

Here is the place to make some observations about anthropomorphism. In the course of my conversion to, and instruction in, the Catholic faith, I used to read warnings against being anthropomorphic about God. They puzzled me: I could not see the likelihood of being so, or indeed what it would be. But some present day English-writing philosophers have shown me. They will write sentences like: 'God must be in the best possible position to form an opinion on such-and-such'. I can hardly believe that a real mind has framed that thought; but it seems at least one has.

However, reverting to my theme, of the argument to prove that if God exists, God must be ill-willed or weak, I have to consider the divine causation of evils. And also the divine permitting of evils. Here I am assuming that there is only one deity; but at present that is a common assumption in Western philosophy—that is, that if there is any deity there is at most one. If it were a living option for us to believe that there are several gods, we might, like the Hindus, believe in a god of destruction as well as a god of creation and a god of preservation. I am not saying there could be no serious consideration of why, or even whether, these are false beliefs; only that I am not going to consider them.

First, then, there is the question whether the sole deity does cause evils. To this the answer must be yes, if creation includes material things. For material substances not merely come into existence but also pass out of existence and the process of the generation of one is the corruption (ceasing to exist) of another, the latter ceasing to exist because it turns into the former; or into the former with some waste material. When you eat an apple or an oyster, you *destroy* it. (This is not indeed your coming to be, but your preservation by nutrition.) Fire burns many things, with the products of combustion as the result. If, then, the completeness of the universe is enhanced if it includes material substances, it is enhanced by including things that perish. If perishing is an evil for what perishes, then the creator of the material world cannot but be a creator of constantly repeated evils, or lacks of the excellence of lasting. You can escape this only by regarding matter itself as an evil, either created by a different divinity, a principle of evil, or as not created at all. Our immersion in matter, our material existence, will then be a sort of evil existence or perhaps a punishment—as we are told Origen thought, believing namely that we were, as it were, angels punished for sin by being given that evil thing, life in matter. Rejecting any such view as fantastical and believing in a divine creator of the material universe, we should say that that creator is the producer of that failure of permanence which is essentially possible for material substances.

Now you might say: something which belongs to the nature of a thing, as perishability does to the nature of material substances, can't be called an evil. 'You don't call it an evil for a stone to fall to the ground and lack the capacity to float in the air'. Well, that is correct enough; we call newborn kittens blind only because they are *im*perfect cats. Cats see: the lack of sight is a stage of development and so only narrowly an evil for kittens. But when an animal goes blind, that is an unhappy evil for it and might be part of a process of total decay. However, so long as it exists, it has the good of existence; and what totally destroys it, however much in the course of nature that is, takes away all its good. So that alone of all the natural developments is a deprivation of all there is to the creature that suffers it.

There are other evils which occur to material substances. Trees, for example, are sometimes cankered: this is a bulgy growth, not proper to the tree, which arises from a disorderly multiplication of cells and is to the tree as cancer is to an animal. There are warts and cataracts and rashes and abscesses as well as cancers. The possibility of these things is the possibility of failure of an organism to work properly, and what is in this sense possible will sometimes be actual. This we see from the fact that the only way we know of these possibilities is by observing their sometimes being actual. The creator of nature is, therefore, their creator. I do not understand the dictum of Aquinas that God, '*quasi per accidens*', causes the corruptions of things; in fact that '*quasi*' suggests that he was a bit doubtful about the '*per accidens*' itself.[23]

We now come to the causation of sin. Here, I believe only one thing stands in the way of our taking the same line as I have taken about things passing away and suffering various forms of disorder and corruption such as warts and cancers and indeed all forms of sickness. Wrong-doing is possible, therefore it happens sometimes—in fact, a lot, but at any rate sometimes. How do we know it is possible? Why, just because it does happen. The creator of nature, therefore, creates its possibility and therefore its actuality, in creating men. It is as human to sin as to make mistakes.

The thing that vividly stands in the way of taking this line is the doctrine of the fall of man: the doctrine of original sin on the part of Adam—the originating original sin—producing a fallen race, a race of rational animals that is not what it was supposed to be.

Some people have thought that it was not just the descendants of Adam and Eve that somehow became what they were not supposed to be—that somehow evil took hold of the earthly creation and made nature 'red in tooth and claw'. We should reject this fantasy. The amiable fancy of the lion lying down with the lamb and a little child leading them, may excite a painter to produce an attractive picture. (Indeed I think I have seen one such in this house.*) I don't deprecate such a thing: nevertheless, I would say that it is, rather, a Hebrew metaphor which I can still call characteristically violent in spite of its

* The reference is to the Dominican House of Studies in Washington, D.C.

[23] *Summa theologiae* 1a q.49, a.2 c.

sweetness. It seems strange to talk of a violent metaphor of peace; but that is what it is. It comes from the same stable as speaking of a camel going through the eye of a needle, of the dead burying their dead. It gives us an image of something against nature, impossible; not of the happy undoing of a way things unhappily are in a damaged world. Nature red in tooth and claw is God's undamaged creation. That sinful men are the result of damage to God's creation *by* an act contrary to the divine will raises up before us the extraordinary picture of unfallen Adam and Eve.

You may ask: Why have I spoken of the originating sin of Adam, and not of Eve? There is a negro spiritual, true to the story, which contains the lines:

> You stole my apples, I believe.
>
> No, Mass'r Lord, I spex it was Eve.

You can't leave Eve out of it; suppose she had not sinned, the story collapses. Between them, they were all the man there was. We believe that they were full of grace and immortal. For by that disobedience 'Came death into the world and all our woe'. Something started, something glorious, as if there were an incredibly beautiful stretch of road, going on for two or three hundred yards—and then no more, but a ditch-like path going sharply away at an acute angle, full of thistles and thorns and dirt and desolation.

That path was the lives of the descendants of Adam's begettings from Eve. We cannot even say how *we* would have been if man had not fallen. We would not have existed. It is indeed an unprofitable exercise to try and imagine the unfallen race of men that might have been. We only know the wonderful Adam and the wonderful Eve who between them spoiled things. What the story tells us is that it would be seemingly false and shallow to treat human sinfulness in the same way as I have treated the mutability and corruptibility of material substances.

What then? Did God cause Adam to sin? No, that is not possible, God can no more cause sins, which are against his will, than he can create evil substances. But evil substances are impossible, there *can* be no such thing. How, then, are sins possible? We know part of the answer: the free creature can act contrary to God's will. The doctrine of the free will of the rational creatures—angels and men—is sometimes used in theodicy, as an answer to the argument which I described, the argument that either there is not deity, or deity is ill-willed or impotent to prevent evil. I incline strongly against this use of it—known as 'the free-will defence'. The freedom of the human will is an outstanding Christian doctrine—reason enough why so many philosophers who hate the Christian religion are keen to argue that it makes no sense. It is, however, a proof of the possibility of sin, not a defence of the creator against the charge of ill will as an alternative to non-existence or relative powerlessness.

If God does not cause sins, these being against the divine will, does that mean that God is not involved in the causation of any free acts? No, it doesn't, and even in sins the sustentation of the sinner, and his power of acting, and even his exercise of that power in his wicked act, come from God. As for acts that are free and good, not bad, we sometimes suppose them to have been the result of *special* action on the mind and will of the creature.

The problem that we have before us, however, is not one of describing how there can be divine action on the mind and free will of a creature—that is no doubt interesting but the proposition asserting that it happens is not a paradoxical one. And it is not my concern here; for I am discussing what to do with that argument for the ill will of God, if God exists and is all-powerful. If all-powerful, then God permits sins, if not causing them—and the latter is impossible. We can now transform the argument we have been considering. It did make the assumption: a benevolent and all-powerful being would have to *prevent* evils. I have discussed the falsehood of this in respect of the constant passing away of material things, and the cankers and abscesses of living material things, which also come into existence and pass away; and I hope to have shown that there is nothing in it, unless you are going to maintain that an all-powerful and benevolent creator simply must not indulge in the creation of a material world.

But now, how about the business of sin? We cannot say that God would not be able to prevent sin. Can we say that if God can, and is benevolent, then God *ought* to prevent sin? This is what has become of the famous argument. And I daresay that there are people who would assent to it. It might seem to have some plausibility, at least if we apply it to ourselves. If we *can* prevent wrong-doing, are we not showing a bad will if we do not at least try to prevent it? And if God, supposedly a rational being, is also a moral being—then will not the same thing hold of God?

No, it is neither true of us, nor of God. There may be a question why we do not interfere to try to prevent some wrong-doings. And there are connections between something's being wrong to do, and its being wrong to do something about it to someone else. If it is wrong to set fire to a cat's tail, having soused it in petrol, it is wrong to try to persuade your little brother to souse a cat's tail with petrol and set fire to it. But we are to consider, not such a proposition, but rather: if something ought not to be done, it ought not to be permitted to be done.

Someone who finds this obvious has not reflected enough on the grammar of 'ought'. Let us suppose that someone, call him Jack, ought to be locked up. And let us also suppose that someone else, call him Tom, does lock Jack up. Can we infer from the fact that Jack ought to be locked up, that Tom ought to lock him up? No; it may for example not be within Tom's authority to lock up someone who nevertheless ought to be locked up. As you can't be locked up without being locked up by someone, we may infer, 'Jack ought to be locked up by someone', from 'Jack ought to be locked up'. But can we infer, 'There is someone who ought to lock Jack up'? No.

These are incipient observations on the grammar—the 'depth grammar'—of the word 'ought' and its equivalent in any language. I say 'depth grammar' because there is an awkward peculiarity in the 'surface grammar' of the verb 'ought' in English. It hasn't got a past tense, or a normally formed future one. In this English is unlike French, Latin, German and even Greek. I will beg permission to say, 'He oughted to...' where I need a past tense for 'ought' in English—for 'He ought to have...' will not always do the job.

One of the rather bad moves in modern analytic philosophy has been to *exclusively* prefer, 'It ought to be the case that Jack is hanged' or 'It ought to be the case that Tom hangs Jack' to 'Jack ought to be hanged' and 'Tom ought to hang Jack'. That may at first sight and in this example seem harmless. But consider the equivalence of 'Jack was hanged by Tom' and 'Tom hanged Jack'. Does it follow that 'It oughted to be that Jack was hanged by Tom' is equivalent to 'It oughted to be that Tom hanged Jack'? It does seem so. But 'Jack oughted to be hanged by Tom' is not therefore equivalent to 'Tom oughted to hang Jack'. (If that seems doubtful, consider 'Jack deserved to be hanged by Tom' and 'Tom deserved to hang Jack'.) 'Ought' with one personal subject does not justify 'ought' with another even though the transformation merely relates to an exchange of active and passive.

These considerations show that if an event, such as Joe's beating John—which is just the same as John's being beaten by Joe—does take place and John oughted to be beaten by Joe, it doesn't follow that Joe oughted to beat John. Only if you think that 'Joe ought to beat John' means simply 'The event of John's being beaten by Joe ought to happen', i.e. if you separate the 'ought' from the person who ought, will you think that 'Joe ought to beat John' follows from 'John ought to be beaten by Joe'. It may be, of course, that John ought to be beaten, but not by Joe. But it may also be that John ought to be beaten by Joe, though Joe ought not to beat John—John has earned a beating from Joe, but Joe has vowed never to beat anyone.

These considerations should lead one to see that the identity of something that both ought to be and ought not to be is not impossible. God permits people to do things which are bad, and in doing which their will is bad. But both what happens by God's action and what happens by God's permission ought to happen.

Therefore, sometimes the same thing both ought to be and ought not to be. For the people ought not to do the bad actions. But you cannot say that they ought not to happen, because they are well and wisely permitted by God if without God's permission they could not happen. In this way, Jesus, being innocent, oughted not to suffer death, nor oughted anyone to inflict it on him; and yet he oughted to suffer it, because he himself wisely and benignly and usefully willed to suffer it. I take this from Anselm, to whose examination of the grammar—the depth grammar—of 'ought' ('*debere*') I am much indebted in what I have already said.

> Who [he asks] will dare to deny that there ought to be what such great wisdom and goodness permits?

His pupil replies:

> Let anyone who dares deny it; I do not dare.

Anselm asks:

> What if you are considering the nature of things as when the nails were pressed into the Lord's body: would you say the fragile flesh ought not to have been penetrated by them, or to have suffered when it was penetrated by sharp iron?

Pupil: I'd be speaking against nature.

Anselm: So it can happen that an action or a being-acted-on ought to happen according to nature, which, if you take the agent or patient, ought not to happen, since neither the one ought to be doing nor the other to be suffering.

Pupil: None of this can I deny.

Anselm: So don't you see that very often it can happen that the same action ought and ought not to happen under different considerations.[24]

With this I end, having derived from Anselm a dose of grammar which gives a famous argument its quietus.

Part IV: God's Exile and Man's Redemption

1. God's Exile

We are taught that God is everywhere and yet that God is present in some special ways in some places or that there is such a thing as being in the presence of God. We believe that Jesus, the Son who is God, is on our altars. The angel Gabriel said 'I am Gabriel, who stands before God'.[25] Zacharias, praising God for the birth of his son John, spoke of serving God 'in holiness and justice, all the days of our life in his presence'.[26] We could multiply examples.

Here we may remember the title of a small book *The Practice of the Presence of God,** which tells us of the things said by a Carmelite brother, Lawrence, who worked in the kitchen of his monastery. People came to see him to ask and learn what he had to say.

The question comes: How can there be a *practice* of the presence of God? We would never speak of a practice of the existence of God—Or might some of us now? There is a movement in a sort of philosophy among those called 'Wittgensteinian', a movement in which there is talk of 'the believer'. Here it is possible that someone might talk about belief in God as an 'attitude', not the sort of belief that can be called true or false, not like things 'in science'. Now such philosophers are not likely to favour speaking of God as existing and

* Brother Lawrence, *The Practice of the Presence of God*; various editions.

[24] St Anselm, *De Veritate* Chap. VIII:
Quis audebit negare debere esse quod tanta sapientia et bonitate permittitur?
D. Neget qui audet; ego vero non audeo.
M. Quid etiam si secundum rerum naturam consideres, ut cum clavi ferrei impressi sunt in corpus domini: an dices fragilem carnem non debuisse penetrari, ut acuto ferro penetratam non debuisse dolere?
D. Contra naturam dicerem.
M. Potest igitur contingere ut debeat esse secundum naturam actio vel passio, quae secundum agentem vel patientem esse non debet, quoniam nec ille agere nec iste debet pati.
D. Nihil horum negare possum.
M. Vides ergo saepissime posse contingere ut eadem actio debeat esse et non debeat esse diversis considerationibus?

[25] *Lk* 1.19.

[26] *Lk* 1.75.

we therefore would not expect them to entertain speaking of 'a practice of the existence of God'. But it seems to me an obvious possibility given the style of talk about 'the believer', which talk is remote from the facts about believers.

So I revert to saying 'No, we would never speak of 'the practice of the existence of God'. What then are we to say of 'the practice of the presence of God'?'

An easy interpretation of the phrase would be that it means constant consciousness of the presence of God. But that would not do. First, it would seem to allow us to speak of existence so, as well as of presence. Second, it supposes answered the question what is meant by 'the presence of God'.

One may sometimes mentally put oneself in the presence of a friend (or enemy), say in order to prevent oneself from talking foolishly. This is a use of the imagination which of course does not involve belief that the person is present. One is only using one's imagination to be conscious e.g. of what it would be like to be talking so if that person were listening—which one knows he is not.

Nevertheless this comparison is not quite useless. It brings out what there was in the first suggestion, of 'constant consciousness of the presence of God'. This now becomes constant consciousness that God sees and hears what we are doing and saying.

It is possible in some sense to believe in deity and not to believe that deity knows or cares what we do. (I have known such belief.) But there is a more ancient and clearer belief that we find in Xenophanes: 'One god, greatest among gods and men, neither in form nor in thought like mortals... He wholly sees, wholly thinks, wholly hears'. And 'Without toil he sways everything by the thought of his mind... and he stays always in the same place; nor does it befit him to go now here, now there'. My dots confess to an assumption on my part of the same subject of all these things. For no reason—or no good one—the English historians of ancient philosophy cannot endure the notion that Xenophanes, Anaxagoras and Aristotle believed in the existence of that deity whose name is 'I am', the ruler of all things and the end of all things, the contemplation and worship of which is the final purpose of wisdom. I can only suppose that there is *a* reason operating: 'We are atheists and proud of it. We do not want to sneer at any ancients. Therefore they certainly were materialists'. The texts, however, do not seem to correspond.

Aristotle, of all these ancients, seems to have been the most explicitly modest and hesitant. In the *Nicomachean Ethics*, Book 10, he quotes another philosopher saying 'Being mortal, we should think mortal thoughts'. But he says No—so far as is possible for us we should be on the side of the immortal—'*dei athanatizein*'. This 'so far as is possible' (1177b 33-4) expresses a modesty about what is possible.

'*Athanatizein*' is a word occurring only here in this active voice (Plato has it again in a single occurrence in the 'middle' voice). It seems to be formed on the model of '*medizien*'—'*to medize*'—i.e. be on the side of the Medes, which would mean being unfaithful to the Greeks. If so, then '*athanatizein*' would mean being unfaithful to mortals, or to their mortality—but the suggestion is made under the condition 'so far as is possible'. But he amplifies a little by saying 'so far as is possible, one should be on the side of the immortal *and* do everything towards living according to the most powerful thing in oneself'.

Thus, then, Aristotle: the others seem not to have thought about '*athanatizein*', but only to have contemplated the divine order of things and to have recommended that contemplation. The thing that is remarkable about these philosophers is not to have had a false picture of deity unless it is to be found in Aristotle's denial that God issues laws for the world. For, as I have already remarked, Aristotle does not derive his ethics from divine law.

Let us return, then, to 'the practice of the presence of God'. This we have seen to be nearly related to 'keeping in mind that God sees and hears us'. It must, however, also be related to the divine ruling of the world. This ruling, in the case of rational animals, includes divine commandments. If so, we are like soldiers whose supreme commanders are constantly aware of what they do. This, in the earthly case, would have a constant effect not only on what we do, but on the spirit in which we did it. In the earthly case, it might sometimes be a spirit, not just of obedience, but of 'mustn't be caught'. In the heavenly case, it would (to put it briefly) hang together with our adjustment as, so to speak, compass needles pointing towards God or away from God.

This is indeed not a matter of what is present to our 'Cartesian consciousness': it is rather a matter of the ultimate reasons we could give, speaking truly, for what we are at any time doing. The 'consciousness' I have spoken of as 'the constant consciousness of the presence of God' would not be a Cartesian *cogitatio*: it would rather relate to that the mention of which is readily elicited from someone who speaks truly when asked what he is doing and why.

This sort of 'consciousness' is here a knowledge of reality *if* the practitioner 'of the presence of God' is truthful in speaking of the practice of that. Being a knowledge of reality it is not like the fantasy of the listening friend: it is itself a form of divine presence to it which the reasonable mind ought always to have. The absence of it, which is all but universal in the human race, is what I call 'God's Exile'. Exile from what exists, even in Hell, is impossible for God. The exile of which I have been trying to speak is not an exile from our physical or mental existence: that too is impossible. It is an exile from our spiritual existence and is the basis of any true accusation of having a dried-up and empty soul.

2. *Man's Redemption*

Almost all who call themselves Christian and mean by this something other than that they are good respectable people, will speak of their Lord as their redeemer; and of his redemption of all other men too by his suffering and death. They might specifically say: by the sacrifice that he was offering to the Father on the cross. This is certainly the doctrine of the Catholic faith. Though the term 'redemption' and the cognate verb doesn't occur in the Apostles' or Nicene Creed, it does occur in the writing of St. Peter and St. Paul; St. Peter speaks of 'your being redeemed, not by corruptible silver or gold, but by the precious blood of Christ, *as of an immaculate Lamb*' (1 *Peter* 1:18-19) and St. Paul says: 'Christ has redeemed us from the curse of the Law, (being) made accursed for us. For it is written 'Cursed is he that hangs on a tree'' (*Galatians* 3:13). The curse of the Law is the curse of guilt under the Law, but is not annihilated by paying the penalty of the Law.

'Redemption' means ransom, and is also used when you redeem something from a pawnbroker. So it may appear that the priestly sacrifice of Christ was a purchase price which he paid to ransom us, to buy us back from someone. There was once a doctrine—I have seen it attributed to St. Gregory of Nyssa—that the human race belonged to the devil and so the price had to be paid *to him* for purchasing us from him. How many held this doctrine, and through what centuries, I do not know. St. Anselm scotched it, referring to it as something 'we are accustomed to say' and saying we should not do so; the devil has not acquired any rights in us and could not possibly do so. I have read in Dick Southern that it was a widely believed doctrine in feudal times, using the notion of feudal overlordship which was the social system before Anselm's day as well as after it, to explain how there was a ransom to pay, a redeeming fee; this notion included that fee's being *owing* to Satan.[27] In some versions Satan was led by a trick to let go his right, and angrily claimed that he had not lost it. All this was successfully discarded by St. Anselm, who was justly regarded as an authority of great weight: he was called the *doctor doctorum*. That he uses the expression '*ut solemus dicere*' of the doctrine that the devil had acquired rights in the human race, I have checked, but do not know otherwise than by reading secondary sources that, or for how long, it was a common doctrine before Anselm. That such a doctrine should have sprung up seems not altogether surprising, because of the meaning of the word 'redemption'. Redeeming, it might be said, is buying back—but from whom? Anselm, and others following him, rejected absolutely that the devil had *rights* in the human race. Did someone else, other than God the Father? It could not be said that the Father had acquired all his right in us through our sins, or that we had to be rescued from his ownership. The notion of 'satisfaction' for sin comes into explanations of the role of Christ's death, and this would seem to be connected with the conception of a sacrifice offered to a deity to somehow make up for human offences. Satisfaction for sins would be a requirement of divine justice. Yet it could not be made by sinners. Not even by someone who never offended, but nevertheless was an heir of Adam's guilt. It must be someone who was not only human, for one who was only a man could not offer a sacrifice which redeemed from that inheritance. On the other hand, only man *owed* satisfaction for sin to the demands of divine justice. Hence the doctrine of Anselm's '*Cur Deus Homo*'?—'*Why the God man*'?, or '*Why did God become a man*'?—'*solus Deus potuit, solus homo debuit*'—'Only man owed it, only God could do it', which proves that the *debt* of satisfaction for sin could be paid only by one who was both God and man—that is, *if* the debt was ever paid, it must have been paid by someone who was both God and man. We have to add: whose humanity was therefore untainted—did not even need rescue from the inheritance from Adam, i.e. a man who as man was not begotten.

If this is correct, then the notion of a purchase price paid to an owner is only a metaphor. 'You rescued me, but at what a price!' one might say to someone who had lost an arm performing the rescue. The metaphor is not objectionable, but we must remember it *is* a metaphor.

---

[27] See R.W. Southern, *Saint Anselm. A Portrait in a Landscape*, Cambridge: Cambridge U.P. 1990: pp. 207ff.

Abandoning the thought of a pawnbroker who has to be paid when one redeems what one has left with him, and who acquires a right in the item on which he lent money—abandoning altogether the thought of a deal with the devil, on which he could press a claim, we should revert to the notion of ransom. If by main force someone has taken you prisoner, then it may be that your only way of getting free is for you or someone else to pay a ransom for you. A society may be such that this is a normal procedure, not limited to gangsters, and people used to this might well think of your captor as having a right to the ransom. However, the notion of a right is not built into that of a ransom and we may reasonably take St. Anselm's objection and still speak of the devils as those from whom we are rescued—and that *by which* we are rescued as an act of ransoming. In speaking so, we are not conceding any right to the captors. On the other hand, it is the captor, or holder of the prisoner, who *is paid* the ransom, and we can still ask: is there any sense in which Lucifer is *paid* by Christ's passion and death? That does not seem to *make sense*—not even a metaphorical sense.

St. Paul says to the Galatians: 'Christ redeemed us from the curse of the Law, being made accursed for us'. I should observe that in the Vulgate the words for 'curse' and 'accursed' are the same—so we might either put 'curse' in both places, 'redeemed us from the curse of the Law, being made a curse for us' or 'accursed' in both places: 'redeemed us from [being] the accursed of the Law, being made accursed for us'. As St. Peter remarks, the writings of his brother Paul contain 'a lot of things that are difficult to understand, and many twist them to their own destruction'.[28] This is a warning: how are we to understand what Paul says? Is it that Christ was made accursed for us by being crucified? He also said that Christ, who knew no sin, was made sin for us (2 *Corinthians* 5:21). How so? From Deuteronomy Paul quoted: 'Cursed is he who hangs on the wood, cursed by God'.[29] That seems to relate to being punished by a most horrible and shameful death. In Spanish America you see statues of the scourged Christ, bloody down his body, legs and arms. One would understand someone looking at that and saying 'Who was cursed with such a penalty?' Indeed the shamefulness and horror of Christ's death is something of which we have little sense; the Apostles will have had a very strong sense of it. He was rendered accursed by the curse of the Law—i.e. he was rendered accursed by suffering

[28] 2 *Pet* 3.16.

[29] *Dt* 21.23.

what the Law counted as being accursed. He was 'made sin' by becoming accursed with the death suffered by the so accursed among sinners. This was the nature of the sacrifice offered to the Father for men which he, Christ, offered, himself the priest but also taking the role of an animal being sacrificed, and being executed in shame and horror.

If this is right, then the condition of mankind, if mankind could only be rescued from it by such an offering in satisfaction for what mankind has made of it's life, must be and have been frightful indeed. There were very wicked people everywhere enjoying the pleasant fruits of their wickedness. To read, say, only the Gospel according to St. Mark and to pay close attention to all that our Lord is recorded as saying, is frightening. But it is not that he was relating especially to a bad time—it relates to mankind anywhere, any time.

One has to understand this, in order to understand a little what Paul meant by being redeemed from the curse of the Law, or from the cursedness of those cursed by the Law. What Law did he mean? Well, clearly the Law of Moses. Remember that the phrase comes in his letter to the Galatians, which letter is much concerned with the trouble about whether the baptised Gentiles were obliged to follow the Law of Moses, as the baptised Jews—or some of them—thought, and some of the baptised Gentiles too. The Mosaic Law will have been much in their consciousness, and it is very like St. Paul to use what he knew was in the consciousness of those he addressed to stamp something further upon their minds.

The redemption now appears as the rescue, through the death of one who by that death was made accursed, from the accursed condition which you are in by the Law—if you will understand the Law. There might be—there were—people who were just and holy; but the stain of original sin, originating in Adam's actual sin and by that origin still in them, meant that there was not yet any release from Hell—until they were redeemed.

The just and holy, still locked up in Hell, but to be released by the harrowing of Hell, include Adam and Eve if we are to believe the tradition embodied in the pictures painted of that event by many classical painters in Europe. I don't know if they recognisably put in Abel—I have not known it; indeed I don't know if anyone recognisably put in any others besides Adam and Eve. But most of the just and holy will have been Jews, who at least had Moses and the prophets to instruct them. Almost all the rest of the world will have been lost because of the exile of God from their hearts and minds. If Paul could speak of the curse of the Law, can we not speak of the curse of the natural law? All over the world, almost, idolatry prevailed and awful laws and customs. And this is still so—at any rate I am inclined to believe it, from the things which from time to time come to light. Certainly there are many millions of idolaters. I am on the whole not well-informed enough to give an account of the miseries and wickedness of mankind with chapter and verse cited in evidence. I don't suppose that I could do it for the circles that I am used to—the world of Anglo-American academic philosophy. I do know that *that* world is possessed extensively by the dogma that there is no God, that there is no such thing as a true religion or a true system of morality, that such things have nothing to do with truth and falsehood—except indeed for the belief that a person of philosophical competence should not believe in God, and that if some do, and indeed if they go so far as to be Catholic Christians, this is very queer of them: how can they possibly reconcile such beliefs with reason and 'science'?

By this latter, in the English language as in the French, people always (or almost always) mean natural science. I also know that the societies that we live in are rapidly becoming more and more murderous; the murderers are mostly highly respectable people; often they are doctors, I mean medical practitioners. And the rest of the people are upon the whole ignorant, apathetic, inert, indifferent.

When I speak of God as an exile, I mean not that no important people use official religious language. I mean rather that the mental world of most people does not include any conception of God as anything to take seriously. The fear of God exists very little. God has been in exile from most men's minds through most of history. The idea of being in a very bad state, and especially of being in a very bad state of guilt which needs forgiveness, is an uncommon one. And this has a lot to do with the matter that I discussed in my second lecture. For even among Catholic Christians there is commonly a bad state of confidence that one is all right—because one's conscience is clear. You can't sin at all quite unwittingly. So if you think you are all right, then you are all right, except no doubt for little venial sins, and those don't matter much and perhaps anyway the notions of mortal and venial sins are nothing very pertinent to our day: they belong to an old-fashioned sort of theology. Mortal sin—if there *is* such a thing—cannot be unconscious and is very rare.

At this point I would like to repeat that this latter belief is false. The calloused conscience, in a grown-up who never thinks seriously about God and sin, is extremely usual and is probably itself an indication of a state of mortal sin. The alternative would be a permanently childish mind that had never seen any light.

We believe in forgiveness. But there is a difficulty about forgiveness being enough. Suppose people go to confession on Shrove Tuesday. On Ash Wednesday there is a prayer said publicly, asking to be cleansed from our sin. Now I do not suppose that the superior of a religious house would decide to leave out that prayer because the people present were all members of the house and had all been to confession the day before. Is this *just in case* some of the confessions had been bad, and so received no absolution or at any rate no valid absolution? Or just in case the interval since the confessions had included sins? I doubt it. So it seems a fair deduction that there is still need for cleansing from sins. Indeed, we might see in this a proof of the doctrine of purgatory: one is not fit for heaven yet, although all one's sins having been forgiven (as one may hope) one is safe from the fires of hell. Seeking light on this matter I looked up the *Summa theologiae* on the justification of the impious—i.e. the justification of sinners. And there (1ª 2ªᵉ q.113, a.1) I learn that the justification of a sinner simply *is* the remission of his sins. There is a transition from a state of injustice—i.e. lack of justice in one's soul—to the state of justice. Now I take it that absolution, if valid, secures forgiveness, if one means one's confession and does not voluntarily leave out anything one ought to include. The work of Christ for that forgiveness was done—it was complete a long, long time ago. What is happening now is that one is availing oneself of it. And so one has obtained forgiveness—and is not that the remission of sins? Yes, surely. And so one is *now* in a state of justice?

At the point at which I gag on this, remembering that Ash Wednesday prayer, which one would not think redundant if one were to pray it in the next minute after receiving absolution—at this point I find St. Thomas saying:

> Because a motion is named for the terminus towards which it is a motion rather than for the other terminus, i.e. its beginning, for this reason the mutation, by which someone is changed from a state of injustice by the remission of sins, is allotted its name from the terminus *towards which* it is a change, and is called the justification of the impious.

This relieves my trouble and puzzlement. It is consonant with this thought of St. Thomas, that the process of justification, i.e. of making *just*, should take time.

Nevertheless I have some doubts about the reassuring thesis that in absolution you have the remission of *all* your sins. I know that this is said to prevent people from being anxious about having forgotten to mention something, and that does not disturb me. And no doubt it may be of some use in dealing with penitents who suffer from scruples, which I gather is a very painful suffering. And if it is a help to remind them that *all* their sins are forgiven by the absolution, well and good—though I guess that if you suffer from scruples you may agonise horribly about whether your confession was sincere, since if not the absolution would be ineffectual. However, I gather that scruples are a very recognisable trouble of soul, and therefore not connected with the difficulty I am feeling after.

Suppose someone has a thoroughly calloused conscience, and it has never occurred to him to think about some matter in which he constantly mistreats people, or robs them, or falsifies information—is there not an equivalence with such callousness of conscience if he feels easy and confident that for sure all his sins are forgiven, accepting that quite commonly made statement about confession and absolution? I strongly incline to think so. A belief which I have run into and which I am sure is false is that people who act badly, very badly, always have pricks of conscience about it—and the same for people who commit great sins of negligence: they have no slightest awareness of this?!—no, it cannot be so, they *must* have pricks of conscience. The earnest priest who assures me of this bases what he says on his experience of people confiding some worry about the past in confession. But this is a special class. The people I am thinking of would not be coming to him with their worry.

In these lectures I have pursued more than one purpose, and discussed more than one problem. One of my purposes I will mention in ending. It was to heighten my awareness of the amazing character of some of the things that we believe. For example, our descent from a first man who was not cumbered with any inheritance of original sin, who walked with God and had grace—and threw it away, bringing it about that the race of men he fathered would be a fallen, damaged race with darkened minds and tendencies to evil. Then again, the astonishing nature of our redemption, if we are redeemed; all that we understand (if we do understand it) about our redeemer being made accursed, being made as it were sin, in order to offer satisfaction for our sins.

I may add something, another thing in this fabulous drama. I was much surprised when talking with a priest not long ago, to hear him say that our Lady, Mary, was necessitated to say 'Yes' to the announcement made to her. He may even have said, though I am not sure, that the angel was announcing to her that she was already pregnant. (This is indeed not according to the Scriptural narrative.) However, I was outraged by the opinion that she had to say 'Yes' and I exclaimed: 'She was free, she had free will as Adam had. She could have said 'No''. The suggestion that *that* was not possible, she had grace, is ineffectual. So did Adam and Eve have grace. She could have said 'No', as they could have too, but did not. Creation trembled, everything was in the balance. And indeed, if her 'Yes' was not free, the place that we give her in our devotions would be utterly unjustified. But no: not only did she not say 'No', she did not turn away at any time. She could have become unfaithful, any time before her death.

Nothing was so crucial as that first 'Yes'. But the picture that I have just conjured up, of her first saying 'Yes' and later regretting it, makes her like a figure in a modern novel. If we first think that she was free in her 'Yes', we are indeed thinking of her purely as an individual. The possibility of one who is God becoming a man depended on such a free acceptance by an individual woman. But this was then more than something in her personal story: *she* was acting as one who represented Israel and mankind. To say this is to say that man cannot be rescued willy-nilly, has to be a party to it for it to happen. This held for the consent of that young girl.

This brings us back to our main theme. Rescued from what? From what was redemption? Here we know no answer but the one long taught: that it was from a captivity, the captivity of sin—its dominance. Whether we know it, and being baptised walk like the unchained prisoners that we are, is another thing.

15*

Two Moral Theologians

Vermeersch's treatise on lying is interesting and learned. The greater part of it is devoted to telling us what other people have thought. With one exception, I'll not be referring to this. Vermeersch** makes clear from the first that his intention, or what he thinks is his intention, is to defend the classical absolute condemnation of lying. Thus he in particular rejects the view that lying is to be condemned because of the social harms involved in or resulting from it. 'An act which of its nature corrupts the one instrument of social communication, which hinders human commerce, nay tends to the overthrow of human society'*** does seem to contain a grave disorder: but in saying this we ought not to forget that lying *as such*—i.e. just any lie, whatever further characteristics it has—is not *eo ipso* a grave sin. Besides, the deduction from consequences is extrinsic, and ineffective for the condemnation of *all* lying; for there are lies which can be socially useful. 'So (the argument) proves too much intensively, and less than it should extensively.'**** Note that we must draw a distinction between saying that a lie as such is *always* wrong, and saying that it is as such always a very seriously wicked act.

* From the text of an unpublished and undated typescript with handwritten corrections by the author.

** Arthur Vermeersch SJ (1858–1936) distinguished Jesuit moral theologian and canonist; taught moral theology and canon law at the Jesuit Faculty of Theology in Louvain, Belgium, 1893–1918; Professor of Moral Theology, Gregorian University, Rome, 1918–1934.

*** A Vermeersch, 'De mendacio et necessitatibus commercii humani', in *Gregorianum* 1(1920), pp. 11–40, 425–74, at p. 30: 'Actus enim qui natura sua corrumpat unicum socialis communicationis instrumentum, qui commercium humanum impediat, immo in eversione humanae societatis tendat, gravem inordinationem continere videtur.'

**** A Vermeersch, *op.cit.*, p. 30: 'Quare [argumentum] *intensive* nimis, *extensive* minus quam oportet probat.'

His own condemnation of lying compares it to contraception as an unnatural act. Speech is the one means of communication among human beings. Mankind should form a unity; being material, they haven't the advantage of angels, each severally possessing its whole nature: no, human nature is divided among indefinitely many individuals and can never exist as an *actual whole*, because there can always be more men. So men have got to be *brought* to a sort of unity and made as it were into *one whole man* by '*caritativa communicatio*'. Original sin, however, and its consequences prevent this; though our nature inclines us to mutual communication as is shown both in the native simplicity of a child and in the shame of being detected in a lie by the person you are lying to.

What he wants, he explains, is to show that the 'order of mutual communication' is *inviolable* for the human race. It follows that a man cannot honestly subordinate that order to himself, but ought to fear (I suppose he means reverence) it as part of the essential order in preserving which he is preserved; or by the preservation of which he is obliged. (I am uncertain how to translate '*quo servando tenetur*').

Having got that far, he reminds us that the badness of lying, as a kind of act, is light. The 'order of speech' gets its necessity from its relation to the 'order of charity', but speech has other functions too, besides social communication. Again, as man is a contingent being and the truth of which he deprives other men by lying is only the truth of his own mind, to know which is very little essential for others, a lie leaves the order of charity towards others substantially intact. Lying will only be deadly from extra circumstances either of hatred or of some obligation of telling, which it violates.

There isn't always evil when the order of something to its end is violated—else we'd sin in eating eggs. There is sin in the violation of an order (*ordo*) *to which we are subordinate*. But, to repeat, grave sin isn't the particular violation of just any *ordo*, but of *the essential ordo* to which that particular one relates. The *ordo* of speech is a particular one, which relates to charity. And so it comes about that although a lie is contrary to the *ordo* of speech, still it isn't *against*, but only *outside* (*praeter*) the order of charity. That is to say, it allows *that* order to be substantially intact. In short, you are violating charity by lying to someone, not by any old lie, but only by a lie out of hatred or a lie where there is something you have an obligation to tell him. This is so, according to Vermeersch, *in spite of* the fact that the point of speech is 'caritative communication' and that *because* of this lying is always wrong. His conclusion seems admirable but his thinking here is a bit odd. If the order of speech is inviolable because and only because speech relates to the 'order of charity', how is it that that doesn't show, not merely that lying is always wrong, but that it is always a violation of the 'order of charity'? Or if it is not always a violation of the 'order of charity', how does its relation to the order of charity manage to show that it is *always* wrong? To repeat, I am not disputing his conclusion that lying is always wrong but not always mortally sinful. I am only criticising the reasons he offers for his conclusion.

He proceeds to deal with the case where it is justified or positively required *not* to tell someone something when he is asking you about it. Here Vermeersch is highly critical of the idea of *restrictio mentalis,* which I take would be wrongly translated 'mental reservation' though that is the only familiar English expression in this context. I take it that '*restrictio mentalis*' means 'a mental restriction' e.g. to *one* sense of an ambiguous expression. His criticism of this idea is partly good, and it is worth noting, as *he* notes, that it is a relatively modern idea. It is the idea that in order not to be lying – i.e. producing speech contrary to your own mind – you restrict your *meaning* to that meaning of the ambiguous expression in which it is true. This is an idea infected by the notion of an act of meaning, the notion that you have to be *thinking* about meaning something in order to be meaning it and not the other thing. Whereas I would suppose that you only had to think, if at all, 'well, it's true in *that* sense, anyway' and the question at issue is whether the fact that you hope and intend that the hearer will take it in the sense in which it is false means that you are telling a lie.

However it is not my business here to defend the position actually in question but to point to the very singular device of Vermeersch in reaching the conclusion that you *aren't* lying. His first observation is the obvious one that not all speech is assertion. This is not because speech may be questions, orders, complaints, and so on. No, his point is that speech may have the form of assertion but not be assertion because for example it is uttered by an actor on a stage or because it is a joke. No one will say the actor or story-teller is lying, says Vermeersch. True enough, and something like that is true about jokes. He now makes the most amazing assertions himself, which alas are not *jokes*. If someone is asked whether she has committed adultery, and she says no, what this means is *not* the assertion that she hasn't, it means: Either I haven't, or I don't want to admit it. And so generally for unwelcome interrogations. Now how much is there in this? Take a criminal trial. It may be a formality that you plead not guilty; so much so that if you refuse to plead, a plea of not guilty is automatically entered by the court. *That*, it can reasonably be argued puts an interpretation on your plea of not guilty when you do make it though you think you know you *are* guilty. This I think we can accept. But that generally if you are being questioned by someone who is persecuting you, you can say that something is the case which is not and *that* not be a lie, not because of the ambiguity but because you *aren't* asserting it, but rather saying 'Either it is the case or I don't want to say it is not' — this is much more nonsense than some of the contentions of the mental restrictioners were.

Now this influential piece by Vermeersch has an interesting family resemblance to the presently very influential book by Bruno Schüller, *Die Begründung sittlicher Urteile.**

When I began to read Schüller's book I was amazed. I knew it was influential; I did not see how it could be regarded as anything but ridiculous. This was because of the way it begins. To put briefly what Schüller spends a lot of ink on: he has noticed that the ten commandments are not statements, but commandments. He produces a word 'Paränese', which he first explains as covering orders and prohibitions and warnings and encouragements. Well and good: it may be useful to have such a word. In English we are used to discussing 'imperatives' which I suppose covers much the same ground, though an imperative is also used for advice. But Schüller has a rhetorical reason for introducing an unfamiliar word; he wishes to characterise the 'paraenetic' in a way which shall be very directive for moral philosophy.

The fact that a commandment is not a statement but a command or prohibition is confused in his mind, it seems, with a non-fact, namely that it has no non-tautological content. So, skipping the first two commandments, he expounds: 'Keep holy the Sabbath day; rest on it'. 'Sabbath day' he says may very well mean 'rest day' and that would mean 'day on which you ought to rest'. So the commandment means 'Rest on the day on which you ought to rest'. That is tautological. The remaining commandments get the same treatment. 'Honour your father and mother'. Well, what does 'father and mother' mean? Not what you might think: it means 'Respektpersonen' i.e. 'people

* Bruno Schüller SJ, *Die Begründung sittlicher Urteile. Typen ethischer Argumentation in der Moraltheologie* (Düsseldorf: Patmos, 1973; second edition 1980). Schüller is an influential German Jesuit moral theologian who advanced a 'proportionalist' (consequentialist) understanding of Christian ethics.

you ought to respect'. 'Thou shall not kill' he tells us, means 'Thou shall not kill wrongfully'. For, he says, people who know Hebrew will tell us that the Hebrew word translated 'kill' means 'wrongful killing' or 'murder'. One understands that they are a bit short of rabbis in Germany these days; but I fear Schüller didn't even try to consult any rabbis. My own experience is that if you ask a Jew who knows Hebrew well, he will tell you that the word is not the ordinary word for killing; you'd use another word for killing in war and another for the work of a butcher. (I have not had the idea—till just now—of seeing whether a word for killing is used in connection with what the 'avenger of blood' might do, or which word is used for what you had done, if you had killed someone accidentally and you had to flee to one of the cities of refuge to escape the avenger of blood.) What I was told was that the word used in the commandment covers what in England we call manslaughter as well as what we call murder. That this shows it means 'wrongful killing', may be maintained by some people but is surely false. An executioner who knowingly executed his own father would thereby be guilty *of wrongful killing* but not of either murder or manslaughter.[1] So 'wrongful killing' is wider *'extensive'*, as Vermeersch would say, than 'murder' or 'murder-and-manslaughter'.

The commandments against stealing, false witness and adultery, get the same sort of treatment.

We are given a *general* thesis about 'ethical exhortation, or Paränese'. (Schüller confines *his* application of Paränese to the ethical.) The general thesis is: 'An important indication (for such sentences) is that if, contrary to their own intention, they are construed as propositions communicating knowledge, they assume the form of tautologies or empty formulae'. Of course he *sees* to it that they do so, by reinterpreting them.

The reason why I was so amazed at these proceedings was that I could not understand how people could be snowed by such writing. What suppression of what they knew could make them accept that 'father and mother' doesn't mean father and mother? How could they suppose that that commandment which contains the week in it: 'Six days shall thou labour and do all that thou hast to do', as it enjoins rest on the seventh day—that this, if transformed into a 'You ought to' proposition, would come out as a tautology?—It is true, as Schüller remarks, that a commandment against adultery could not be given to people who had no institution of marriage; equally a

[1] I owe this observation to Dr. M. C. Geach.

commandment against theft presupposes some custom of property. It is true then that disapproval of theft and adultery is also to some degree presupposed. I learned from a Jewish surgeon that the traditional vital application of 'Honour your father and mother' was: not to leave them to die by the wayside in the desert travel of the children of Israel. Schüller thinks that anything he calls 'paraenetic' conforms to an already totally and utterly unquestioningly received morality. Well he can restrict his term like that if he likes; it is then not open to him to assume that the ten commandments were what he called 'paraenetic'. This sliding in of something which, given the way in which a term has been introduced, may very well not be so, is I fear characteristic.

Reading the rest of the book I perceived why, having somehow swallowed or skipped this first chapter, people might be impressed. The book is learned especially in Anglo-American moral philosophy. However, the purpose of the first chapter becomes clear: it provides a very fundamental defence against a protest: But we *know* that certain things are required, certain others wrong. We know some of these from the commandments.

As I said, there is a curious resemblance to Vermeersch. Remember Vermeersch's innocent and obvious observation that not all that has the grammatical form of assertion *is* assertion. (I put it in my terms, but it is clearly what he means from the example of the actors in a stage play.) Well and good. From that he slides to saying that you haven't asserted that you have not committed adultery if you say you have not when your husband asks or accuses you: that 'the amiable Saint Francis', when he said 'The man hasn't passed this way' was actually saying 'Either the man hasn't passed this way or if he has I don't want to betray him'.* Our two moral theologians both play Humpty Dumpty with words and both use well known facts, which do make their topic more difficult than a naïf person would think, to justify themselves. There the similarity ends: Vermeersch *thinks* he is strictly maintaining a strict doctrine; Schüller's bent is to make hay of any strict doctrine.

Schüller's book is also quite interesting reading. But you do have to be watchful. He writes *as if* there were only two possibilities when

* A Vermeersch, *op.cit.*, p. 463. 'Et amabilis S. Franciscus, dum vitam servare voluit hominis quem insectabantur, ut sine mendacio responderet: 'Non hac transivit', opus non habuit, manu manicam suam indicare vel pede locum designare cui insistebat; responsum de se hanc ambiguitatem ferebat: Vel *non transit*, vel *non prodo hominem*.'

there are evidently, or likely to be, more. About lying, for example. If you must preserve a secret, are asked a question about it and 'silence will betray'; well then—to betray the secret is excluded; so you must *either* lie *or* if you think you must not lie you must *give an answer* which *is* an answer but which doesn't betray; in giving it you use a restrictive concept of lying so that what you say, by that concept, doesn't count as a lie. Schüller's comment is that the restriction imposed on the concept of lying brings the people who are supposedly 'deontological' as near as makes no odds to what he calls a 'teleological' view. If I am to translate this, it seems to mean (a) that they think what you do here *is* justified by the good result of not betraying the secret, and (b) that the alleged purpose—*not to lie*—is a put-up job. But the effort to give an account of how you can give an answer and yet avoid a lie seems to distinguish such a person from a 'teleologist', if the latter judges one should be willing to lie for a good purpose.

That in an actual situation there may be possibilities not mentioned, like feigning a faint or a fit of madness, making a distracting joke or producing some other red herring, is a feature of discussions of this topic, of Schüller's no less than others'. That if you can see no possibility except to give some information you must not give, or to lie, you will do better to lie than, say, to betray the unjustly persecuted fugitive—this is sufficiently obvious but does not get mentioned. The most that is mentioned is that you may not be clever enough, which is unfair. For the discussions are all about how to *avoid any sin* at all. But the truth is: you might not be good enough to do that.

Schüller explains or accepts a defining contrast between what he calls 'deontologists' and what he calls 'teleologists': a 'teleologist' thinks that actions are to be judged only by their consequences, or their tendency to produce good or bad consequences; and a 'deontologist' (of the more savage sort) thinks that some actions are wrong (or right and obligatory) no matter what the consequences. The milder sort of 'deontologist' thinks that *all* actions are to be judged always *partly*, but not always *only* by their consequences. Schüller maintains that 'teleological' ethics is the right Catholic sort.

The terminology is not invented by Schüller, though it is strange to me, who have quite different meanings for these terms. However, accepting them for the sake of proceeding, I can say: there *is* a crucial difference between moral philosophers according as they think or do not think that some kinds of actions one should not do—not for any advantage to be gained or evil to be avoided.

Now lying is one of the candidates. This makes the discussion of it rather interesting.

I said one should lie about the thing *rather* that give the fugitive away. How come? Isn't that doing something bad for the sake of avoiding an evil?—namely the evil of the fugitive being caught? This must be what incites Schüller to say that the devices invented to show what would *not* be a lie come as near as anything to teleology. Aren't we going by consequences?

People may easily be incited to say that the devices invented to show that something would *not* be a lie come as near as you like to saying 'Lie for the good purpose, or to avoid the evil, and I'll tell you a way of muddling your mind into thinking it isn't a lie'. Now *aren't* we just going by consequences here?

No, and the point is important. If it is absolutely clear that someone can't be persuaded to avoid wrongdoing altogether in some matter, it is good to persuade him to commit some lesser sin than what he is minded to do. If you *cannot* see any alternative to committing one sin or another, you act better if you chose the lesser sin. And you may not have time or cleverness to find out a better possibility. To betray the fugitive, we will suppose, is a gravely wicked thing to do. Telling the pursuers he is there *is* betraying him. So in this case telling that truth is a wicked act—more than telling the lie that he is not there. But suppose that somebody else threatened that *he* would give the fugitive away unless you told some lie? That case would be different. If you are a consequentialist, you are likely to say you should tell that lie just as much as the other one. But I didn't say you *should* tell the other one, only that you should do it *rather* than commit an act of betrayal by what you tell the pursuers. If you are a consequentialist you will hold that you are responsible for all the consequences of your acts and omissions and therefore that you are responsible for the capture of the fugitive if he was caught because you refused to tell the lie demanded by the person who betrayed him—just as much as if you betrayed him.

Now I am not quite clear to what extent Schüller is a consequentialist. He sometimes I think forgets the totality of opinion involved in defining the 'teleologist'—a 'teleologist' thinks *all* acts are determined in their moral character by their consequences or tendency to produce certain consequences. The latter phrase may suggest *kinds of act* as what are being considered. In general, the people who are 'deontologists' think there are some *kinds* of act such that acts of that kind are wicked regardless of consequences in a particular case. As a 'teleologist' is one who holds the view that contradicts this, he thinks there are not any such *kinds* of act. This would seem to lead to his thinking that if any particular act is wicked, it is not as being of such and such a kind. Now Schüller objects to attacks by 'deontologists' on 'teleologists' which run like this: 'Am I to defraud someone because I could do better things with the money I owe him, than by giving it him? If you go by consequences only, justice and fairness go overboard'. With what justification, asks Schüller, are justice and fairness not to be counted among the consequences of your act? Well, he certainly is given to taking rather unimpressive statements of opposing positions. However, this is a very interesting one. If you do pay what you owe, justice is satisfied as far as that transaction is concerned. So that's part of the consequences. And it may outweigh the advantage of what you might have done with the money. What if it doesn't? Well, it's not clear that you intend the permanent defrauding of the other party, so if some really serious need for the money here and now makes you say 'Sorry, can't pay you today', justice isn't flouted, its demands are merely postponed and will that be objectionable? – Well what we want is not such a case – it is a poor case to put forward. We want a case where the consequences of a lie, or of an intentional adultery, or of deliberately killing a baby, are held by a 'teleologist' to justify the action, i.e. to make it out to have been a good action in spite of its having those characters. Why I put in lying as an example ought to be clear from what I have said in the matter of betraying the fugitive. We ought not to take a case where one of the things would at any rate be *less bad* to do than any alternative you can think of. 'Such', you may say, 'can always be imagined.' But no; it would be too fanciful to think out e.g. a case where you are irresistibly tempted either to commit adultery *or* to murder someone, so you choose the adultery as the lesser sin. You can only introduce cases plausibly if you construct a set-up such that this action will have such-and-such consequences and refusing to do it will mean those consequences don't occur. Let the consequences be greatly desirable, the to-be-expected alternative dreadful and miserable. Is the weight of the badness of the act something to put into the calculus of the total value or disvalue of the consequences – as Schüller in effect says justice and fairness would be?

Moore argued that everyone has to be a consequentialist – has to accept his analysis of rightness and wrongness of action – who has a moral view at all. For, he says, your action must have consequences, and if you say: they don't matter, such-and-such an action is wrong, what you *have to* mean is that the sum of their value is never such as to outweigh the sum of disvalue when this includes the intrinsic evil of the act. Moore says that anyone who thinks of ethics at all must think this, and in this way he accommodates to his own general theory the views of those who say e.g. 'Deliberately procuring abortion is wrong; whatever the consequences, you must not do that'.

If Moore were right, then the difference between a 'deontologist' and a 'teleologist' would be ill-expressed by contrasting the views so labelled: it would be a matter of including or not including the value or disvalue of consequences. Or, more seriously, the difference might be between people who think that the disvalue of an intrinsically wrong act is *eo ipso* so great that it could not be outweighed, and those who think that no kind of act is in that sense intrinsically wrong. As Schüller does seem to think there is a serious difference, and that the right ethic is 'teleological', it follows that he is among those who do *not* think any kind of action intrinsically wrong and so irredeemable by, say, the spirit in which, or the further purposes for which, you do it. In fact, it is quite clear that he is among such thinkers.

His thesis that traditional Catholic morality is 'teleological' is a startling impudence.

Comparing Vermeersch and Schüller, I have found a certain likeness between them in that they both play Humpty Dumpty with words. They do this, in the example I have cited, for different purposes: Schüller to anaesthetise his readers against the effect of knowing the ten commandments, Vermeersch to justify lying in response to unwelcome interrogation. As he thinks he is maintaining a strict classical doctrine that lying is always wrong, he may seem rather to contrast with Schüller who does not desire even an appearance of holding any absolutist positions like that. However, as I hope to have shown, the absolutism is something of a self deception on Vermeersch's part.

Let us return to another topic to show Vermeersch in his world-pleasing role. He discusses killing by a private person in self defence. He is admirable in his criticism of one who thinks to find the 'principle of double effect' in St. Thomas's article on this subject (*Summa theologiae* 2^{a} 2^{ae}, q.64, a.7). St. Thomas thinks that even in self defence one may not kill on purpose: 'Illicitum est quod homo intendat occidere ut se defendat'. How remarkable it would have been, Vermeersch remarks, if the principle of double effect had no force in the one passage of the *Summa* where St. Thomas was formally formulating it!—i.e. he is doing no such thing.

All the same, St. Thomas' rigorous doctrine has its difficulties. If in a struggle on the edge of a cliff you push your assailant over the edge, it is reasonable to say you are intentionally exerting enough force to push him away from you, and so it may well be true that you didn't intend his death.—But suppose you shoot him and that kills him? (Or, to make the point more strongly, you throw a hand grenade, which is all you've got to repel one who is advancing on you with a machine gun?) 'How, several have asked', says Vermeersch 'is the killing of the aggressor not direct, not chosen as a means to saving yourself?'* Here he makes a suggestion which is worth careful thought:

> The unjust aggression itself morally alters the action of exploding (shooting) the gun. Without that present attack, the explosion (shooting) of the gun neither would nor could be anything but a direct killing. But now that aggression, persisting for some time, makes it fall under the conception of defence, and of a defence the intention of which is directed to saving yourself. This shows why actual (present) attack has to be stipulated among the conditions of bloody defence. For when the actual attack stops, the action would simply fall under the concept of killing for an end, perhaps a good end: but it isn't permissible to do evil for the sake of good.**

If the main thing Vermeersch means by this passage is respectable, it can't be that in such a case you are justified because you *aren't* engaged in intentional direct killing. I would rather understand him as saying that an attack which makes your shooting fall under the concept (gives it the *ratio*) of immediate defence, is a counter-

* A. Vermeersch, *op.cit.*, p. 466: 'Quo modo tunc, sic non nulli interrogant, occisio aggressoris non est directa, non est electa ut medium salutis propriae?'

** *loc.cit.*: 'Verum id attendendum est, actionem explodendi sclopetum ipsa iniusta aggressione moraliter mutari. Separata ab hac invasione praesenti, explosio sclopeti non foret nec esse posset nisi directa occisio. Nunc autem aggressio ista, quam diu perseverat, eidem rationem tribuit defensionis, et defensionis cuius intentio ad salutem propriam dirigitur. Hinc etiam probe perspicitur cur actualis aggressio inter condiciones cruentae defensionis ponenda sit. Cessante enim actuali aggressione, actio non haberet iam nisi rationem occisionis propter finem fortasse bonum: sed non licet facere mala ut eveniant bona.'

example to the prohibition of 'direct', i.e. intentional, killing. This is worthy of more exploration.

I fear, however, that he meant worse. As in the case of lying, he thought he was adhering to a classically rigorous principle. But look how he goes on (in small print):

> But there is no lack of other examples in which an action, physically very clearly direct, is nevertheless held to be morally purely permissive, because it goes with another physical effectiveness, which alone is intended. Thus, as everybody admits, the burning of innocent people is merely being permitted by one 'who burns innocents in a tower along with nocents... because by the intention of the agent the action only looks to the burning of the nocents, although here and now the burning of these cannot be separated from the burning of the others'; thus someone who transfixes a nocent by piercing an innocent placed between is judged neither to have intended nor to have chosen the killing of that innocent. In the same way the unjust attack here conferred a double immediate effectiveness on the explosion of the gun: one being the defence of the man being attacked, which alone is chosen and intended, the other the killing, which is only being permitted'.*

This doctrine is introduced for the sake of an application to lying:

> Someone who requires us to disclose a matter we have a right to keep secret is an unjust aggressor: materially or formally so, according as he is or is not conscious of his importunity. This makes no difference as it is all right to repel an attack with the same kind of defence, whether it is materially or formally blameworthy... In themselves, the words would be nothing but a signification of what is false. But the unjust attack of the other has the effect that they are at the same time a defence of oneself. Where they are so applied, the false signification is merely permitted.

* *loc.cit.*: 'Ceterum non desunt alia exempla in quibus actio quae physice est manifestissime directa, moraliter tamen pro mere permissive habetur, quia concurrit cum alia physica efficientia quae sola intenditur. Sic, ut omnes fatentur, combustionem innocentium mere permittit, 'qui comburit innocentes in turri simul cum nocentibus ... quia actio, ex intentione agentis, solum tendit ad comburendos nocentes, licet hic et nunc non posit combustio horum separari a combustione illorum'; sic, qui per innocentem interpositum transfigit nocentem, innocentis occisionem nec intendisse nec elegisse censetur. Non aliter hic aggressio iniusta explosioni sclopeti duplicem efficientiam immediatam tribuit: alteram hominem invasum defendendi, quae sola eligitur et intenditur, altera occidendi, quae sola permittitur.'

> Hence the fault of lying is absent in our case, for the same reason as the concept of homicide does not apply in the other.*

I would have to know more history than I do to say whether Vermeersch is sounding a new note. Certainly the earlier casuistry on the subject of lying seemed to me to have been inspired by a traditional concern that one not sin against the truth, which is what assertion is for. (For this last, see St. Anselm, *De Veritate* cap.II.) This concern appears in Vermeersch only as a concern that one as it were find a legal loophole to get out of a charge of lying. As for the matters he adduces as parallels, they seem sinister indeed. Perhaps they were already there in a tradition in which he writes. Whether this is so or not, there is a strong atmosphere of one using his quite powerful talents to go along with the world, to reassure and flatter it. This characteristic is raised to a higher degree in Schüller's *Die Begründung sittlicher Urteile*.

* *op.cit.* p.467: 'Qui a nobis postulat revelationem rei quam ius nobis est secreto tegere, est iniustus aggressor: materialiter aut formaliter, prout importunitas suae est conscius vel non. Hoc ceterum non refert, cum eodem defensionis genere aggressionem formaliter et materialiter tantum culpandam repellere liceat ... Secundum se, verba ista non essent nisi significatio falsi. Iniusta alterius aggressio efficit ut sint simul propria defensio. Qua talia adhibentur falsa significatio mere permittitur. Quare, labes mendacii abest in nostra casu, simili prorsus ratione qua, in altero, ratio homicidii.'

16*

Contraception and Chastity

I

I will first ask you to contemplate a familiar point: the fantastic change that has come about in people's situation in respect of having children because of the invention of efficient contraceptives. You see, what can't be otherwise we accept; and so we accept death and its unhappiness. But possibility destroys mere acceptance. And so it is with the possibility of having intercourse and preventing conception. This power is now placed in a woman's hands; she needn't have children when she doesn't want to and she can still have her man! This can make the former state of things look intolerable, so that one wonders why they were so pleased about weddings in former times and why the wedding day was supposed to be such a fine day for the bride.

There always used to be a colossal strain in ancient times between heathen morality and Christian morality, and one of the things pagan converts had to be told about the way they were entering on was that they must abstain from fornication. This peculiarity of Christian life was taught in a precept issued by the Council of Jerusalem, the very first council of the Christian Church. The prohibition was issued in the same breath as the merely temporary retention of Judaic laws prohibiting the eating of blood—no black pudding!—and the prohibition on eating the flesh of animals that had been

* First published by the Catholic Truth Society (London) in 1975. Reprinted with the permission of the Catholic Truth Society. The text is a revised version of a paper delivered to the Bristol Newman Circle, published in its original form in *The Human World* No.7 (May 1972), pp. 9–30. It attracted criticism in a subsequent number of that journal (No.9, November 1972) from Peter Winch and from Bernard Williams and Michael Tanner (pp. 41–48) to which Anscombe replied (pp. 48–51).

sacrificed to idols. And in one way these may have been psychologically the same sort of prohibition to a pagan convert. The Christian life simply imposed these peculiar restrictions on you. All the same, the prohibition on fornication must have stood out; it must have meant a very serious change of life to many, as it would today. Christian life meant a separation from the standards of that world: you couldn't be a Baal-worshipper, you couldn't sacrifice to idols, be a sodomite, practise infanticide, compatibly with the Christian allegiance. That is not to say that Christians were good; we humans are a bad lot and our lives as Christians even if not blackly and grossly wicked are usually very mediocre. But the Catholic Christian badge now again means separation, even for such poor mediocrities, from what the unchristian world in the West approves and professes.

Christianity was at odds with the heathen world, not only about fornication, infanticide and idolatry but also about marriage. Christians were taught that husband and wife had equal rights in one another's bodies; a wife is *wronged* by her husband's adultery as well as a husband by his wife's. And Christianity involved non-acceptance of the contemptible role of the female partner in fornication, calling the prostitute to repentance and repudiating respectable concubinage. And finally for Christians divorce was excluded. These differences *were* the measure, great enough, of the separation between Christianity and the pagan world in these matters. By now, Christian teaching is, of course, *known* all over the world; and it goes without saying for those in the West that what they call 'accepting traditional morals' means counting fornication as wrong—it's just not a respectable thing. But we ought to be conscious that, like the objection to infanticide, this is a Jewish-Christian inheritance. And we should realise that heathen humanity tends to have a different attitude towards both. In Christian teaching a value is set on every human life and on men's chastity as well as on women's and this as part of the ordinary calling of a Christian, not just in connexion with the austerity of monks. Faithfulness, by which a man turned only to his spouse, forswearing all other women, was counted as one of *the* great goods of marriage.

But the quarrel is far greater between Christianity and the present-day heathen, post-Christian, morality that has sprung up as a result of contraception. In one word: Christianity taught that men ought to be as chaste as pagans thought honest women ought to be; the contraceptive morality teaches that women need to be as little chaste as pagans thought men need be.

And if there is nothing intrinsically wrong with contraceptive intercourse, and if it could become general practice everywhere when there is intercourse but ought to be no begetting, then it's very difficult to see the objection to this morality; for the ground of objection to fornication and adultery was that sexual intercourse is only right in the *sort* of set-up that typically provides children with a father and mother to care for them. If you can turn intercourse into something other than the reproductive type of act (I don't mean of course that every act is reproductive any more than every acorn leads to an oak tree but it's the reproductive type of act) then why, if you can change it, should it be restricted to the married? Restricted, that is, to partners bound in a formal, legal union whose fundamental purpose is the bringing up of children? For if that is not its fundamental purpose there is no reason why for example 'marriage' should have to be between people of opposite sexes. But then, of course, it becomes unclear why you should have a ceremony, why you should have a formality at all. And so we must grant that children are in this general way the main point of the existence of such an arrangement. But if sexual union can be deliberately and totally divorced from fertility, then we may wonder why sexual union has got to be married union. If the expression of love between the partners is the point, then it shouldn't be so narrowly confined.

The only objection, then, to the new heathen, contraceptive morality will be that the second condition I mentioned—near-universality of contraception where there ought to be no begetting—simply won't be fulfilled. Against the background of a society with that morality, more and more people will have intercourse with little feeling of responsibility, little restraint, and *yet* they just won't be so careful about always using contraceptives. And so the widespread use of contraceptives naturally leads to more and more rather than less and less abortion.[1] Indeed, abortion is now being recommended as a population control measure—a second line of defence.

Now if this—that you won't get this universal 'taking care'—is the only objection then it's a pretty miserable outlook. Because, like the fear of venereal disease, it's an objection that's little capable of moving people or inspiring them as a positive ideal of chastity may.

The Christian Church has taught such an ideal of chastity: in a narrower sense, and in a broader sense in which chastity is simply the

[1] The exception to this in the short term is where abortion has been encouraged and contraceptives not available; making contraceptives available then produces an immediate but only temporary reduction in abortions.

virtue whose topic is sex, just as courage is the virtue whose topic is danger and difficulty. In the narrower sense chastity means continence, abstention. I have to say something about this—though I'm reduced to stammering because I am a mediocre worldly person leading an ordinary sort of worldly life; nevertheless I'll try to say it even with stammering.

What people are for is, we believe, like guided missiles, to home in on God, God who is the one truth it is infinitely worth knowing, the possession of which you could never get tired of, like the water which if you have you can never thirst again, because your thirst is slaked forever and always. It's this potentiality, this incredible possibility, of the knowledge of God of such a kind as even to be sharing in his nature, which Christianity holds out to people; and because of this potentiality every life, right up to the last, must be treated as precious. Its potentialities in all things the world cares about may be slight; but there is always the possibility of what it's for. We can't ever know that the time of possibility of gaining eternal life is over, however old, wretched, 'useless' someone has become.

Now there are some people who want this so much that they want to be totally concerned with it and to die to their own worldly, earthly and fleshly desires. It is people who are so filled with this enormous desire and are able to follow it, who pursue the course of chastity in the narrow sense—this is the point, the glory, of Christian celibacy and virginity and of vows of chastity. I think one has to know about it in order to appreciate the teachings of Christianity about chastity in a wide sense. But, as I say, I speak stammeringly because I'm not very well qualified.

II

Turning to chastity not in the narrower sense but in the sense in which it is simply the virtue connected with sex, the Christian Church has always set its face against contraception from the earliest time as a grave breach of chastity. It inherited from Israel the objection to 'base ways of copulating for the avoidance of conception', to quote St. Augustine. In a document of the third century a Christian author wrote of the use of contraceptives by freeborn Christian women in Rome. These women sometimes married slaves so as to have Christian husbands but they were under a severe temptation because if the father was a slave the child was a slave by Roman law and this was a deterrent to having children; and they practised some form of contraception. This was the occasion of the earliest recorded explicit Christian observation on the subject. The author writes like a person mentioning a practice which Christians at large must obviously regard as shameful.

From then on the received teaching of Christianity has been constant. We need only mention two landmarks which have stood as signposts in Christian teaching — the teaching of Augustine and that of Thomas Aquinas. St. Augustine wrote against the Manicheans. The Manicheans were people who thought all sex evil. They thought procreation was worse than sex; so if one must have sex let it be without procreation which imprisoned a soul in flesh. So they first aimed to restrict intercourse altogether to what they thought were infertile times and also to use contraceptive drugs so as if possible never to have children. If they did conceive they used drugs to procure abortions; finally, if that failed, in their cruel lust or lustful cruelty, as St. Augustine says, they might put the child out to die.* (The appetite for killing children is a rather common characteristic in the human race.)

All these actions Augustine condemned and he argued strongly against their teaching. Sex couldn't possibly be evil; it is the source of human society and life is God's good creation. On the other hand it is a familiar point that there is some grimness in Augustine's view of sex. He regards it as more corrupted by the fall than our other faculties. Intercourse for the sake of getting children is good but the need for sexual intercourse otherwise, he thought, is an infirmity. However, 'husband and wife' (I quote) 'owe one another not only the faithful association of sexual union for the sake of getting children — which makes the first society of the human race in this our mortality — but more than that a kind of mutual service of bearing the burden of one another's weakness, so as to prevent unlawful intercourse'.**

Augustine holds up as an ideal something which he must have known didn't happen at all much: the life of married people who no longer seeking children are able to live in continence. He considers it a weakness that few ever do this. There's a sort of servitude to fleshly desire in not being able so to abstain. But marriage is so great a good, he said, that it altogether takes vice out of this; and what's bad about our weakness is thereby excused. If one partner demands sexual

* St Augustine, *De nuptiis et concupiscentia* [*Marriage and Concupiscence*] I, 17.

** St Augustine, *De Bono Coniugali [The Good of Marriage]*, chapter 6.

intercourse out of the pressure of sexual desire, he says, the other does right in according it. But there is at least venial sin in demanding it from this motive, and if one's very intemperate, mortal sin.

All this part of his teaching is very uncongenial to our time. But we must notice that it has been a bit misrepresented. It has been said that for Augustine sexual intercourse not for the sake of getting children involves actual sin, though not mortal sin—a little bit of sin—on the part of at least one partner, the partner who demands it. What he seems to say however is not that, but something different; that if one seeks it out of mere fleshly desire for the sake of pleasure, there is such sin; and this latter teaching has in fact been constant among all the saints and doctors of the Church who have written on the matter at all. (I will be coming back to this.)

St. Augustine indeed didn't write explicitly of any other motive than mere sensuality in seeking intercourse where procreation isn't aimed at. What he says doesn't exclude the possibility of a different motive. There's the germ of an account of the motive called by theologians 'rendering the marriage debt' in his observation that married people owe to one another a kind of mutual service. Aquinas made two contributions, the first of which concerns this point: he makes the remark that a man ought to pay the marriage debt if he can see his wife wants it without her having to ask him. And he ought to notice if she does want it.* This is an apt gloss on Augustine's 'mutual service', and it destroys the basis for the picture which some have had of intercourse not for the sake of children as necessarily a little bit sinful on one side, since one must be 'demanding', and not for any worthy motive but purely 'out of desire for pleasure'. One could hardly say that being diagnosable as wanting intercourse was a sin! St. Thomas, of course, speaks of the matter rather from the man's side, but the same thing could be said from the woman's, too; the only difference being that her role would be more that of encouragement and invitation. (It's somewhat modern to make this comment. We are much more conscious nowadays of people's complexities and hang-ups than earlier writers seem to have been.)

St. Thomas follows St. Augustine and all other traditional teachers in holding that intercourse sought out of lust, only for the sake of pleasure, is sin, though it is venial if the intemperance isn't great, and in type this is the least of the sins against chastity.

* See *Summa theologiae, Supp.* q.64, a.2c [= IV *Sent.* d.32, a.2 sol. 1c]

His second contribution was his definition of the 'sin against nature'. This phrase relates to deviant acts, such as sodomy and bestiality. He defines this type of sin as a sexual act of such a kind as to be intrinsically unfit for generation.* The definition has been colossally important. It was, indeed, perfectly in line with St. Augustine's reference to copulating in a 'base' way so as not to procreate, thus to identify some ways of contraception practised in former times as forms of unnatural vice. For they would, most of them, be deviant sexual acts.

Contraception by medical methods, however, as well as abortion, had previously been characterised as homicide throughout the dark ages. And this seems a monstrously unreasonable stretching of the idea of homicide. Not unreasonable in the case of abortion; though some may doubt (it's a rather academic question, I think, an intensely academic question) the good sense of calling a fertilised ovum a human being. But soon there is something of a human shape; and anyway this is the definite beginning of a human being (or beings in the case of a split—where you get twins—the split occurs soon, at least within two weeks), and if you perform an abortion at that early stage all the same you are destroying that human beginning.

But of course the notion of homicide is just not extendable to most forms of contraception. The reason why it seemed to be so in the dark ages (by the 'dark ages' I mean roughly from the 4th-5th centuries on to the 12th, say—I won't make an apology for using the expression—scientifically it was pretty dark) was that it was taken for granted that medical methods were all abortifacient in type. We have to remember that no one knew about the ovum. Then, and in more primitive times, as language itself reveals with its talk of 'seed', the woman's body was thought of as being like the ground in which seed was planted. And thus the perishing of the seed once planted would be judged by people of those times to be the same sort of event as we would judge the perishing of a fertilised ovum to be and hence the deliberate bringing about of the one would be just like the deliberate bringing about of the other. So that is the explanation of the curiosity that historically medical contraception was equated with homicide—it was equated with homicide because they thought it was that sort of thing, the sort of thing that destroying a fertilised ovum is.

* *Summa theologiae* 2a 2ae q.154, a.1c; a.11c.

When Aristotle's philosophy became dominant in the thirteenth century a new (but still erroneous) picture replaced that ancient one: namely that the woman provided the *matter*; and the man the formative principle of a new conception. This already made that extended notion of 'homicide' look untenable—contraception that would prevent the formation would obviously not be destroying something that was already the beginning of new human life. With modern physiological knowledge contraception by medical methods could be clearly distinguished from early abortion, though some contraceptive methods might be abortifacient.

On the other hand intercourse using contraception by mechanical methods was fairly easy to assimilate to the 'sin against nature' as defined by St. Thomas. Looking at it like this is aided by the following consideration: suppose that somebody's contraceptive method were to adopt some clearly perverse mode of copulation, one wouldn't want to say he committed two distinct sins, one of perversion and the other of contraception: there'd be just the one evil deed, precisely because the perversity of the mode consists in the physical act being changed so as to be not the sort of act that gets a child at all.

And so the theologians tried to extend the notion of the evil as one of perversity—speaking, for example, of the 'perverse use of a faculty'—so as to cover all types of contraception including medical ones which after all don't change the mere physical act into one of the type: 'sin against nature'.

For with contraception becoming common in this country and the Protestants approving it in the end, the Popes reiterated the condemnation of it. It was clear that the condemnation was of deliberately contraceptive intercourse as a breach of chastity, as 'a shameful thing'. But the rationale offered by the theologians was not satisfactory. The situation was intellectually extremely distressing. On the one hand, it would have been absurd, wouldn't it? to approve douches, say, while forbidding condoms. On the other hand, the extension of the notion of a perverse act, a deviant act, seemed strained.

Furthermore, while one doesn't *have* to be learned (nobody has to be learned) or able to give a convincing account of the reasons for a teaching—for remember that the Church teaches with the authority of a divine commission, and the Pope has a prophetical office, not a chair of science or moral philosophy or theology—all the same the moral teaching of the Church, by her own claims, is supposed to be reasonable. Christian moral teachings aren't revealed mysteries like the Trinity. The lack of clear accounts of the reason in the teaching was disturbing to many people. Especially, I believe, to many of the clergy whose job it was to give the teaching to the people.

Again, with the effective contraceptive techniques and real physiological knowledge available, a new question came to the fore. I mean that of the rational limitation of families. Because of ignorance, people in former times who did not choose continence could effect such limitation only by obviously vile and disreputable methods. So no one envisaged a policy of seeking to have just a reasonable number of children (by any method other than continence over sufficient periods) as a policy compatible with chastity. Indeed the very notion 'a reasonable number of children' could hardly be formulated compatibly with thinking at once decently and realistically. It had to be left to God what children one had.

With society becoming more and more contraceptive, the pressure felt by Catholic married people became great. The restriction of intercourse to infertile periods 'for grave reasons' was offered to them as a recourse—at first in a rather gingerly way (as is intelligible in view of the mental background I have sketched) and then with increasing recommendation of it. For in this method the act of copulation was not itself adapted in any way so as to render it infertile, and so the condemnation of acts of contraceptive intercourse as somehow perverse and so as grave breaches of chastity, did not apply to this. All other methods, Catholics were very emphatically taught, were 'against the natural law'.

Now I'd better pause a bit about this expression 'against the natural law'. We should notice it as a curiosity that in popular discussion there's usually more mention of 'natural law' in connexion with the Catholic prohibition on contraception than in connexion with any other matters. One even hears people talk of 'the argument from natural law'. It's probable that there's a very strong association of words here: on the one hand through the contrast 'artificial'/'natural' and on the other through the terms 'unnatural vice' or 'sin against nature' which are labels for a particular range of sins against chastity; that is those acts which are wrong of their kind, which aren't wrong just from the circumstances that the persons aren't married: they're not doing what would be all right if they were married and had good motives—they're doing something really different. That's the range of sins against chastity which got this label 'sins against nature'.

In fact there's no greater connexion of 'natural law' with the prohibition on contraception than with any other part of morality. Any type of wrong action is 'against the natural law': stealing is, framing someone is, oppressing people is. 'Natural law' is simply a way of speaking about the whole of morality, used by Catholic thinkers because they believe the general precepts of morality are *laws* promulgated by God our Creator in the enlightened human understanding when it is thinking in general terms about what are good and what are bad actions. That is to say, the discoveries of reflection and reasoning when we think straight about these things *are* God's legislation to us (whether we realise this or not).

In thinking about conduct we have to advert to laws of nature in another sense. That is, to very general and very well-known facts of nature, and also to ascertained scientific laws. For example, the resources of the earth have to be worked on to supply our needs and enhance our lives: this is a general and well-known fact of nature. Hence there needs to be control over resources by definite owners, be they tribes or states or cities or corporations or clubs or individual people: and this is the institution of property. Laws of nature in a scientific sense will affect the rules about control that it is reasonable to have. The type of installations we need if electricity is to be made available, for example, and the way they work, will be taken into account in framing the laws of the country or city about control of this resource. The institution of property has as its corollary the 'law of nature' in the ethical sense, the sense of a law of morality, which forbids stealing. It's useful, very useful, to get clear about all this; it should help us to think and act justly and not to be too mad about property, too.

It was in these various ways that the Pope spoke of natural laws in *Humanae Vitae** — the expression occurs in all these senses — and the topic of natural law in the ethical sense has not any greater relevance to contraception than to anything else. In particular, it is not because there is a *natural* law that something *artificial* is condemned.

The substantive, hard teaching of the Church which all Catholics were given up to 1964 was clear enough: all artificial methods of birth control were taught to be gravely wrong if, before, after, or during intercourse you do something intended to turn that intercourse into an infertile act if it would otherwise have been fertile.

* Pope Paul VI, *Encyclical Letter on Regulating Human Procreation Rightly* [*Humanae Vitae*], July 25 1968; most recent English translation — by John Finnis — published by the Catholic Truth Society, London, 2008.

At that time there had already been set up by Pope John in his lifetime a commission to enquire into these things. The commission consisted of economists, doctors and other lay people as well as theologians. Pope John, by the way, spoke of contraception just as damningly as his predecessor: it's a mere lie to suggest he favoured it. Pope Paul removed the matter from the competency of the Council and reserved to the Pope that new judgement on it which the modern situation and the new discoveries—above all, of oral contraceptives—made necessary.

From 1964 onwards there was an immense amount of propaganda for the reversal of previous teaching. You will remember it. Then, with the whole world baying at him to change, the Pope acted as Peter. 'Simon, Simon,' Our Lord said to Peter, 'Satan has wanted to have you to sift like wheat, but I have prayed for thee that thy faith should not fail: and thou, being once converted, strengthen thy brethren.' Thus Paul confirmed the only doctrine which had ever appeared as the teaching of the Church on these things; and in so doing incurred the execration of the world.

But Athenagoras, the Ecumenical Patriarch, who has the primacy of the Orthodox Church, immediately spoke up and confirmed that this was Christian teaching, the only possible Christian teaching.

III

Among those who hoped for a change there was an instant reaction that the Pope's teaching was false, and was not authoritative because it lacked the formal character of an infallible document. Now as to that, the Pope was pretty solemnly confirming the only and constant teaching of the Church. The fact that an encyclical is not an infallible kind of document only shows that one argument for the truth of its teaching is lacking. It does not show that the substantive hard message of this encyclical may perhaps be wrong—any more than the fact that memory of phone numbers isn't the *sort* of thing that you *can't* be wrong about shows that you don't actually know your own telephone number.

At this point one may hear the enquiry: 'But isn't there room for development? Hasn't the situation changed?' And the answer to that is: 'Yes—there had to be development and there was'. That, no doubt, was why Pope John thought a commission necessary and why it took the Pope four years to formulate the teaching. We have to remember that, as Newman says, developments 'which do but contradict and reverse the course of doctrine which has been developed before them, and out of which they spring, are certainly corrupt'. No other development would have been a true one. But certainly the final condemnation of oral contraceptives *is* development—and so are some other points in the encyclical.

Development was necessary, partly because of the new physiological knowledge and the oral contraceptives and partly because of social changes, especially concerning women. The new knowledge, indeed, does give the best argument I know of that can be devised for allowing that contraceptives are after all permissible according to traditional Christian morals. The argument would run like this: There is not *much* ancient tradition condemning contraception as a distinct sin. The condemnations which you can find from earliest times were *almost* all of early abortion (called homicide) or of unnatural vice. But contraception, if it is an evil thing to do, is distinct from these, and so the question is really open. The authority of the teaching against it, so it is argued, is really only the authority of some recent papal encyclicals and of the pastoral practice of modern times.

Well, this argument has force only to prove the need for development, a need which was really there. It doesn't prove that it was open to the Pope to teach the permissibility of contraceptive intercourse. For how could he depart from the tradition forbidding unnatural vice on the one hand, and deliberate abortion, however early, on the other? On the other hand to say: 'It's an evil practice if you do these things; but you may, without evil, practise such forms of contraception as are neither of them'—wouldn't that have been ridiculous? For example, 'You shouldn't use withdrawal or a condom, or again an intrauterine device. For the former involve you in acts of unnatural vice, and the latter is abortifacient in its manner of working. But you may after all use a douche or a cap or a sterilising pill.' This would have been absurd teaching; nor have the innovators ever proposed it.

We have seen that the theological defence of the Church's teaching in modern times did not assimilate contraception to abortion but characterised it as a sort of perversion of the order of nature. The arguments about this were rather uneasy, because it is not in general wrong to interfere with natural processes. So long, however, as contraception took the form of monkeying around with the organs of intercourse or the act itself, there was some plausibility about the position because it really amounted to assimilating contraceptive intercourse to acts of unnatural vice (as some of them were), and so it was thought of.

But this plausibility diminished with the invention of more and more sophisticated female contraceptives; it vanished away entirely with the invention of the contraceptive pill. For it was obvious that if a woman just happened to be in the physical state which such a contraceptive brings her into by art no theologian would have thought the fact, or the knowledge of it, or the use of the knowledge of it, straightaway made intercourse bad. Or, again, if a woman took an anovulant pill for a while to check dysmenorrhoea no one would have thought this prohibited intercourse. So, clearly, it was the contraceptive intention that was bad, if contraceptive *intercourse* was: it is not that the sexual act in these circumstances is physically distorted. This had to be thought out, and it was thought out in the encyclical *Humanae Vitae*.

Here, however, people still feel intensely confused. Because the intention where oral contraceptives are taken seems to be just the same as when intercourse is deliberately restricted to infertile periods. In one way this is true, and its truth is actually pointed out by *Humanae Vitae*, in a passage I will quote in a moment. But in another way it's not true.

The reason why people are confused about intention, and why they sometimes think there is no difference between contraceptive intercourse and the use of infertile times to avoid conception, is this: they don't notice the difference between 'intention' when it means the intentionalness of the thing you're doing—that you're doing *this* on purpose—and when it means a *further* or *accompanying* intention *with* which you are doing the thing. For example, I make a table: that's an intentional action because I am doing just *that* on purpose. I have the *further* intention of, say, earning my living, doing my job *by* making the table. Contraceptive intercourse and intercourse using infertile times may be alike in respect of further intention, and these further intentions may be good, justified, excellent. This the Pope has noted. He sketched such a situation and said: 'It cannot be denied that in both cases the married couple, for acceptable reasons,' (for that's how he imagined the case) 'are perfectly clear in their intention to avoid children and mean to secure that none will be born.'* This is a comment on the two things: contraceptive intercourse on the one hand and intercourse using infertile times on the other, for the sake of the limitation of the family.

* *Humanae Vitae* §16.

But contraceptive intercourse is faulted, not on account of this further intention, but because of the kind of intentional action you are doing. The action is not left by you as the kind of act by which life is transmitted, but is purposely rendered infertile, and so changed to another sort of act altogether.

In considering an action, we need always to judge several things about ourselves. First: is the *sort* of act we contemplate doing something that it's all right to do? Second: are our further or surrounding intentions all right? Third: is the spirit in which we do it all right? Contraceptive intercourse fails on the first count; and to intend such an act is not to intend a marriage act at all, whether or not we're married. An act of ordinary intercourse in marriage at an infertile time, though, is a perfectly ordinary act of marital intercourse, and it will be bad, if it is bad, only on the second or third counts.

It may help you to see that the intentional act itself counts, as well as the further or accompanying intentions, if you think of an obvious example like forging a cheque to steal from somebody in order to get funds for a good purpose. The intentional action, presenting a cheque we've forged, is on the face of it a dishonest action, not to be vindicated by the good further intention.

If contraceptive intercourse is permissible, then what objection could there be after all to mutual masturbation, or copulation *in vase indebito*, sodomy, buggery,[2] when normal copulation is impossible or inadvisable (or in any case, according to taste)? It can't be the mere pattern of bodily behaviour in which the stimulation is procured that makes all the difference! But if such things are all right, it becomes perfectly impossible to see anything wrong with homosexual intercourse, for example. I am not saying: if you think contraception is all right you will do these other things; not at all. The habit of respectability persists and old prejudices die hard. But I am saying: you will have no solid reason against these things. You will have no answer to someone who proclaims, as many do, that they are good too. You cannot point to the known fact that Christianity drew people out of the pagan world, always saying no to these things. Because, if you are defending contraception, you will have rejected Christian tradition.

People quite alienated from this tradition are likely to see that my argument holds: that if contraceptive intercourse is all right then so are all forms of sexual activity. To them that is no argument against

[2] I should perhaps remark that I am using a *legal* term here—not indulging in bad language.

contraception; to their minds anything is permitted, so long as that's what people want to do. Well, Catholics, I think, are likely to know, or feel, that these other things are bad. Only, in the confusion of our time, they may fail to see that contraceptive intercourse, though much less of a deviation, and though it may not at all involve *physical* deviant acts, yet does fall under the same condemnation. For in contraceptive intercourse you intend to perform a sexual act which, if it has a chance of being fertile, you render infertile. *Qua* your intentional action, then, what you do *is* something intrinsically unapt for generation, and that is why it does fall under that condemnation. There's all the world of difference between this and the use of the 'rhythm' method. For you use the rhythm method not just by having intercourse now, but by not having it next week, say; and not having it next week isn't something that does something to today's intercourse to turn it into an infertile act; today's intercourse *is* an ordinary act of intercourse, an ordinary marriage act. It's only if, in getting married, you proposed (like the Manicheans) to confine intercourse to infertile periods, that you'd be falsifying marriage and entering a mere concubinage. Or if for mere love of ease and hatred of burdens you determined by this means never to have another child, you would then be dishonouring your marriage.

We may be helped to see the distinction by thinking about the difference between sabotage and working-to-rule. Suppose a case where either course will have some typical aim of 'industrial action' in view. Whether the aim is justified: that is the first question. But, given that it is justified, it's not all one how it is pursued.

If a man is working to rule, that does no doubt make *a* difference to the customary actions he performs in carrying out the work he does. It makes them also into actions in pursuit of such-and-such a policy. This is a matter of 'further intention with which' he does what he does; admittedly it reflects back on his action in the way I have stated. That is to say: we judge that any end or policy gives a new characterisation of the means or of the detailed things done in executing it. All the same he is still, say, driving this vehicle to this place, which is part of his job.

If, however, he tries to sabotage his actions—he louses up a machine he is purporting to work, for example—that means that *qua* intentional action here and now his performance in 'operating' the machine is *not* a doing of this part of his job. This holds quite without our having to point to the further intention (of industial warfare) as reflecting back on his action. (And, *N.B.* it holds whether or not such sabotage is justified.)

Thus the distinction we make to show that the 'rhythm method' may be justified though contraceptive intercourse is not, is a distinction needed in other contexts too.

The anger of the propagandists for contraception is indeed a proof that the limitation of conception by the 'rhythm' method is hateful to their spirit. It's derided for not working. But it does work for many. And there were exclamations against the Pope for pressing medical experts to find out more, so that there could be certainty here. The anger I think speaks to an obscure recognition of the difference between ordinary intercourse with abstention at fertile times when you are justified in seeking not to conceive at present, and the practice of contraceptive intercourse.

Biologically speaking, sexual intercourse is *the* reproductive act just as the organs are named generative organs from their role. Humanly speaking, the good and the point of a sexual act is marriage. Sexual acts that are not true marriage acts either are mere lasciviousness, or an Ersatz, an attempt to achieve that special unitedness which only a real commitment, marriage, can promise. For we don't invent marriage, as we may invent the terms of an association or club, any more than we invent human language. It is part of the creation of humanity and if we're lucky we find it available to us and can enter into it. If we are very unlucky we may live in a society that has wrecked or deformed this human thing.

This—that the good and the point of a sexual act is marriage—is why only what is capable of being a marriage act is natural sex. It's this that makes the division between straightforward fornication or adultery and the wickedness of the sins against nature and of contraceptive intercourse. Hence contraceptive intercourse within marriage is a graver offence *against chastity* than is straightforward fornication or adultery. For it is not even a proper act of intercourse, and *therefore* is not a true marriage act. To marry is not to enter into a pact of mutual complicity in no matter what sexual activity upon one another's bodies. (Why on earth should a ceremony like that of a wedding be needed or relevant if that's what's in question?) Marriage is a mutual commitment in which each side ceases to be autonomous, in various ways and also sexually: the sexual liberty in agreement together is great; here, so long as they are not immoderate so as to become the slaves of sensuality, nothing is shameful, if the complete act—the ones involving ejaculation of the man's seed—that they engage in, are true and real marriage acts.

IV

That is how a Christian will understand his duty in relation to this small, but very important, part of married life. It's so important in marriage, and quite generally, simply because there just is no such thing as a casual, non-significant sexual act. This in turn arises from the fact that sex concerns the transmission of human life. (Hence the picture that some have formed and even welcomed, of intercourse now, in this contraceptive day, losing its deep significance: becoming no more than a sort of extreme kiss, which it might be rather rude to refuse. But they forget, I think, the rewardless trouble of spirit associated with the sort of sexual activity which from its type is guaranteed sterile: the solitary or again the homosexual sort.)

There is no such thing as a casual, non-significant sexual act; everyone knows this. Contrast sex with eating—you're strolling along a lane, you see a mushroom on a bank as you pass by, you know about mushrooms, you pick it and you eat it quite casually—sex is never like that. That's why virtue in connection with eating is basically a matter only of the *pattern* of one's eating habits. But virtue in sex—chastity—is not *only* a matter of such a pattern, that is of its role in a pair of lives. A single sexual action can be bad even without regard to its context, its further intention and its motives.

Those who try to make room for sex as mere casual enjoyment pay the penalty: they become shallow. At any rate the talk that reflects and commends this attitude is always shallow. They dishonour their own bodies; holding cheap what is naturally connected with the origination of human life. There is an opposite extreme, which perhaps we shall see in our day: making sex a religious mystery. This Christians do not do. Despite some rather solemn nonsense that's talked this is obvious. We wouldn't, for example, make the sexual organs objects of a cultic veneration; or perform sexual acts as part of religious rituals; or prepare ourselves for sexual intercourse as for a sacrament.

As often holds, there is here a Christian mean between two possible extremes. It is: never to change sexual actions so they are deprived of that character which makes sex so profoundly significant, so deep-going in human life. Hence we would not think of contraceptive intercourse as an exercise of *responsibility* in regard to sex! Responsibility involves keeping our sexual acts as that kind of act, and recognising that they are that kind of act by engaging in them with good-hearted wisdom about the getting of children. This is the standard of chastity for a married Christian. But it should not be thought that it is against wisdom for poor people willingly to have many children. That is 'the wisdom of the flesh, and it is death'[3] (there's a lot of this death around at present).

Sexual acts are not sacred actions. But the perception of the dishonour done to the body in treating them as the casual satisfaction of desire is certainly a mystical perception. I don't mean, in calling it a mystical perception, that it's out of the ordinary. It's as ordinary as the feeling for the respect due to a man's dead body: the knowledge that a dead body isn't something to be put out for the collectors of refuse to pick up. This, too, is mystical; though it's as common as humanity.

I'm making this point because I want to draw a contrast between two different types of virtue. Some virtues, like honesty about property, and sobriety, are fundamentally utilitarian in character. The very point of them is just the obvious material well-ordering of human life that is promoted if people have these virtues. Some, though indeed profitable, are supra-utilitarian and hence mystical. You can argue truly enough, for example, that general respect for the prohibitions on murder makes life more commodious. If people really respect the prohibition against murder life is pleasanter for all of us—but this argument is exceedingly comic. Because utility presupposes the *life* of those who are to be convenienced, and everybody perceives quite clearly that the wrong done in murder is done first and foremost to the victim, whose life is not inconvenienced, it just isn't there any more. He isn't there to complain: so the utilitarian argument has to be on behalf of the rest of us. Therefore, though true, it is highly comic and is not the foundation: the objection to murder is supra-utilitarian.

And so the value of chastity. Not that this virtue isn't useful: it's highly useful. If Christian standards of chastity were widely observed the world would be enormously much happier. Our world, for example, is littered with deserted wives—partly through that fantastic con that went on for such a long time about how it was part of liberation for women to have dead easy divorce: amazing—these wives often struggling to bring up young children or abandoned to loneliness in middle age. And how many miseries and

---

[3] *Romans* 8.6.

hang-ups are associated with loss of innocence in youth! What miserable messes people keep on making, to their own and others' grief, by dishonourable sexual relationships! The Devil has scored a great propaganda victory: everywhere it's suggested that the troubles connected with sex are all to do with frustration, with abstinence, with society's cruel and conventional disapproval. As if, if we could only do away with these things, it would be a happy and life-enhancing romp for everyone; and as if all who were chaste were unhappy, not only unhappy but hard-hearted and censorious and nasty. It fitted the temper of the times (this is a rather comic episode) that when psychiatrists were asked to diagnose the unidentified Boston Strangler, they suggested he was a *sex-starved* individual. Ludicrous error! The idea lacks any foundation, that the people who are bent upon and who get a lot of sexual enjoyment are more gentle, merciful and kind than those who live in voluntary continence.

The trouble about the Christian standard of chastity is that it isn't and never has been generally lived by; *not* that it would be profitless if it were. Quite the contrary: it would be colossally productive of earthly happiness.

All the same it is a virtue, not like temperance in eating and drinking, not like honesty about property, for these have a purely utilitarian justification. But it, like the respect for life, is a supra-utilitarian value, connected with the substance of life, and this is what comes out in the perception that the life of lust is one in which we dishonour our bodies. Implicitly, lasciviousness is over and over again treated as hateful, even by those who would dislike such an explicit judgement on it. Just listen, witness the scurrility when it's hinted at; disgust when it's portrayed as the stuff of life; shame when it is exposed, the leer of complicity when it's approved. You don't get these attitudes with everybody all of the time; but you do get them with everybody. (It's too much hard work to keep up the façade of the Playboy philosophy, according to which all this is just an unfortunate mistake, to be replaced by healthy-minded wholehearted praise of sexual fun.)

And here we're in the region of that constant Christian teaching, which we've noticed, that intercourse 'merely for the sake of pleasure' is wrong.

This can mislead and perturb. For when is intercourse purely for the sake of pleasure? Some have thought this must mean when it's not for the sake of getting a child. And so, I believe, I have been told, some Catholic women have actually feared the pleasure of orgasm and thought it wrong, or thought it wrong to look for it or allow oneself to respond to feelings of physical desire. But this is unreasonable and ungrateful to God. Copulation, like eating, is of itself a good kind of action: it preserves human existence. An individual act of eating or copulation, then, can be bad only because something about it or the circumstances of it make it bad. And all the pleasure specific to it will be just as good as *it* is.

A severe morality holds that intercourse (and may hold this of eating, too) has something wrong about it if it is ever done except explicitly as being *required* for that preservation of human life which is what makes intercourse a good kind of action. But this involves a thoroughly faulty moral psychology. God gave us our physical appetite, and its arousal without our calculation is part of the working of our sort of life. Given moderation and right circumstances, acts prompted by inclination can be taken in a general way to accomplish what makes them good in kind and there's no need for them to be individually necessary or useful for the end that makes them good kinds of action. Intercourse is a normal part of married life through the whole life of the partners in a marriage and is normally engaged in without any distinct purpose other than to have it, just *as* such a part of married life.

Such acts will usually take place only when desire prompts, and desire is for intercourse as pleasurable; the pleasure, as Aristotle says, perfects the act. But that does not mean that it is done 'purely for pleasure'. For what that expression means is that sensuality is in command: but that one has intercourse when desire prompts and the desire is for pleasure, does not prove, does not mean, that sensuality is in command. One may rightly and reasonably be willing to respond to the promptings of desire. When that is so, the act is governed by a reasonable mind, even though no considering or reasoning is going on. The fact that one is thus having intercourse when, as one knows, there's nothing against it, makes it a good and a chaste marriage act and a rendering of the marriage debt.

There is indeed such a thing in marriage as intercourse 'purely for pleasure': this is what the Christian tradition did condemn. Marks of it could be: immoderate pursuit of or preoccupation with sexual pleasure; succumbing to desire against wisdom; insisting against *serious* reluctance of one's partner. In all these cases but the last both parties may of course be consenting. For human beings often tend to be disorderly and extreme in their sensuality. A simple test of whether one is so is this: could one do without for a few weeks or months in case of need? For anyone *may* be faced with a situation in which he ought to do without; and he should watch that he does not get into a state in which it is impossible for him.

But we ought to remember also, what isn't always remembered, that insensibility and unjustified abstention is *also* a sin against moderation, and is a defrauding of one's partner.

Well now, people raise the cry of 'legalism' (one of the regular accusations of the present day) against this idea which I have taken from the old theologians of 'rendering what is owing', the giving the other person this part of married life, which is owing. It embodies the one notion, I would say, that is honest, truthful and quite general. People would rather speak of the expression of mutual love. But what do they mean by 'love'? Do they mean 'being in love'? Do they mean a natural conjugal affection?

Either of these may be lacking or onesided. If a kind of love cannot be commanded, we can't build our moral theology of marriage on the presumption that it will be present. Its absence is sad, but this sadness exists; it is very common. We should avoid, I think, using the indicative mood for what is really a commandment like the Scout Law ('A Boy Scout is kind to animals'—it means a Boy Scout ought to be kind to animals). For if we hear: 'a Christian couple grow in grace and love together' doesn't the question arise 'supposing they don't?' It clears the air to substitute the bite of what is *clearly* a precept for the sweetness of a rosy picture. The command to a Christian couple is: 'Grow in grace and love together.' But a joint command can only be jointly obeyed. Suppose it isn't? Well, there remains the separate precept to each and in an irremediably unhappy marriage one ought still to love the other, though not perhaps feeling the affection that cannot be commanded. Thus the notion of the 'marriage debt' is a very necessary one, and it alone is realistic: because it makes no assumption as to the state of the affections.

Looking at the rightness of the marriage act like this will help in another way. It will prevent us from assuming that the pleasant affection which exists between a happy and congenial pair *is* the fulfilment of the precept of love. (It may after all only be a complacent hiving off together in a narrow love.) We ought absolutely not to give out a teaching which is flattering to the lucky, and irrelevant to the unhappy. Looked at carefully, too, such a teaching is altogether too rigorist in a new direction. People who are not quite happily married, not lucky in their married life, but nevertheless have a loyalty to the bond, are not, therefore bound to abstain from intercourse.

The meaning of this teaching 'not purely for pleasure' should, I think, have a great appeal for the Catholic thinking of today that is greatly concerned for the laity. We want to stress nowadays that the one *vocation* that is spoken of in the New Testament is the calling of a Christian. All are called with the same calling. The life of monks and nuns and of celibate priesthood is a higher kind of life than that of the married, not because there are two grades of Christian, but because their form of life is one in which one has a greater chance of living according to truth and the laws of goodness; by their profession, those who take the vows of religion have set out to please God alone. But we lay people are not less called to the Christian life, in which the critical question is: 'Where does the compass-needle of your mind and will point?' This is tested above all by our reactions when it costs or threatens to cost something to be a Christian. One should be glad if it does, rather than complain! If we will not let it cost anything; if we succumb to the threat of 'losing our life', then our religion is indistinguishable from pure worldliness.

This is very far-reaching. But in the matter at hand, it means that we have got not to be the servants of our sensuality but to bring it into subjection. Thus, those who marry have, as we have the right to do, chosen a life in which, as St. Paul drily says:the husband aims to please his wife rather than the Lord, and the wife her husband, rather than the Lord* — but although we have chosen a life to please ourselves and one another, still we know we are called with that special calling, and are bound not to be conformed to the world, friendship to which is enmity with God.

And so also we ought to help one another and have cooperative pools of help: help people who are stuck in family difficulties; and have practical resources in our parishes for one another's needs when we get into difficult patches.

The teaching which I have rehearsed is indeed against the grain of the world, against the current of our time. But that, after all, is what the Church as teacher is for. The truths that are acceptable to a time — as, that we owe it as a debt of justice to provide out of our superfluity for the destitute and the starving — these will be proclaimed not only by the Church: the Church teaches *also* those truths that are hateful to the spirit of an age.

* See *I Corinthians* 7. 32–34.

17*

On Humanae Vitae

I first read *Humanae Vitae,* of course, when it first came out. At that time everyone, including myself, homed in almost exclusively on the declaration about contraception. Not just the fact of the condemnation interested me. I had indeed feared there was going to be a silent slide, traditional teaching getting abandoned by default; but if there was going to be a pronouncement at all, I was confident that it would condemn contraceptive intercourse. But the precise formulation of the condemnation interested me intensely. The invention of the contraceptive pill had in a way put moral theologians in a difficulty and it often led to the collapse of their former views. There had long been a characterisation of the use of contraceptives as involving a sort of perversion in sexual acts. Now the physical act of sexual intercourse was not itself 'distorted', as they put it, if you used a pill. And suppose that sort of pill were prescribed for something else *bona fide* (for endometriosis, say: I have known it be prescribed for that), it wouldn't have been thought wrong to use the period of infertility that it gave. So where *was* the wrong? It became clear that it lay in the aspect of *intention*. But here again people felt an immediate difficulty because they had not thought enough about intention. The intention, they said at once, was to have intercourse without getting a child. But *that* intention had long been declared possibly acceptable. It was so declared in Pius XI's teaching of the allowability 'for grave reasons' of confining intercourse to infertile times, quite methodically, with a view to avoiding conception.**

* Text of a paper delivered in February 1978 to an International Conference at the University of Melbourne on *Humanae Vitae* and the Ovulation Method of Natural Family Planning. Published in J N Santamaria and John J Billings (eds) *Human Love and Human Life* (Melbourne: The Polding Press, 1979), pp.121–27.

** Pope Pius XI's Encyclical *Casti Connubii* at §59 speaks of the acceptability of marital intercourse when 'on account of natural reasons either of time or of certain defects new life cannot be brought forth'; but it contains no teaching about *methodically* confining intercourse to infertile periods in the woman's cycle. The

As a professional philosopher, and quite independently of this subject, I had for a long time been very much interested in intention—so interested, indeed, that I wrote a book simply about it in 1956.* This interest had helped me to concentrate on the aspect of intention in thinking about contraception and the 'rhythm' method of birth control.

The first thing to get clear about is that there is a mistake in speaking of '*the* intention' in an act. Whenever you do anything, there are, as you might put it, lots of things you do. Take an example: you endorse a cheque which someone produces for you to do that. What are you doing? You are depositing ink on a bit of paper, you are writing your name, you are signing a cheque on its back, you are perhaps thereby paying a bill for someone; you are, we'll suppose, thereby doing a kindness to the person whose debt it is. All these might be comprised in your one act. And *all* of them would be intentional, though there may be others that you are doing in the very same act, which are unintentional—like marking the table under the cheque as you press down with your pen.

And there is also your *objective*. You do the kindness, perhaps, in order to improve family relations. *That* lies in the future: it is a further intention, perhaps *the* main one, the end or goal, of doing all those other things. But there may be side intentions too, like impressing someone with your gold pen by using it to endorse the cheque.

So we can ask this question about what you do: 'What is the character, or rather, what are the characters, of the act, as intentional, at the time when it is done?' What are you doing, and doing on purpose? And there is also the question: 'What are the further intentions with which your act is done? What is its goal?' These are different questions. The first *always* has several answers. The second may have only one.

Suppose a couple's situation to be one in which it is right and honest to have intercourse but avoid conception. This goal, that there be intercourse but no conception is *an* intention (a further intention) *with* which the act is performed, and in the case in hand it is common to two different couples whom we'll imagine: one couple use contraceptives, the other infertile times. The goal we have mentioned makes no difference between them, and we are assuming their situation to be one in which it deserves no reproach. But the act of the con-

relevant teaching which Anscombe surely had in mind is to be found in the *Allocution to Italian midwives* (29 October, 1951) of Pope Pius XII.

* G E M Anscombe, *Intention* (Oxford: Basil Blackwell, 1957).

traceptive pair has *a* different character from the act of the other pair. For one of the descriptions true of their act is: that it is an act of sexual intercourse deliberately rendered infertile (if it should by chance be fertile otherwise). And this is the immediate significant difference between them and the other pair. For the other pair are performing an act of the generative kind – what the Pope calls an act with procreative significance – nothing having been done in order to change it from that. Now the difference in *these* characters of the intentional acts, between their intentions at *this* level, is a difference between wrong and right. Why it is so remains to be seen.

This point, about the identity of goal, but difference in character of the act of intercourse, was made very clear in paragraph 16 of *Humanae Vitae*. The translation we have is bad. It should run: 'It is true in the two cases the couples are alike in meaning to avoid children for acceptable reasons'. But it goes on, 'in the former case they make legitimate use of a natural disposition'.

When considering an action you need to know whether your goal in doing it is all right, but also whether the act itself is all right, and the former might be all right while the latter was not.

This point about intention, which is put so clearly, was the first thing I observed at that time of first reading. The second was the Pope's exhortation to get more knowledge. This I found truly instructive. (The other only confirmed what was already clear to me.)

In earlier days, when Catholics were generally rather firm and clear in their rejection of contraception, they were *not* really clear about the *status* of the permissibility of using the 'safe period', the 'rhythm method', which was the only way they knew. Was it perhaps divinely ordained that it be uncertain and risky? Was it morally destructive to be secure? Should one's begettings and conceivings be hardly *more* within one's control than intercourse itself? Should they perhaps not be fully voluntary but arise from nature?

When the Pope said: 'Go to it, get all the knowledge you can, obtain certainty about the times of fertility', this was very enlightening. We were not to assume that knowledge was impossible, that ignorance was part of God's plan, we were not to treat involuntariness as a divinely ordained necessity in these matters. Sanctified ignorance was not to be our badge. This was good and instructive news. It is splendid that the knowledge has been obtained.

I have only recently reread the encyclical. Originally those were the two things I saw in it. An encyclical is always full of proper sentiments, generally edifying material together with repetition of familiar points of doctrine. All this I thought of as the 'blurb' surrounding the hard definite stuff, and I fear I didn't pay much attention to it. Rereading it, I find I misjudged it: there is very much material for reflection in it.

First, there is the opening, with its observations on the changes in the world and the new questions that have arisen.

There is surely an implicit acknowledgement that rapid development of population is capable of proving a problem which it can be right to consider in considering how many children to try and have. Note, however, that the Pope was too cautious to commit himself to any views on the existence of over-population anywhere. (Our world has gone mad on this.)

Second, there is note taken of the change 'in the manner of considering the person of a woman and her place in society, and in the value to be attributed to conjugal love in marriage, and also in the judgement of the meaning of conjugal acts in relation to that love'.[1]

That paragraph could receive a *lot* of expansion and reflection. Note that it contains no nostalgia for the past, no lamenting in favour of times when women were thought of as *obviously* not equal *citizens*, not suitable witnesses in a law court, for example (as St. Thomas remarks somewhere)—let alone judges etc. We are familiar with a kind of nostalgia about former times 'when women *were* women'. But no such note is struck here.

The idea of a new valuation of conjugal love is strange to me. But maybe the old great valuations of it in Homer, in Proverbs, in Confucius, which I should think are paralleled in most cultures, are nevertheless exceptional, and standard attitudes have usually been more ignoble.

The changes in the appreciation of the meaning of conjugal acts in relation to the love of married couples might, I suppose, be described like this: formerly such things, so long as they were acts of proper sexual intercourse, not acts done in vile disreputable ways, were just left to take care of themselves. They were part of life; nothing much to do or think about them except to do or abstain. A wife was supposed to be treated with respect, not used like a prostitute. But a man would use his wife, perhaps, without its occurring to him to consider how she felt about it. I don't know how universally this was so; but it may have been very widespread.

---

[1] *Humanae Vitae*, §2.

I have heard from young men that it is intolerable travelling with a female companion (not your wife) in Arab countries, because it is apt to be regarded as the most obvious form of politeness, of quite superficial friendliness, to hand her over for sexual use. Unwillingness, and the idea that she might have something to say in the matter, is simply not understood. Well, the whole situation I am describing would very likely be, and would certainly be assumed to be, one of fornication, so it is not so easy to make observations out of Christian morality which speak directly to this point. Nevertheless we can make a sort of transposition of the theme to marriage. The idea that the woman is for use (licit or illicit doesn't make a difference to the point we are addressing) and that what she may be thinking about it is nothing of which to take much account (her task is to be available and amenable) – *that*, I suppose, is the attitude that is disappearing; and with that, the assumption that a wife could never have the right to say 'no' for sufficient reason. In suggesting this right, I am not denying the teaching of St. Paul. But remember that his doctrine on *this* point was absolutely symmetrical and egalitarian between the two partners. I take it no one interprets it so that it would be out of the question for a husband to say 'No' on a particular occasion too, even though he 'has not the power over his own body, but his wife has'.[2] Can he be too busy? Think it unwise and be firm? Then so can she.

Pope Paul himself has done much in this encyclical to contribute to the 'appreciation of the relation of conjugal acts to married love'. The principal way has been by his speaking of the 'significance' of such acts. He has taught that conjugal acts have a 'procreative significance' and a 'unitive significance' which cannot be separated from one another.

This takes a good deal of thinking about. First it is clear that 'procreative significance' does not entail that the act be actually procreative. It has the significance of being that type of act, whether it procreates or not: these acts are what we *call* the 'generative acts'. It is the same sort of point to say that the acorn is the seed of the oak tree – though most acorns don't grow into oaks. To take steps to render the act infertile in case it should be fertile is to denature it in your intention.

But not only does a normal sexual act have procreative significance without necessarily procreating – in fact, few of them are actu-

[2] 1*Corinthians* 7.4.

ally procreative – but, *if* the Pope is right about the 'inseparability' of the procreative and unitive significance, an act could actually *be* procreative and yet *lack* 'procreative significance'. If it were performed by a man's squirting his semen into a tube, which conducted the sperm so that conception resulted, that would not have been an act of procreation on his part. He might well say 'I didn't beget, I only – –'. Begetting is a personal act involving actual union of man and woman. It is not the provision of sperm which then is conveyed to an ovum, even if there should then be conception as a result. If that is so, then equally there can be acts of physical union which lack unitive significance. This deserves much reflection. What it has to do with is not how united people feel themselves to be in the moment, but with the actual profound union of the married state. These are the acts that have a significance deriving from the significance of married life.

Make no mistake: it is the whole Catholic Christian idea of chastity that is under fire in the modern world. It is also under fire from those Catholics who reject *Humanae Vitae*. I used to think you could argue, sufficiently to convince a Catholic, that no sort of sexual acts could be excluded if once you admitted contraceptive intercourse. But the enemies of *Humanae Vitae* seem now to embrace that conclusion. Not indeed without any restriction, but at least as far as concerns sexual activity between two people; I suppose adult people. For though I know Catholics who solemnly defend and commend homosexual activity, I don't know any who make propaganda for bestiality, group-sex or paedophilia. No doubt, however, all that will come as the world at large becomes accepting of these things.

Therefore we need to think very hard about this 'unitive significance' of which *Humanae Vitae* treated. That the unitiveness has to do with marriage, gets its character from marriage, is clear. But more needs to be said about it in order to present the strong and shining virtue of chastity as understood by the Catholic Church. I can't say more about this here. It is a programme for thought.

Briefly, I will end by pointing to its connexion with human dignity. That conception we used to have called to our attention every day at Mass:

> Deus, qui humanae substantiae dignitatem mirabiliter condidisti et mirabilius reformasti ...

and I wish the prayer had not got relegated to Christmas Day only. For the idea of human dignity *is* a popular one, pro tem., nowadays. A young African friend of mine (not a Catholic) when *Humanae Vitae* came out, said 'The Pope has struck a great blow for human dignity!' and I was glad to learn from him.

Well, but there are two pictures of it. That of the Church, and of the world. In the world's picture, however, human beings can more and more be killed so that others can have the life they think they want: human dignity is not a fact to make you behave with reverence before any human life, but rather a standard which it is demanded life should reach. And the dignity and honour of human sexuality rightly conducted equally does not enter into the world's picture of human dignity: *this* is not, for the world, the place to set up a standard. Then the world and the Church are precisely opposite in their tendency. The Church makes no requirement of a standard before it reverences human life, and sets up a standard to which we must conform in our sexuality if we are to use it to reflect and not blaspheme the dignity of human nature. But the world will set up standards, partly standards of satisfaction (where?), not meeting which human life doesn't deserve to be respected; while it reveres sexuality unmeasured by standards, as we do life.

18*

Address to the Clergy: On Contraception and Natural Family Planning

There was a question addressed to Mr Madden when he was on the panel the other day: 'What's the difference between Natural family Planning and Family Planning, inasmuch as both are Family Planning?' Mr Madden replied by analogy of Natural Weight Loss, which he contrasted with Artificial Weight Loss. A good answer as far as it went, especially in what it implied. For the thought in the questioner's mind seems to be: 'Given that it's Family Planning, why should you mind what sort of Family Planning it is? Why should it be a question of anything but convenience?' That is, he is assuming that 'Family Planning' is an action description rather like 'Abortion'. So he is saying: I'll understand you if you are going to object to just *any* activity of this sort, but if that is not your stance, I don't understand. It's like saying that abortion is a course of action you'll entertain, but never on Tuesdays and Thursdays, or never with instruments as opposed to drugs, or *vice versa*.

Let us first clear away one source of confusion. Someone may have the thought: 'If it's all right to procure a certain significant effect *at all*, it can't matter *how* you do it'. Now, *this* idea doesn't stand up for a moment. It might be all right to execute a criminal who has been caught, had a fair trial, and been found guilty. It would not follow that it was all right to starve or torture him to death, or to leave a suggestive noose hanging on a nail in his cell. Or it may be all right to try and arrange that some bore and nuisance won't come to a meeting that he has a right to attend: this objective itself may be fine. That's

* Evidently a supplementary contribution to the Melbourne conference at which the previous paper was delivered. Unpublished typescript.

not to say you can do it by lying to him or by locking him up, effective as these means would be. But it could be quite acceptable to fix the time of the meeting cunningly, so that he can't conveniently get to it. So that is the first point: means obviously can matter.

But the objector has a point to his question which I think was not met. He was told what the difference was—but he wants to know why it matters. He might say: 'I see the difference, but I don't see what difference *that* difference makes to the morality of your Family Planning activity.' And if that is his point, he is in a position which is very common indeed. I've noticed that all speakers at this conference who've referred to the matter at all, have obviously found the difference clear; natural and artificial methods are to them as different as chalk from cheese, and it has been obvious to them that contraceptive acts are illicit, even when the purpose of adopting contraceptive methods is good and justified. This was also the message of *Humanae Vitae*: you must not do evil that good may come. But what *was* the evil in question? I believe that people who live rightly perceive the difference: they have what the scholastics call 'connatural knowledge'—the instinct of a thoroughly honest person for what is honest is an example. Such a person may not be able to give much explanation *why* such-and-such an act is dishonest, may not be armed with a theoretical account; he merely has a good sense of what is honest and what is not. But reason demands that there be an account; and those who don't live rightly, and so have not got this 'knowledge of connaturality', badly need an explanation.

I myself formerly attempted a back-handed sort of explanation. What was involved, I said, was in principle and intention that special form of unchastity known as 'unnatural vice'.

Before elaborating this answer, I will say a word about this characterisation 'unnatural vice' for homosexual intercourse, mutual masturbation, bestiality and so on. It is a *label* for a recognisable range of sins. But it's not that other sins are 'according to nature' in the sense that as far as *nature* goes, they're all right. *All* sins are contrary to the Law of Nature. But that particular label attaches to some forms of sin because the order of nature that is violated in them is a pattern of use of bodily parts and functions not specific to man but generally animal. The 'unnaturalness' is positively biological, not a violation of some specifically human order as are lying, stealing, or adultery. Adultery is *also* a sin against nature, but against nature as specifically human, not as generically animal, so it doesn't get called that.

This is not a total explanation because the sins so labelled all have to do with generation or the use of the human generative apparatus. A doctor who was a friend of mine once said to me 'Isn't deliberately making meals of totally un-nutritive food a form of unnatural vice?' I could see his point, but such acts are not called that, nor even necessarily condemned. This is a point of great interest, but I can't take it further at present.

To return to my theme: I argued that *if* it is all right to change the character of your intended sexual act from being an act of the generative type to something else, by rendering it infertile (if it would otherwise be fertile), precisely for the sake of the intercourse, *then* it is very difficult to see anything wrong with those other acts, acts of mutual masturbation, say, or of homosexual intercourse. They would only be somewhat more deviant. I thought that Catholics at least—to whom the argument was addressed—would be pretty clear that *those* acts were acts of gross unchastity, and so that they could infer that *these* acts of contraceptive intercourse were, in intention, marked by the same sort of unchastity.

Many have accepted this; it is a more or less familiar argument. But to my astonishment I have also met the following reaction: 'Yes, the argument is sound enough; it shows that the whole picture of 'unnatural sin' hangs together. But why should we accept any of it?' Someone who says this is likely to maintain that homosexual activities, and indeed any mutually acceptable form of sexual satisfaction between two people (I'm not sure why it should be just two actually) are all right so long as they are 'expressions of love' between the parties. This is what Dr Billings would call regarding men as 'superbeasts'; but his description would itself be rejected.

What we have here of course is a thorough rejection of the whole Catholic Christian doctrine of chastity. A sympathetic pagan friend of mine questioned me about what sort of embraces between the unmarried, say, (not involving intercourse) a Catholic regarded as permissible. I said that embracing on purpose in a manner to produce genital excitement, and dwelling on that, staying with it deliberately if it occurred, were excluded: that, indeed, one should only engage in such embraces with complete acts of licit sexual intercourse in view. To my surprise, she showed surprise, remarking that a vast amount of the embracing that goes on would be condemned by that rule, and that embracing so as to produce orgasm and ejaculation, without proper intercourse, was a very usual thing. Now I think we know for sure that this *is* contrary to the virtue of chastity.

But, the critics say, what's wrong with it? Why isn't it good? If it's contrary to chastity, why should we have any regard for chastity?

Now I think that *Humanae Vitae* offered an answer to the general question about chastity, even though its considerations were restricted to the context of marriage and contraceptive intercourse within marriage. The considerations have in them the seeds of an answer along the whole front. In that answer will be delineated the badge of chastity which in ancient pagan times was one of the distinctions of a good Christian life: not a rare, all but impossible virtue, but something practicable by ordinary people.

The Pope said that the conjugal act has two meanings, the unitive and the procreative, and that there was an inseparable connexion between them. We must look at this teaching closely.

The 'inseparable connexion' is not said to be between being unitive and being procreative, but between having unitive meaning and having procreative meaning. Now if these 'meanings' are inseparable, it follows that if you have an act which manages to be procreative (i.e. to procreate) without being an act of union, it will *not* have 'the procreative significance of the conjugal act'. Such might be an act of ejaculation into a tube leading to the right spot for causing conception.

And equally it means that if you have an act which manages to be unitive, i.e. to join the partners up, while its character as a generative type of act is destroyed, that act has not 'the unitive meaning of the conjugal act'.

This teaching has been criticised on the ground that an act can be unitive though procreation is excluded. But the symmetry I have indicated shows that that is irrelevant. Obviously an act can equally be *procreative* though union is excluded. If it would nevertheless lack 'the procreative meaning' its being unitive though procreation was excluded would not show that it didn't still lack 'the unitive meaning'.

We would very well understand someone who said: '*I* didn't do any act of begetting, I didn't *beget,* I merely discharged my semen into that tube they offered me'—even though the sperm had got home and a conception resulted.

(We know that the Church says that children are to be begotten, not produced in any other way.)

So we can understand the 'lack of procreative meaning' in an act which does procreate without union; can we understand the lack of unitive meaning in an act of union which is intentionally rendered *incapable* of procreative meaning?

We say that it has unitive meaning *only* if it is a marriage act, that is: such an act as demands marriage as its appropriate setting. A complete sex-act—an ejaculation—accomplished in the course of mutual masturbation, for example, has nothing about it to suggest that its proper home is a marriage. Only acts of the generative type have that character of belonging properly in a marriage. And that is why such acts, done within a marriage, are no derogation of human dignity—whereas all others, including these ones *outside* a marriage, violate the dignity of human nature.

It is, I believe, universal to regard marriage as having a sort of honourableness and dignity about it. This is obviously connected with its role in reproducing and rearing children.

Dr Billings has already made out the connexion between his programme* and the value of chastity, the virtue of the conduct of one's sexuality *according to right reason*. For a multitude of reasons the pride and glory of that virtue have not been prominent in present day Western culture. People think of chastity as nothing but abstinence; even if they admire it, they think of it only in connexion with priests, nuns and monks. Christian celibacy is indeed a glorious thing—but it is specially appropriate to our day (because of its special temptations) to charge into battle with the banner of the chastity of married people. It is the greatest thing, to my mind, about this programme that it develops this virtue. We have witnessed it, heard perhaps unconscious but very clear testimony of it. The more teaching of the ovulation method there is the more chance people are going to get to learn this virtue and to shine out before the world. There is a legend of a young woman called Thecla, who was so ravished by St. Paul's preaching of chastity, which she overheard by the accident of the position of her house, that she forthwith took baptism and embraced virginity. This sort of enthusiasm is rare—now. We reverence real voluntary poverty when we see it far more than the other vows. But the flame should be kindled again, and the place, the opportunity, for kindling it is among the married. Among the contraceptive Catholic populations there is an awful spiritual deadness, which will last until they are weaned from their vices. The virtues of married chastity can be joyfully preached as never before.

I don't know if it is necessary to add a warning. For the populations which are really suffering from the pressure of large families in

* i.e. of natural family planning: the Billings ovulation method.

hunger, natural family planning must be a boon in the possibility of regulating births without doing violence to human nature. Among the contraceptive populations of the West, I believe that the message ought to be 'Get having babies! – you are going to ruin your country and often your personal future, by regarding, say, two as quite enough, when you have no great excuse. Remember that it had to be for *grave* reasons that you adopted a policy of extreme limitation not just for ease in your lives'. There is already a ghastly dearth of children in the West because of the present fashion.

I have been impressed by the claim that natural family planning does not go with a restriction for insufficient reason on having children. I can see that it operates in favour of acceptance of a child if it comes, and I can also see a particular reason why people say it 'doesn't work' – namely that with people abstaining because on the whole they'd rather not have a baby again just yet, this resolution is quite likely to break down. I think therefore that it is worth asking people what they mean by 'it's not working' – it may turn out that they mean just that. Now that is a rather good form of 'not working', and people show their chastity by their willing acceptance of a child when it comes.

But for pretty self-controlled people it would be possible to abstain from having children, for insufficient reason, by this method. Back in the nineteen-fifties, I think, there was a controversy in the correspondence columns of the London *Times*, about contraception. The Catholic parties to the debate declared the ancientness and constancy of the Church's teaching, citing St. Augustine to prove their point. At that juncture, someone wrote saying: 'But St. Augustine condemned the use of the safe period to avoid conception!' There was a dead silence from the Catholic side. This made me read St. Augustine. What I found was that he condemned the Manicheans' attempts in various ways never to have any children at all. Their methods included the use of what they took to be infertile times, as well as abortifacient drugs.

Doctrine has not changed; St. Augustine's view still prevails. A determination never to have any children nullifies a marriage. This will of course be the reason for the new marriage services, in which the couple profess their willingness to accept children. If one determined never to have children, one could not flatter oneself that one was obeying Divine Law and following the teaching of the Church, just because one was successfully seeking to avoid children by rhythm or the ovulation method, and never never using contraceptives. The whole spirit in which one had sexual relations would be contrary to that law and that teaching. However, relatively speaking, rather few people will have that attitude, and it matters where you are coming from and what you are moving towards. At present it would be a tremendous push in the direction of virtue and Christian living to wean contraceptive populations from their vices by leading them into the practice of natural family planning.

Here the clergy are important. The clergy I'd like to speak to are, I believe, not here: the other ones, who do the big cop-out, I mean the great evasion, who despise the teaching of the Church and tell anyone who asks them 'It's just a matter of private conscience'. This is cowardly, and careless of people's souls. Such clergy do not reflect how much damage they may be doing. There *are* things that are a 'matter of private conscience': for me it means one thing (for example) to treat such-and-such a person with conventional respect, for you it would mean another. But such matters are necessarily subject to reassessment according to circumstances, and a husband, say, who will not accept contraception when his wife is very keen on it might well be made to look an arrogant stubborn beast by his insistence on following his own 'private' conscience. I have known such cases.

How such clergy can be stirred up I don't know. Clearly the bishops are in the strongest position to urge them to stop saying that, to become more serious and shoulder their pastoral task.

19*

Contraception, Chastity and the Vocation of Marriage

Let me indulge in a day-dream. The time is 1968. The Encyclical** has just been issued. Everywhere where contraception has got a hold, the bishops speak out boldly and repeatedly. Their message runs something like this: 'Christian people! The Holy Father requested that this issue not be discussed in this past four years. In that time, the enemies of the Church's teaching have not been silent. They have done everything to persuade you, dear people, that you could change your minds, forget the former teaching, and be wholly conformed to the world in this matter. But that you cannot be. The times have come again, the times of the ancient world, when it is apparent to everyone that the mere calling of a Christian separates you from the world even though leaving you in it. In the centuries of Christian history, the Church educated your forefathers into at least an acknowledgment of God's laws. Then open wickedness seldom pretended to be virtue itself, and, what especially affects everyone, the common lot of marriage was generally regular Christian marriage. No wonder, then, that in these times the common calling of a Christian was often hardly perceived as a calling *not to be of this world*. No wonder that Christian people at large were regarded as a sort of Christian lumpenproletariat. No wonder the entry into a monastic life was characterised as almost a second baptism. No wonder marriage was thought of as belonging to the common worldly life. But now, in these decades of the twentieth century, all that has changed. It has become visible to everyone that a Catholic Christian is called

* Text of an untitled manuscript; no date.

** The reference is to Pope Paul VI's encyclical letter *Humanae Vitae*.

not to be conformed to the world and, though the religious life remain higher, you need enter no monastery to manifest this. Where unchastity is recommended on all sides as the norm, you are to accept a different norm. The law of chastity, which the world hates, you know is this: only in marriage to seek the satisfaction of genital desire; outside marriage your behaviour is to be free. For the conventions of genital solicitation are a sort of slavery in the world, poisoning many relations, rendering us incapable of many gestures and affections, and of all this you ought to be free. Marry if you are willing to have children; then, without anxiety rejoice in one another in the flesh. Performing true marriage acts as mutual inclination prompts you, you will normally have children without having to direct your intention especially to getting them; for they normally will come from this form of life. Do not be immoderate; but then whatever does no harm and that you mutually desire is permitted you, so long as the ejaculation of the man's seed is only in the woman's vagina, and you do nothing to render these acts infertile, if they would otherwise have been fertile. You may not marry with the intention of having no children, for that is not marriage but only an agreement in concubinage. If you have a just reason later on to avoid children, you still have rights in the form of married life, rights in one another's bodies, and you may seek out infertile times for intercourse. But make sure that the reason is a just one and not laziness, love of ease or mere worldliness.

'Against these laws of marriage the world rages, crying out in particular that this permission is absurd, if you are not allowed artificial contraception. But the very rage of the world is the proof of the difference: for they are angry at the law of holiness, at the different ideal of life that you have before you. Under this law, the obsessive fire of sensual preoccupation need not burn you, running uselessly in your veins. The erotic fire will burn on a domestic hearth: tamed, it will warm you, and you can thank God for it, for so it helps to forge the bond of the first, and still the strongest, society of the human race. But you will not live like your neighbours, defiling your marriages, and above all you will welcome children if you are able to have them.'

This message, so far as I know, was not given. In many places the bishops were visibly taken aback by the encyclical. Poor men, they too had been affected by the great onslaught through the media and otherwise. And the best that was said was 'No change, after all. So defend, and live according to, the rules as well as you can.' And pretty heavy hints were given to the faithful that they could find easy accommodation for their vices if they really didn't want to go along with the Pope.

I accuse the bishops and the parish clergy of failure to teach. Indeed, who would be a bishop? The responsibility is frightful, the danger of hell much greater than for the rest of us. This teaching was needed not once or twice; it was not enough that people should know at the back of their minds that this *was* the official teaching. They needed to be taught to take it seriously, to be taught in season, out of season. The great Irish Dominican of the English Province, Father Vincent McNabb, who died before these things happened, predicted that this century would see great struggles in the Church, not about dogma, but about morals: he was surely right. As things were, those lay people who were faithful in their lives were, humanly, in a sense alone. I am grateful that I wasn't put to the test of these times. They had to lean upon God, not upon the encouragement of their pastors. A deathly silence from the clergy, I mean from those who did not actually dissent, was pretty discouraging. And spirituality dried up. All this was perhaps out of fear of driving people out of the Church. Well, it has often meant that the process was accomplished in two stages. First, you decide to reject the teaching about contraception. Then you become more and more watery in the dogmatic content of your faith. Then, very often, it fades out altogether. Or it settles down to a total worldliness.

That cunning and sapient man, Soren Kierkegaard, once wrote: 'The danger for the degeneration of Protestantism is shallow worldliness; of Catholicism, sanctimonious hypocrisy'. What insight! But see how things have changed: the shallow worldliness, happily identified as very religiousness, is now much more our form of degeneration than formerly. For, note, the degeneration was not supposed to be a falling away, but a degenerate form of religiosity. The cause is the failure to embrace the Papal teaching—to embrace it with real enthusiasm, not grudgingly, and to proclaim it strongly. It was more important than we knew.

How you are paying for it now, you bishops and clergy! How many baptisms are there in your parishes? Have they not in many places declined far more than the birth rate has itself? You were short sighted and cowardly. And how about adult baptisms? In England there used to be 12,000 converts a year; now there are hardly any.

It was in 1963, late I am sure, that I became aware of the peculiar dreadful miasma of the present day that was spreading over the

Church. It was then that an acquaintance showed me an article by some quite well-know priestly writer from Europe, in an American periodical. I forget its content, which was boring, except for the way it ended. It ended with a joyful celebration of the fact that the conception of the 'embattled Church' was now out of date. This I saw with a sort of numbness, a passive scepticism at what seemed an odd opinion. How could it be? Out of date—just when the formerly Christian world was more and more *explicitly* rejecting the whole of Christian teaching? How strange if the concept of the embattled Church was appropriate all through the centuries of ostensibly Christian culture!—and just when that collapses it becomes out of date! Hearing of the way the voices of the clergy were going along with the world, the artist David Jones exclaimed: 'Oh, they should have called out the guards!' But where were the guards? The analogue of the Jesuits of the Counter-Reformation?

What can be done? If you want to repair the situation, you will have to preach chastity, the whole doctrine of the Church: the whole package. For it all hangs together.

They say we are 'anti sex': this astounds us at first for we know our war against the Manichees, our unfailing rejection of the loathsome heresy that the flesh is evil.

But the truth is, we *are* what *they call* 'anti sex'. To set a value on virginity voluntarily maintained, and on the religious vow of chastity, to commend abstinence from time to time even for the married—that *is* to be anti sex. We are accused of thinking that sexual intercourse needs an excuse, and that it is excused only by being for procreation. Of course if you look at it like that, the Papal teaching becomes incomprehensible. And I feel forced to admit that there is a *hint* of this in the Augustinian tradition. In that tradition, St Paul's speaking of something as being matter of pardon or excuse, not of command, was taken to mean that *intercourse* was pardoned or excused; whereas it would seem to me a more natural understanding of that text that deliberate abstentions for a time 'to give yourselves to prayer', are permissible, though not commanded.* If this *is* the more correct interpretation, then it has to be granted that there is a *strain* of a *false* idea that intercourse needs excuse in our tradition. But what concerned St Augustine was really the feeling of a peculiar disorder in our sexuality. And about that, I think he was right. This disorder, he thought, was excused and made up for by the excellence of marriage. The doctrine is more subtle than would be one that 'inter-

* See *I Corinthians* 7. 5–6

course needs excuse'. And the idea that procreation is the needed excuse for intercourse is exactly like the idea that nourishment is the needed excuse for eating. The reason why that sounds funny is that it is the inbuilt teleology of the *kind* of activity not an external justification. You can see this by asking how you would identify sexual differentiation and genital organs in another species. This inbuilt teleology does not mean that every act must be intended to procreate: rather, engaging in these acts as part of your form of life is what, in people of suitable age, is geared to procreation, and you don't have to think about that in connection with each act. Responsibility is first of all in making that life a permanent married life, and thereafter it is a matter of detail.

If it were not for the disorder that Augustine perceived, we would not need to guard against anything but excess (and, more rarely, defect), i.e. sins against moderation, in matters of genital activity and excitement. This is how it is with eating. But the strange obsessiveness and the mad pervasive *atmospherics* of disorderly sexuality as it infects a culture and a place point to something different. This is *a* reason, though I don't know whether it is the only reason, why there's something wrong with treating sexuality just as an appetite that needs regulating according to principles of moderation. I believe the Greek way of classifying chastity—i.e. as a subspecies of temperance—was always inadequate. It would really not account for the mystical value and character of virginity which even the Greeks were aware of.

Failure of moderation—in either direction—on the part of married people is the least of sins against chastity. It is fairly easy to identify by the following criterion: could we do without, if need arose?—as, for example, it very well might in case of illness. The practice of abstinence in natural family planning is of course a practice in moderation.

But the world rejects the whole of Catholic teaching. Here let me remark that the idea that contraceptive practices are alright within marriage, but we should worry about the supply of contraceptives to the unmarried, is quite ludicrous. Contraception is a defilement of marriage. That idea is one of mere worldly respectability: I hope it may disappear.

Rejecting the Church's teaching on contraception, people have naturally enough come to accept homosexual genital practices, as was warned by the minority report.* We thought it enough to say: if you reject the teaching on contraception you'll have no reason not to reject the other teaching too. But it isn't enough. Now there are Catholic homosexuals making earnest propaganda, and saying 'We agree it all hangs together, and we reject the whole deal.'

So we are having to consider the whole question of chastity. There are broadly speaking three possible views: one, there is no sense in the idea of such a virtue at all. Sexual pleasure, genital pleasure, need not be restrained; no moral law requires it, there are no forms that are objectionable (unless the sadistic forms are excepted). Let us dismiss this; it seems too crazy. But then there is the view which associates genital union with love, and so sees that it should be between humans, and perhaps is even inclined to think it should be restricted to loving *couples*. I don't really know why the latter.

Here we have the Pope's teaching that there is an inseparable connection between procreative and unitive *significance*. It is implicit in that that you can have procreation without the act having procreative *significance*—as when it is dissociated from union or unitive significance. And the other side of the coin is that you can have union without unitive significance—as when it is dissociated from procreation or procreative significance. It will then be essential to the Catholic teaching that the legitimate use of infertile times does not dissociate the act from procreative significance. That of course would not be the case if infertile times were chosen, as they were by the Manichees throughout a marriage, or, I should say rather, throughout an arrangement for concubinage, with a view to avoiding children altogether.

The homosexual will perhaps claim that his unions have unitive significance. We may contemplate the contrast, between the most ideal form of this, and the form of marriage in which the couple are joined in the work of bringing up the children that result from their union to serve and love God. It is not difficult to see that the one is a poor imitation of the other, and that the reason for the particular love to be confined to a pair is lacking. The reason in the married pair is the background of responsible love required for children. Some philosophic speculators now entertain the idea of sexual groups, with wives and husbands in common; but there is an obvious objec-

* The reference is to a 1966 memorandum by a group of four moral theologians who were part of the Papal Commission for the Study of Problems of the Family, Population and Birth Rate, originally established by Pope John XXIII, and reconstituted with a greatly increased membership by Pope Paul VI.

tion: the cry 'It wasn't my job' would be inevitable in connexion with a diffuse responsibility.

All this shows why chastity as understood by the Catholic Church is a useful virtue. For even the unitive significance as described is useful. But there is more to explore, hinted at in our references to the mystical significance of virginity.

Chastity, though a solid, practical, useful sort of virtue, is perhaps not of the greatest worth, perhaps isn't even the real thing—I don't know—unless it is one particular form or aspect of purity. I mean purity of heart.

Now this may seem nebulous and difficult to make anything of. One can perhaps *practise* various virtues, like truthfulness, moderation, hospitality. How would one *practise* purity of heart? Isn't it a character which one has or not? 'Blessed are the pure of heart for they shall see God.' How credible that sounds! But if one's heart is *not* pure, does one just look with helpless admiration, perhaps hopeless longing, at the spectacle of those who manifest purity of heart? I think this *is* a common frame of mind.

Well, but St Paul says, 'Purify your hearts'. So there must be something that can be done. Purity is perhaps the end product, rather than a practice. But how does one purify one's heart?

I suppose that a great part of the training of a religious, if it is a good training, is a training in the purification of the heart. We need instructions from those who know. I cannot say much. But I would think that declining to act from contemptible motives—motives of vanity, for example—must be part of it, together with a lack of enslavement to sensuality, and also a determination to trust God. Trust in God is most constantly derided—it's indicated that the priest hypocritically said 'Trust in God' and the deluded victim tried it and it didn't work. That is one of the most common bits of propaganda. And I suppose that a priest who is himself rather comfortable and is not humble and not obedient in spirit, is in an awkward position in telling some hard pressed person to trust God. Nevertheless that vulgar attack *is* an attack on the roots of religion, and the proof of it is this: Everyone knows that the picture of one who continued to suffer greatly, but who continued to trust God, is *not* a picture of someone trying something that doesn't work. Rather the story: 'I trusted God, and see, I got a job promotion!' demands rather special circumstances not to be a bad joke.

What, then, is needed? Constant teaching—teaching of the whole faith as if to children who have never been taught it. People often haven't: and those who have it will be built up and not irritated by such teaching. And, in this particular matter: the teaching needs to take the form: Do not be conformed to the world, and: Purify your hearts. Embark upon marriage with a will to have children, and a determination not to defile your marriage with acts which make it a sort of concubinage, a setting for proceedings not unlike those of active homosexuals. And trust God if you are afflicted. It is not for nothing that you are a Christian: you cannot demand that it cost you nothing or that it not separate you from the world you live in.

20*

The Early Embryo

Theoretical Doubts and Practical Certainties

Although impressed by the opinion of such a man as Jérôme Lejeune, and also to a certain extent by the numbers of people who share that opinion, I still have doubts about whether a single cell or the collection of cells resulting from its earliest divisions, the product of conception, can possibly be a human being, i.e. a *homo*, a *Mensch*, an *anthropos*. Here I avail myself of languages which do have a distinct word simply meaning 'human being', i.e. an individual member of the human species. In English 'man' does sometimes have this sense, e.g. if we say that men and beasts were among the few prime movers used before the industrial revolution, or 'What a wondrous work of God is man'. But it is not at all restricted to this sense and perhaps most often means 'grown-up male human being'. I regard this as a misfortune for users of English. I will often use the word 'human' as a substantive because 'man' is not tied down to this one meaning. It is a disadvantage to have to do this, because 'human' as a substantive is not old and so lacks what the old words have. However, using it I repeat my doubt by saying that I doubt whether a human set of cells, the product of conception, having unity but not organs, can be a human. The same doubt would of course apply to the zygote which is just one cell, to the two cells it splits into, and the three cells which are the result of the next division. I do not mean to suggest that in a conceptus which is a set of cells but has as yet no organs, there is no differentiation, no organisation and no being a single thing.

* This paper was commissioned and produced in 1990 for a volume on the Human Embryo which failed to appear.

It is (or certainly has long been) Professor Lejeune's opinion that a human zygote which is going to twin is somehow already two (or more, for he uses the word 'twin' also when there are more than two). In the early 1970s he said there was no proof of this. I have not heard that any proof of it has been found. At that time he thought that in a certain species of armadillo there was a proof that the conceptus was four from the start, because they always produced four at each birth. But with humans, he said, we do not know. Nevertheless, it is pretty clear that he has always believed that identical twins were, so to speak, written into the human conceptus from the very beginning. I don't know what would count as proof of this. It might count as disproof if embryologists succeeded in causing a fertilised ovum in a dish, after a number of divisions, to twin. This twinning might appear to be a sort of random accident which someone had found out how to bring about.

There is a variety of possible views about identical twinning. One, that of Jérôme Lejeune. Another, the random accident that some apparently would like to prove. Another, that the conceptus is always a single human to start with, and as it were grows a sprout, which may become physically separate. Then if one could identify one twin as the sprout, there would not be the curious problem of identity: these are two distinct humans, i.e. not identical with one another, so which of them is in fact the same human as was there first of all? For one could say, 'In principle, and keeping constant track, we could tell'. A different explanation: what started as one human being sometimes naturally divides into two, a method of reproduction well known in the amoeba. . The original one, of course, no longer exists, having become two. Now if being two is not written into the conceptus from the first, this 'one becoming two through division' (more often than not complete) is just what does happen when there are identical twins. If the conceptus is ordinarily (when there isn't twinning) a single human from the first, then it may be natural for some people to assume that when there is twinning, and one twin is not as it were a sprout from the other, the conceptus did start (like an ordinary human conceptus) as a single human who then split into two humans. It would not be necessary to hold this; it might be thought that a conceptus that was going to twin was not *a* human, but that two humans came about through a foreordained splitting. This would imply that there was something abnormal about the conceptus that was going to twin, though it would not be equivalent to Lejeune's view that the two-ness is already written in. For I take him to have meant that such a conceptus is already two human beings.

These are only fairly ignorant speculations on the matter of identical twinning, a matter which originally aroused my interest in the question when 'hominisation' can be reasonably held to have occurred in the development of a conceptus of human origin. This is perhaps the place to say that I would equally have doubts whether a sheep zygote is yet a sheep, and similarly for other animals, the ones that rarely twin, or ones in whom there is always a particular number of offspring from one impregnation—or again, where there are usually several such offspring, but no particular number as a rule.

People sometimes speak of 'ensoulment' or ask 'When does life begin?' The question has an obvious answer: There is a first product of conception: that conceptus is alive. I would also recommend the Aristotelian philosophy strongly enough to say: anything alive has a soul, the soul being its principle of life. That is the same thing as the principle of unity of a living thing which has disparate parts: even an amoeba is in that sense an organism. So the question people are really trying to ask is 'When does a product of conception begin to be a human being?'

Aquinas thought that the male contribution was not any material in the conceptus but that it gingered up what in the female was alive only with as it were sleeping vegetative life.[1] It causes the female-supplied material to start living with active vegetative life. Rather naturally and like many who had thoughts on the subject up till rather recent centuries, he thought the female contribution in humans was blood. The blood of the menses which cease in pregnancy might be as it were the soil in which the seed grew; for an Aristotelian it would rather be the matter of the newly developing being. The conceptus is at first alive only with vegetative life: it has nutrition and growth. Moderns can add 'reproduction' because we know the cells multiply by division. Once the conceptus moves about and has sensation, it is alive with animal life; but that does not mean that it is yet an actual *member* of any species of animal. Somewhat later the rational soul is created in the conceptus. For sure Aquinas never believed that the male contribution was a tiny human—a 'homunculus'—which grew in the soil of the woman's blood. In just

---

[1] *Summa theologiae* 1a, q.118, a.1, especially ad 4.

one case he believed that the conceptus *was* a complete tiny human being: this was Jesus.[2]

It is noticeable that he relies on criteria consisting of what the ordinary embryo does as criteria for its living with animal life. Not so for its living with human life, i.e. for its principle of life being a rational soul. Because of this contrast, I assume that he would rely on the human appearance of the baby for saying that it was now a human being. In a rather similar way, I incline to rely on its outward form and its having the human organs. In fact, I suppose that the period of animal but not yet human life must be very short. I have seen it reported that a six-week-old conceptus has been observed to swim vigorously with a breast stroke. (This, I have also heard, was an ectopic pregnancy.) The amniotic sac was in the hand of the doctor who observed the swimming. Certainly the old idea that babies only move about when the mother can feel them doing so, which used to be called the 'quickening'—i.e. the coming alive—was a complete mistake.

I do not find St Thomas's ideas absurd, though we must think his physiology rather quaint. What is most interesting is his thesis that in the process of production, there is a stage of living with animal life without being e.g. a man or a horse. (His example.[3]) This is quite astonishing. One would expect a 'good Aristotelian' to say 'Of course not' in answer to the question 'Can something be just an animal without being a member of a particular species?' However, Aquinas is evidently not that sort of 'good Aristotelian'. But neither was Aristotle himself: St Thomas gets this account of the matter from Aristotle's *Generation of Animals*.[4]

If, however, he can think that surprising thing, it appears to me that he need not think that the changes from vegetative to animal to rational life have to be seen as substantial changes. I had worried myself, thinking about this. 'Surely', I thought, 'for some 'what' I am the same somewhat as that zygote that I once was, even if when I was a zygote I wasn't yet a human.' Here I am asking for a general term in answer to the question 'what?' It did not suffice to say I was the same *thing*; the concept 'thing' does not properly lend itself to being so used. Reflexion however led me to say 'Why can't I say that I am the

---

[2] *Summa theologiae* 3a, q.33, a.2 ad 2.

[3] *Summa theologiae* 1a, q.119, a.2 corp: 'prius generatur animal, quam homo vel equus.' See also Aristotle's *Generation of Animals* 736b.

[4] See reference in previous footnote.

same *living thing* as that zygote?' If in its development it could come alive with animal life without having the substantial form of any particular kind of animal, then why should we respect the argument that the change from vegetative to animal life is a substantial change, and therefore involves the cessation of what is changed and the start—the coming to be—of the new thing it is changed into? After discovering what Aquinas was prepared to say about a certain stage of animal life, he seemed to me to be unjustified in inferring a substantial change in the way I have indicated. For his topic is: the matter (the blood of the *menses*) gradually becoming first actively vegetative and then animal in its operation.

I have referred to him partly because I think he is intrinsically worth referring to in this context; and also having read him precisely because I knew he was what is ineptly called a 'mediate animationist' and I was myself inclined to be what is meant by that.

In the horror of our time, when people are willing to kill babies, and others to approve or seek the same, I note that those stalwarts who resolutely oppose abortion (what a pity we use that obfuscating word!) almost universally hold that the human zygote is a human being, and therefore that killing it is murder. Indeed, it is certain that most killing of unborn babies is murder, the killing being done at a stage where the baby is, if only seen, visibly a human being. But I feel uneasy about relying so confidently on a thesis—that a conceptus is a human from the first moment—in order to oppose the killing of early conceptuses. Suppose the thesis *were* proved wrong? Would all those stalwarts say: 'Oh well, then, up to four weeks, say, you can kill it'? I do not think they would want to, and yet they have in a certain sense painted themselves into a corner.

At this point I shall be asked 'What then is wrong with procuring early abortion, abortion before there is a human with the human organs?' The answer is: 'If you kill an early human conceptus, you are killing an individual living thing whose life is at a stage in the development of one or more human lives, the coming human life (or lives) of that very same living thing as you are proposing to kill'. This at least is certain, amid the uncertainties I have mentioned. You cannot speak *so* of the sperm or the ovum; neither is itself a beginning human or a beginning set of humans. Nor is a pair of them. This is obvious from the fact that even given the pair you have not yet got a particular single being, as you have once there is a zygote. The ovum can combine with any one of many sperms; the sperm could have combined with various ova in different women.

I believe that modern discoveries in genetics, filtering through to the common run of people, have a considerable influence on our thought. We think of all those genes and chromosomes—all the 'information' they carry. In them is determined what colour eyes a person will have, whether they'll be at least liable to be tall or short, curly or straight haired, albino or otherwise, heavily pigmented in their skin or not, and a host of other things. Jérôme Lejeune, skilful and urbane under cross-questioning in a court of Tennessee,* said there will be a linguistic component in the human cell, though whether it develops as Japanese or some other speech of course depends on what surroundings the baby is brought up in. This made me wonder why he thought there was a linguistic component in the cells. Conscious of his enormous knowledge of things I am ignorant of, I nevertheless dare to express the suspicion that he thinks it is so because he thinks it must be so. The potentiality of language is after all part of what it is to be a human even if damage blocks its development.

However, whatever the number of characteristics thought or known to be predetermined, barring accidents, by the genetic constitution of the zygote (human or other), it appears to me (possibly from insufficient knowledge of the details of experimentation when geneticists 'play with cells' or of other details of investigation) that saying 'This is what determines sex as male' must be a matter of correlation. I am not calling it in question. I do not doubt it. But what can it be based on but discovered correlation? What is for sure implied in the correlation is indeed very, very interesting: it is that there is something about the observed genetic item (the XY pair of chromosomes) that already is maleness or makes maleness in the developed animal. To say, however, that this first cell, which includes the relevant thing in its constitution, is a male human would appear to me to be a reading back into the early stage of what can certainly be said at a later stage.

* The reference here is to the expert witness testimony Professor Lejeune gave in February 1989 before Judge W Dale Young in Blount County, Tennessee, in a case concerning the fate of seven frozen embryos of a couple who were divorcing and who disagreed about what should happen to their progeny. The story of the case and an account of Professor Lejeune's testimony were subsequently published in Jérôme Lejeune, *The Concentration Can: When Does Human Life Begin?* (San Francisco: Ignatius Press, 1992). A transcript of Lejeune's testimony was widely available before the publication of this volume and Professor Anscombe would have read that.

The zygote of human conception is of course a *human* zygote. That is however not enough to prove that it is a human, any more than a human bone is or a human hair. The significant difference is that these are parts, whereas the zygote is a whole living thing. So if one holds that its humanness means that it is *a human*, the crucial thing must be the single wholeness, and not just the fact that the adjective 'human' can be applied to it. Here there is something to think about; for some parts—hearts, for example—can be kept alive after separation from the body. I will not pause to consider this, but only to note it in passing as a topic for consideration. The human zygote is not a separated part but a natural whole. Nevertheless, there is a certain lack of determinateness. This one zygote will very likely develop, if all goes well, into one single human being, but it may also develop into more. That we originate in an undetermined state ought not to be surprising, in view of the great differentiation and enormous multiplication of cells and all the development that has to take place.

However, proceeding in this line of thought, I come to the suggestion it offers that there is a confusion of final with formal causality in the belief that the human zygote is a human. To believe that is to believe that a human soul or principle of life of a new human is governing the unified development of the beginning cells into what will be equipped with finally differentiated and organised organ-cells. Now who can doubt that something is doing this?—though as far as I know even the beginning of cell differentiation and organisation is as yet a mystery unpenetrated by natural scientists. But when we say: 'Something is doing this', we may call to mind the origin of these reproductive cells and take it that the species of the parents is relevant. And that must be right. But to say that there is here an individualised actual form so operative that we can say of the zygote 'Here is a human' seems to me too bold. The form that is to be, if development is normal—that is surely what is governing the development at least until you are really justified in saying 'This is a human'. Now a form that is to be is, as governing a development, precisely a final cause.

I am not saying that final and formal cause are never the same: on the contrary, they are when for example a foal runs about doing things doing which is part of being a horse, and for the sake of that horse-life. But, to justify saying that, the little horse must already be there. And that is why I suggest that in saying 'The human zygote is already a human' there is a confusion of what are here distinct—namely formal and final causes.

On the account that I am suggesting, the set of genes and chromosomes would be the proximate matter for the unifying principles of the life of the living thing, which is at first a zygote; or for the unifying principles of the lives of living things which jointly were once a single zygote.

The major practical certainty about procuring an abortion is that it is gravely wrong. The reason for this is what I have already stated—the proposal to procure an abortion is a proposal to kill either a growing human baby, or, if it should be so early that there can be some doubt—as I have expounded—whether it is reasonable yet to call it *a* human, it is a proposal to kill a living individual whole whose life is—all going well—to be the life of one or lives of more than one human being.

The immediate inference, that *if* this latter supposition is true, then the killing of the conceptus would not be murder, is of course based on a rigid definition of murder as the (wilful and unjust) killing of a human being. One need not stick to this in an obstinate fashion. To apply the description 'murder' to wilfully destroying the beginning of a new human life would seem to be an unpedantic deviation from that definition: rather does an insistence on the definition itself appear to be pedantic in this context. In the present article, then, I am warning against (a) sticking to the definition together with (b) insisting that the product of conception, all going normally, is at least one human being from the first moment, in order to justify a firm objection to procuring abortion. The purpose I applaud; the method I fear might prove to be essentially based on a mistake. Even if it *is* a mistake, so long as there is a doubt about the matter anyone proposing to procure an abortion should indeed be deterred by the possibility that they are killing a human being. But also, even if it were certain that, for example, a week-old conceptus is not yet a human being, the act of killing what is in the earliest stages of human life has evidently the same sort of malice as killing it later on when it is unquestionably a human, or more than one.

There are some developments of a conceptus that are definitely not stages in the life of a human being—e.g. when it turns into a lethal cancer. There are also carneous moles, of which I have heard that they are probably each a development of a 'blighted ovum'. I presume that a blighted ovum is a product of conception. But it, as well as a cancer and its antecedent, is evidently *not* a human being; it is a proof that you cannot reason that just *any* product of conception is one or more humans.

Here it is worth observing the change that has come about in the last forty years in the meaning of the term 'abortion'. 'An abortion' used to mean 'a miscarriage': the abominable act was to procure it, wilfully to bring it about. Now our language has changed: 'having an abortion' no longer means suffering a miscarriage but having an operation to kill one's baby (or beginning of a baby). It sounds, however, like something of the same family as 'having injections against rabies' or 'having one's appendix out'. Truth nevertheless speaks: why are Rescue operators—whose object is by persuasion to save the life of any baby they can—described as harassing women 'on perhaps the worst day in their lives'? Such a description I have seen. Why might it be such a bad day in one's life? Obviously because of the dreadful thing that one is doing. To see this clearly, imagine demonstrations outside dentists' surgeries, with placards showing teeth and announcing 'Here *teeth* are pulled out!'

Much work is done by language changes. People who kill them will speak of fetuses, not babies. But I heard Hymie Gordon, the head of genetics at the Mayo Clinic, saying: 'I have talked with lots of mothers who were consulting me, and I have never heard one of them ask "How is my fetus getting on?"'*

A further practical certainty is one about which lies are often told. The Catholic Church has never taught that procuring an abortion in the first few weeks of pregnancy was permissible. The lies that are told about this are often based on an assumed scholastic acceptance of Aristotle's theories about when 'hominisation' occurred. But that would prove nothing about its being permissible to procure abortion in the early stages. To the condemnation of such action, we can add that the Catholic Church has never committed herself to the thesis that the rational soul of a human being is there from the first moment of conception. Even the doctrine of the Immaculate Conception of the Virgin Mary—that from the first moment of conception she was freed from the taint of original sin by the coming redemption—does not have any such implication, though people sometimes think it does. The opinion of St Thomas, that original sin as originated is in the human conceptus by inheritance from Adam, from whose begetting of his children, and their begetting of theirs and so on, every

* Dr Hymie Gordon (1926-1995), first Professor of Medical Genetics (1972-1989) at the Mayo Medical School, Rochester, Minnesota. Professor John Dolan, in his eulogy for Hymie Gordon, recalls the following version of the statement to which Professor Anscombe refers: 'I have been practising medicine for more than forty years and have delivered babies on three continents and never once has a woman said to me "Doctor, how is my fetus doing?"'

subsequent human life springs except that of Christ, is not universally accepted by modern theologians; but it appears the most reasonable. It shows the connexion of the originated original sin with the originating original sin of Adam's disobedience. The inheritors of original sin are not guilty of disobedience or of any actual sin in having the taint of original sin; but this originated original sin is not in the specially created rational soul of each individual but in the physical inheritance. That physical inheritance was rendered clear of original sin in the Blessed Virgin by the as-it-were promissory note of the redemptive death of her son. Thus the doctrine of the Immaculate Conception of our Lady does not involve the presence in St Anne of a human at the first moment of conception, only of a human zygote.

Two points especially interested me in *Donum Vitae*, issued by the Congregation for the Doctrine of the Faith in 1987. In a paragraph on prenatal diagnosis[5], it warned against having this done, or recommending it, with a view to abortion's being procured if there was something wrong with the embryo or fetus. It spoke of the grave wrong of having or carrying out an investigation with that intention, the wrong to the unborn child. This was enlightening to me: of course you would be wronging the prospective human being even by something done to him at a stage—if there is such a stage—so early that he was not yet one. Living in Baltimore, I was struck by the fancy of a damaged adult suing a doctor or hospital for damage done to him at that early stage. (The USA is a litigious country.) It was obvious that even if it had somehow been proved that a man was not *yet* a human being at the stage at which what caused the damage was done, that should certainly not lead to the rejection of his suit. Thus it became obvious that you can wrong someone by what you do to, say, an early cell cluster which was a stage in his development. I was also pleased to note that the document says that the Magisterium of the Church has not 'committed itself to an affirmation of a philosophical nature'.* It has, in short, not claimed to decide difficult philosophical questions in this area.

* In regard to whether there is an individual human being at the earliest stages of embryological development. *Op.cit.* Section I, 1.

---

[5] Congregation for the Doctrine of the Faith, *Instruction on Respect for Human Life in its Origin and on the Dignity of Procreation [Donum Vitae]* Section I, 2.

21*

The Moral Environment of the Child

What is the 'moral environment' of a child? – Everything in its environment that speaks to it and to which it itself reacts with intelligence and feeling.

When I say 'everything that speaks to it' I don't mean only everything that addresses the child, but rather whatever tells it anything. Whatever the child gets purely from existing with its senses and its human intelligence in nature, we cannot estimate it. In any case what it gets from nature is modified by its human culture. Largely by talking to it the surrounding humans teach it human speech. The rest of their behaviour also tells the child a great deal and this, first and foremost, in the same way as speech does, by showing it forms of behaviour which it will understand and some of which it will imitate. Just as a child has an innate capacity to learn whatever language it hears regularly, so also it is able to learn the inwardness of all sorts of ways of going on. Of feeding animals, for example, of greeting people, of giving gifts, of cleaning things; of hiding, storing, throwing away; of dancing; of many gestures; of hurrying or delaying. The list is endless; and all of these descriptions are *interpretations* of behaviour, or rather of the elementary movements and happenings that constitute behaviour.

All this is natural history. We can say: it belongs to the natural history of man that he has a moral environment. No one could decide that in a particular case of a human infant this was not to be so. Not, at any rate, if he proposes that the infant shall be brought up. I suppose an infant, once weaned, might be kept on chicken litter in a box, with food and water put within its reach, but no human communication; the litter being changed and the food and water appearing

* From an unpublished and undated typescript.

automatically. But this would not be bringing the child up and it would surely die. This is at least present opinion; for so evil an experiment is not tried.

Now the 'telling' that is inescapably done in bringing a child up so that it has language and can move around in its own society — so that roughly speaking it *knows its way about* — this minimal telling is not what anyone would call moral training. So it might be asked why I call it part of the child's moral environment. The reason is that it supplies the raw material, the matter of which the ethical is the form. Look for example at the ten commandments, at the concepts that are involved in them. All of them refer to activities or to facts which are not just natural events or states of affairs; to covet what *belongs to* someone else; to *bear witness against* someone; to commit *adultery*; to *murder*; to *steal*; to *honour* someone; *to take a name in vain*; to *keep holy*; to make *idols* and *bow down* to them; to *have a god*. Every italicised phrase here signifies, not as do words for physical processes, characteristics and relations, or immediate experiences or feelings. The descriptions are all high-level interpretations of what goes on. It will be seen that I have referred to the commandment against murder not in the form in which it is so often cited: 'Thou shalt not kill', but in the more correct form 'Thou shalt do no murder'. The Hebrew word means murder, not killing. Otherwise that commandment would be a counter example to what I have been saying; killing need not even be a human act, since a lion or a rock may kill. 'Killing' is a relatively low-level description of an action, without much specifically human reference about it.

No one could have the concepts corresponding to the words used in the commandments, if he had not lived in an environment in which he learns the inwardness of all sorts of ways of going on: he must live a specifically human life with human practices.

Moral action descriptions are not natural event descriptions. But it is part of the natural history of mankind that the human young acquire concepts corresponding to them, or in some cases, at least concepts in which they are rooted, as adultery is in that of marriage, or stealing in that of property. Some notion of property will be picked up by anyone in the course of his upbringing, and almost certainly some notion of stealing in its train. Quite generally: to grow up as a child of normal intelligence in a human society is *eo ipso* to be equipped with a range of concepts which form the raw material for moral action descriptions, and in many cases to acquire these as well, at least in a rough inchoate form.

To say this is not to say that to grow up in a human way is to acquire moral convictions and sentiments. That is something else. We can easily imagine someone with a full grasp of human language, yet not participating in many moral notions, even not participating in any of a certain range: the ones, I mean, connected with condemnation.

This is no doubt unusual. As St Paul says, people reveal what is written in their hearts by their way of making accusations and excuses. I am imagining someone who does not seek to be justified or ask others to justify themselves. He is not defective in his grasp of language. He functions mentally as a juryman, who can say what has been done; never as a judge, who condemns or discharges the accused person.

In short a human being of normal intelligence can't grow up without being able to use a host of descriptions which are either already moral descriptions or the basis for moral descriptions. But he can do so without acquiring the habit of either condemning or exonerating, accusing or excusing either himself or anyone else. Usually he learns to do these things; but he need not. His subjectivity need not be called into play except as that of a being with feelings and objectives.

This division is important. It means that a human subjectivity is trained or formed ethically in two different ways. One way is the formation of the will and the education of the emotions. The other is the training in justification, in judgement of good and evil in human action, and in what is called 'conscience'. The separability of these is the source of many philosophical problems, which are not my concern here. But it, and partly those problems themselves, are also the source of the widespread conviction nowadays, that a man's ethics is purely subjective, in the sense that it is up to him to determine what he is to call right and wrong. This is even the basis of some educational theory in England.

The development of the will and the schooling of the emotions are largely effected without any definite intention on the part of the adults who are responsible for a child's upbringing. The child is born with a will which is at first fixed on necessities and on comfort and attention. Later, as individual differences appear, they seem not to be of our making. Still later, a child can be encouraged to have certain ends and concerns by the attitudes of its adults, and sometimes by being associated with the adults in promoting and pursuing them. This may be done with intent; as is a training in manners, which at least suggest certain attitudes.

But there is an important sense in which *velle non discitur*: willing is not taught. Suppose, for example, that the adult would like to train the child to help people who are poor and wretched. He can do quite a lot. He can teach it, give it information, including forms of thought on the subject. I am referring to the sort of thing that is said about the people to be helped, the style which shows attitudes. He can give the child relevant moral teaching, rising up from minimal teaching on the duty of almsgiving. He can get the child to join with him in some of the things that he does. He can direct the child to do certain things which are means to his objectives; as King Wenceslas told the page in the carol: 'Bring me flesh and bring me wine, Bring me pine logs hither, Thou and I shall see him dine'. No doubt all of this will sometimes be effective and the child then becomes an adult who has that sort of concern at heart, has such objectives quite often in the course of his life. But it is not something that can be guaranteed, as you can guarantee that a normal ten year old will learn a foreign language if placed only among speakers of it for a few months. The only sort of moral action that can be pretty well guaranteed by training, by upbringing, is such as is counted absolutely obligatory in a society and whose performance or non performance is quite open and visible: like the prayers at fixed times in a strict Muslim town or the supply of small coins for beggars in their shops.

It is much like the following case: you can teach a child to pray in the sense that you teach it its prayers, have it say the prayers with you and make a regular habit of this. But if the child does not then pray by itself and off its own bat, this is not necessarily a failure on your part in the teaching of anything that can be taught. The most that can be said is that if you clearly pray yourself with some sincerity and clearly mean the expressions of the pertinent beliefs in which you embed the training, the child will *probably* pray on its own. But its own will is a spontaneous new source of action, and cannot itself be taught to operate. (What can be taught are capacities, knowledge of how to do things.) The nearest thing to a training of the will itself is a training in supervised habits. But there comes the time when the child is autonomous and may not maintain the former habits. Again, though it is of value to teach a child its prayers, there is a sense in which it is already autonomous: your teaching does not secure that it really prays, as opposed to joining in those compulsory recitations. Or again, take going to confession. Here the child is already autonomous, already on its own and responsible. No one can give it a piece to say, saying which it will have managed to do what is in question.

A child's first going to confession is a spiritual weaning of a very explicit sort.

Thus the training of the will, so far as such a thing is possible, is a training by causing the child habitually to do certain things, and for the rest it occurs by circumstances which inform it and call attention to the possibilities – the possible objects of its will. When St Hugh of Lincoln was seven years old his mother died and his father divided his estate between his two grown-up sons and withdrew with Hugh to a monastery. There no doubt certain possibilities were made apparent to the boy, which in the world would have been more remotely heard of. The story has an alarming character. Was not Hugh's father betting on a response of the will of the boy, which could by no means be predicted? But then, don't we all do that? No: we don't take such worldly risks.

The training of the will – so far as such a thing is possible – is likely to be most effective where the child is following practices which its adults also follow. This is the training by example of which so much is always made. It is mostly implicit and inevitable. Here also is found the training of the emotions; it is difficult to see how this can be much more than implicit. The expression of attitudes for the sake of inculcating them, which one manifestly does not have in practice, had better be accompanied by an admission. Otherwise the training is likely to be a training in hypocrisy. It is very difficult to avoid this, in any case.

Here it is worth saying that it is of enormous value in demanding the obedience of children, to be manifestly oneself under obedience. And it is necessary to require obedience from children in bringing them up. The scope of this reduces gradually; but not to demand obedience is to inflict a great wrong on the child. Everybody can see that when what is in question is the avoidance of gross physical dangers. But it ought to be clear too in connection with the performance of those tasks in which the child's capacities are trained and developed. Here there has been some deleterious educational opinion rife in my country and elsewhere: as if a child would develop algebra, grammar and a knowledge of history, or at least an effective appetite for these things, if left to itself with no teaching forced upon it. Of course the word 'forced' sounds like a situation of stress and tension; that the children have to do their exercises is something which should be taken for granted without any tension. This requires that obedience be the assumption.

In moral matters there has been an even greater loss of nerve. Now I think one of the sources, perhaps even the main source, of this is the feeling that adults are just laying their own arbitrary requirements on children: and what right have they, really, to do that? This is why no difficulty is felt about the requirement of obedience to avoid manifest physical danger; it is not a question, here, of the child's having to obey the arbitrary inclination of the parent and it doesn't look like that to anyone. But otherwise, in ways of spending time, in choice of companions, in taking and using things—if the adult feels uncertain in giving any moral teaching, it becomes more and more like a mere imposition when he demands obedience.

I have spoken so far of the training of the will and of the emotions. The other area of ethical training is the training of ideas of obligation and guilt and justification. Praise and blame of behaviour, moral approval and disapproval, accusation; excuses and justifications and beliefs of the form 'It is right to ...', and 'It is wrong to ...' are what come in here.

There is in the names of virtues and vices, as also of wrongful acts, a bridge between the two divisions I have made of my subject. The will can be inclined against (or, indeed towards) wicked acts like murder, theft or adultery; it can be inclined towards or against virtues and vices. Thus courage excites admiration and someone may very well want to be brave and therefore not want to have it told of him that *he ran away* in a certain situation. 'Running away', unlike mere 'running', is one of those high-level descriptions which is a basis for a moral action description and hence provides, as I described at the beginning, the raw material of the ethical.

There are indeed other forms for courage to take besides not running away from dangers and pains that one needs to face and endure. But such not running away is one of the most intelligible forms of courage. To bring up a child without a training in courage is to do it a great wrong; for it cannot live without getting into situations in which it needs courage. A training which includes training in courage comes as near as possible to direct training of the will—for the child who has got to do what is difficult, to pick himself up after set-backs, is actually performing acts of fortitude.

The bridge of which I just spoke is like this: virtues and vices are acquired in the pursuit of the objects of the will, and with the help of the development of the emotions. But virtues and vices are also praised and condemned. In a training in virtues, then, the two things—pursuit of worthy objects of the will, and the ideas of justification and condemnation—will be combined. When we condemn something, we name the vice that it seems to be an act of; we say: that's unjust, untruthful, cowardly, indecent, greedy.

Virtues, however, may be means rather than ends. Indeed Christians *must* regard them as such, for we have an end proposed to us, namely the vision of God, and participation in the life of God, which is not a state or practice of moral virtue. And we don't even think it is attained by the practice of the moral virtues—only that the failure to practise them greatly endangers its attainment.

Nevertheless there is in human minds this strong theme of right and wrong, obligation and guilt, accusation and justification. We must notice that they are in themselves contentless, however compelling. It is indeed the notions of the virtues, of good and bad types of action, such as feeding the hungry or killing the innocent, that give them any content. A strong sense of duty, uncombined with a true moral code, is alas, a real possibility. But it is likely to be extremely harmful: to 'justify' the commission of many wrongs.

Think of a man such as a Nazi with a strong sense of duty, or a soldier under Nazi command. A saving lack or failure of *such* a sense of duty preserved the city of Paris at the end of the Second World War. Or, again, think of the common conviction that you must 'act for the best', act to secure the best possible consequences. These are two different ways of giving a sense of duty some content. For a sense of duty must of course be accompanied by *some* way of conceiving something as your duty. Thus it can be filled out with a notion of party loyalty, military obligation to obedience, or of acting for the best consequences, and in all these cases leads to very evil actions. Only if it is combined with truth in the moral code can it be trusted to lead to good actions. Similarly, someone who 'always tries to do what is right', but has not such truth, will not succeed in acting well.

In practice, in education, the contentless notion of wrong is given content by 'It is wrong because it is a lie', 'because it is stealing', 'because it is dishonouring your parents', and a lot of explicit moral teaching consists in telling children what kinds of action are wrong.

A child who is taught truth in a moral code by its own adults, will of course have them—these adults—only as part of its human moral environment. Others will tend to teach it contrary things. If you have truth to communicate to your child here, it is good to prepare it also to hear lies, telling it: 'People do these things and think it right to do them; don't be surprised'. Then when the child encounters it he is forewarned.

For a Christian, the training in ideas of justification and accusation *ought* to be first and foremost a training of the conscience, that is, a training in self-examination before God. The questions asked in the self-examination concern one's past actions, and whether they have been wrong, and also one's proposed actions. In this enquiry, one cannot leave out the spirit in which one has acted or proposes to act; but that is not the first question. The first question concerns objective conformity to the standards of the commandments.

Catholic Christianity teaches a strict moral code. (The time is past, I think, when many thought it rather lax!) One form of strictness lies in the exactness and absoluteness of its prohibitions of actions, prohibitions of idolatry, murder, adultery and false witness. It has, by the way, been a long time since it was necessary to stress the prohibition on idolatry, except for occasional curbing of superstition relating to particular statues or shrines. It is becoming rather more relevant now: with present fashions, some of our young people are being drawn into spiritual cults which include the worship of Shiva and Krishna and other deities of the Hindu pantheon, including image worship; but in any case it is clear that these are (false) gods. The other prohibitions are extremely familiar. We are known as 'absolutists' and described as thinking that these absolute rules tell you what to do. This is peculiarly thoughtless, as it is evident that a prohibition only tells you *not to* do something. A morality which consisted solely of absolute prohibitions on fairly definitely described actions would leave you free to do anything else whatever. Such in fact is not our morality; we have absolute prohibitions indeed, but you would not be guaranteed to do no wrong purely by abstaining from what they positively prohibited. Take lying. If you are not to lie, that doesn't tell you what you are to do in a particular situation: tell the truth? Mislead in some other way? Turn the subject? Make a joke? Say nothing? Lose your temper? Or whatever else might be a good course of action.

Nor is it always clear what committing the offending action is. In England there is a line that children have got to work out their own ethics. This is a mere fraud. I have seen a television programme in which this comes out clearly. Four children acted out the part of someone in a factory who had just received a letter telling him that a fellow-employee had been found guilty of theft as a young teenager. He is then asked his opinion of the proposed promotion of this person. Does he 'know anything against him?' Two of the children told of the letter, two said they didn't know anything against the person.

In discussing this later it was called a lie without further investigation, and the case was used to illustrate the difference between absolutists who think you may not lie and others who 'go by the situation'. This was card-forcing on the part of the producers and commentators. *Was* it a lie? The case is not at all clearly made out.

Even when we are concerned with absolute rules, the question 'Is this a case of the prohibited action?' is one to be approached with judgement; and here something really can be taught. In the past, we would perhaps have been likely to ask a priest, assuming him to be trained in casuistry; nowadays we would feel much less confident, though it would still be a sensible thing to try. Lay people plunge bald-headed towards the opinion that strikes them as plausible; very many priests still have at least the appearance of having learned some principles and methods of consideration which make them more judicious and cautious.

Suppose, however, that it is clear what the application of an absolute rule is in the particular case. When the rule is a prohibition that still doesn't tell you what actually to do. And it may be that it matters a good deal what you actually do; and you need wisdom to know. Here is a case: a young man is reconverted to the Catholic religion and is full of enthusiasm. He says to his wife: 'Right! No more contraception!' It is easy to imagine how the marriage gets smashed up. Clearly it mattered a great deal how he approached the thing. A cunning wisdom might have made him extremely cautious about revealing his new attitude. 'Darling, let's have another baby! — the one we have is so wonderful' might be a successful line, and that would give an interval in which much could be done. I tell such a story to illustrate how the absolute prohibitory rules, with their application to the particular case clearly ascertained, do not exhaust morality: one may do wrong in one important way of handling a situation and good instincts and practical wisdom are necessary.

Fairly young children often steal and it is fortunate for them if this is discovered by a sensible parent and not by any other authority, for another authority may have to take very stringent measures against such a child and yet this is a fault which it may very well grow out of — an infantile fault, even in a twelve year old. It is important not to make too great a disgrace of it, but, if it is possible, to insist on restitution. (Maybe without making any admissions: often money can be conveyed to the victim of a theft without the culprit having to disgrace himself.) If direct restitution is impossible, there should be insistence on a substitute restitution. But it is important not to call theft anything that is mere disobedience and greed within a family; I fear this mistake is often made.

Articulateness and willingness to talk with one's children is of enormous importance. It is often said that parents tend to leave the teaching of religion to schools. This is deplored, but not enough. The school to which this has been left cannot do anything, ordinarily, but an inadequate repair job. If children don't pray with their families for example, it's luck if prayer can be instilled at school. But schools are often faced with the following problem: how to impart the truth without inciting the children to a condemnation of their parents? Now that is not allowed: not because they are parents—for in this regard they are to be looked on as neighbours—but because we are not allowed to judge—i.e. condemn—others. The state of mind that is right for a child of unconscientious and irreligious parents who nevertheless want it to be brought up a Christian, must be one that is very difficult to achieve. But the matter is already notorious. It is not to be solved, however, by sliding along in silence. What is needed is much clear and explicit teaching and the encouragement of reflection. The Christian ethical tradition is extremely rich, powerful and subtle and the mind of a child that has been impregnated with it is more likely to resist the alluring and facile judgements which are so common in the world. Clear and true teaching on these matters—teaching concerning the moral code and justification and the end of man—is intrinsically interesting, appealing and enriching. It is an important component of any *good* moral environment for a child as it grows up. As I said at the beginning, no child who grows in a human environment can fail to have *some* moral environment, even if it is a bad one. But even if it is a bad one, it will be full of matter which provides the raw material for the ethical.

22*

Christians and Nuclear Weapons Designed for the Destruction of Cities

It is anciently human to speak of loving your friends and hating your enemies; also, of giving them their due. The due is good things for the friends and evil for the enemies. Now friendship can mean many things; from the intimate love of people who love one another for their own sakes, who know one another and like to be together, who have unanimity and are good; for if they are not good they will only like one another for advantage or pleasure. This personal friendship is the most important kind for individuals generally but there are lesser friendships: there are friendships of advantage or pleasure, the friendships of fellows in an association, of fellow workers and of fellow citizens—and also of fellow men, as would make its appearance if fear did not when two humans alone find one another in the desert. And between states it is the same except that there may be an hostility to strangers who are felt to threaten the society that they approach; and if not hostility, at least caution in case they should turn into enemies. As, upon the whole, people are not good, it comes about that friendship between states is only friendship of advantage and so it changes very easily.

This feature of hostility between states and between societies is fostered by something in corrupt human nature which lies at the base of the following story. A party of German academics was visiting a university in New Zealand. They were discussing human rights, for these were Germans of the post-war era and those of them

* From an undated manuscript.

who were young enough had been brought up on a human rights ethic. They were debating what was the first human right and coming to the statement that it was the right to life. Suddenly one of their hosts, an aged Maori professor, said 'What nonsense! It is for a man to kill!' (When told this story I understood that what he meant by 'man' was 'Mann', not 'Mensch', 'vir' not 'homo', i.e. male human being, not human being.) The Germans were rather thrown by this utterance, being accustomed to the purveying of unchallenged human rights theory, and they couldn't think what to say. I asked the teller of the story 'To kill whom? Not just anyone, anytime, I suppose?' He replied that presumably it was to kill strangers, not members of your own family, for example; but it sounded as if the Maori were coming out with his native ethos, perhaps comparable, - well, certainly comparable, and perhaps quite *like*—that of ancient Macedon, where you emerged from boyhood and assumed the status of a *man* once you had killed your first wild boar and your first man. This wasn't a license for casual domestic or civic murder; but quarrels on the road are things that readily happen, and I suppose the spirited youth would feel that his pride was at stake on such an occasion, and find in it the opportunity to attain to manhood. If there is this streak in human *nature* (for though it would not be natural to women to have such a rule for *themselves*, presumably they approved and applauded it) then we may see in it something that fosters an inclination to quarrels, to finding enemies in strangers, and to regarding the enemies of your society in warfare as suitable objects of hate. In ancient times a common rule was for the victorious side to kill all the men and enslave the women and children; but in extreme pride and confidence you might kill the whole lot, as the Athenians killed the people of Melos. Or, even in not so ancient times there might be the feeling that these people are so atrocious they must *all* be wiped out, down to the children themselves. This was done, according to the story, when the cause of disappearance of travellers was found, somewhere in Scotland under James VI. There was a family, a tribe of several generations, living in a cave or caves, and waylaying travellers, whom they killed and ate. Not all at once; human hams were found preserved and hanging up in their cave. When found they were *all* seized and slaughtered without any suggestion of a trial.

And similarly in warfare where we have the means of destroying cities; the sentiment is around that all are enemies, all are participants, just by being members of that hated society. There is, I surmise, an *appetite* for massacre, not itself *based* on that sentiment. Witness the saying of Simon de Montfort when he stormed and captured an Albigensian city and ordered that everyone should be slaughtered. His war was against the Albigensians and no doubt also stimulated by the stories of *their* wickedness. But it was pointed out to him that the city, though in the hands of the Albigenses, was not by any means exclusively Albigensian; there were plenty of Catholics there. What did he say? He stuck to the order he had given. As to the Catholics—'The Lord will know his own'. This is clearly the story of a man who is out for massacre, and so are his troops.

This appetite for massacre is with us still, though only occasionally is it quite blatantly expressed in what is said. It was so expressed by the U.S. people who spoke up favouring Calley when he was found guilty in respect of a little massacre—by hand—of Vietnamese villagers. It was because he did it by hand that it was thought an atrocity. Massacre by advanced technology would never get you into trouble in modern warfare—unless you fell into the hands of the population you were bombing.

The preparation for massacre is reckoned a necessary part of defence policy. This preparation is of course both ways—it is preparation against attempted and in part successful massacres of our own people by an enemy—or, rather, *the* enemy; and preparation *to* massacre *their* people. A vast amount is spent—and this emerged years ago, in the time of Harold Wilson's government, I think—on the sophisticated system of weaponry which we are prepared to deploy to countervail against the sophisticated system of defence of the city of Moscow. And presumably they are in a like position in relation to London and other cities.

There is long and much argument about whether we should or should not go in for unilateral nuclear disarmament. Those who are against this say it is crazy, for obvious reasons. You don't throw your gun out of the window when your enemy is at your door with a gun. Those who are for it say that the obvious reasons aren't as good as they seem—we in the UK at least have a merely token *force de frappe* with such weapons, for example; we insist on having them in order to strut among the Great Powers, thinking perhaps to have an influence on policy.

I wouldn't have the knowledge to enter such an argument. I note that it doesn't touch the soundness of U.S. policy in trying to be equal or superior to Russia. I don't know how U.S. people argue when they wish to maintain that it's *not good policy*, apart from rhetoric about the craziness of the arms race. What seems to me quite certain is that the governments will go on as they have been going on, short of some great and unimaginable cause of change.

The question for us, if I am right, is not: to make up our minds about the right policy for *our* government. That I incline to regard as a waste of time.

To take that seriously—I mean, to take seriously the thesis that that is a waste of time—is to make what ought to seem a pretty big decision. We have assumed for a long time, we Catholics, that if we are allowed to, we ought to be participators in government and its policies. At least, so far as we can compatibly with our religion; we can't so participate in its abortion policies, for example. But defence policy, war policy, what's involved in decisions which may lead to your being called up to fight for your country—in all that sort of thing we have assumed that if *we* aren't cut off by the country from participation in public life, we, or some of us at any rate, *should* be participating. Particular decisions may indeed be mistaken or wrongful, but that doesn't mean that we should be cut off from participation in decision making, or in the formation of public policy.

But now—if the essential decision about public policy has been taken and won't be reversed—won't any Catholic who is involved be implementing and maintaining that decision? Just like a Catholic who was engaged in giving directives about the employment of gynaecologists, anaesthetists and psychiatrists in the National Health Service?

It may be argued that it is not necessarily wicked to threaten what it would be wicked to do. And that I do not deny. If you are an individual threatening the like to someone who has his guns sighted on your family, and this can make him desist, maybe you are justified in making your threat, even though it would be wicked to carry it out. But then you can—perhaps—know that you do not mean to carry it out.

If it's a government and not an individual that is in question, the threat can only be made in reliance on there being a lot of people who *are* prepared to carry it out. So in our analogy we have to change the individual into one who has a lot of plug-uglies at his command who are perfectly prepared to kill his enemy's family. His position begins to look a bit more dubious. Could we argue that it *is* all right? or: that it *is* all right if he knows the plug-uglies will only shoot on his orders, and he is not going to give *that* order? (He isn't going to affect their being plug-uglies, anyway.)

I do not know the answer to that question.

But what it's supposed to be an analogue of is rather different. What corresponds to the plug-uglies is going to be a large number of highly respectable people who think it is all right actually to engage in massacre, and who are necessarily sustained and strengthened in that conviction by their role in the preparedness which is part of making the threat. You can't pretend the threat is not meant. In those circumstances you might say: Well, as far as government—i.e. the top deciders—are concerned, it's rather like Russian roulette. The man who plays Russian roulette doesn't *mean* to shoot himself, only to incur the risk of doing so. But remember that in the analogue the machinery he doesn't positively *mean* to set off—or only conditionally *means* to set off—is a machinery of people who mean to play their part as much as the hammer in the pistol is set to operate. And, anyway, is it all right 'conditionally to mean' to commit massacres?

These considerations lead me to think that Christians have to regard themselves as *not* contributing to the debate on policy, and as people who mustn't get into the position of having to be willing to set off certain sorts of destructive apparatus; just as they ought to regard themselves as excluded from dropping bombs on cities.

23*

Simony in Africa

> When Simon saw that the Holy Ghost was given through the laying on of the apostles' hands, he offered them money, saying 'Give me this power too ...'. But Peter said to him, 'Your silver perish with you, because you have thought to obtain the gift of God with money. You have no part or lot in this word. For your heart is not right in face of God. Repent of your wickedness, then, and ask God, if the intent of your heart may be forgiven you. For I see that you are into the gall of bitterness and the bond of iniquity.' Simon said in answer: 'Pray for me to the Lord, so that none of what you have said may come upon me.' (*Acts* 8: 18-24)

In the autumn of 1969 there appeared a short article 'Schism in Kenya', signed P H Dirwen MHM, in the little magazine *Missions and Missionaries*. This is about a movement or body which started in Kenya in 1963, in the first place through the action of a woman, Gaudencia Aoko, of the tribe of the Luo, who are an agricultural and pastoral people living around the eastern shores of Lake Victoria.

> They accepted Christianity eagerly when it was presented to them some sixty years ago by the Mill Hill Missionaries ... The Missionaries, handicapped by an acute shortage of personnel, and deeply involved in the school system, had not enough time for the adequate pastoral care of the constantly increasing number of converts. As a result, many were converts in name only and did not practice their religion[1]; others returned to their pagan practices.

Gaudencia Aoko promised two things in particular, to cure people of illnesses by driving out the devils and thus expose the frauds of

* Undated typescript of a paper given at a meeting of the Common Room Society of the Beda College, Rome, probably in October 1978 (and not later than January 1979).

[1] This circumstance, of course, having no parallel in *our* European society!

the expensive witch-doctors, and *to give free baptisms*. 'I don't charge anything', she said, 'it is all free. *I don't believe anyone should charge* for a gift given to him or her by God. Our people are very poor and can't afford to pay to be rescued from the clutches of the devils.' Her message, the author says, was 'one of hope to many who were ... victims, too, of the demands of the Church for a period of instruction before baptism *and of a small contribution towards the upkeep of their Church*; victims, moreover, of involvement in polygamy, bringing with it denial of baptism and the sacraments.'

What developed was a separate church called the 'Maria Legio'. Gaudencia Aoko had wanted people to take their instruction from the Catholic missionaries, but a man, Simeon Ondeto, developed a new church, with himself as Pope: a colourful organization with cardinals and bishops and numerous priests to assist him. Gaudencia Aoko 'resents the fact that her original plan of sending those baptised by the Maria Legio to the Catholic missions for instruction has been thwarted by Simeon'.

The passages I have italicised in these extracts from the article prompted an enquiry by a member of my family of the then editor of *Missions and Missionaries*. Was it really true that people had to pay in order to be baptised? The answer was a rap over the knuckles: one must be very ill-instructed not to know that Catholics had a duty of supporting their church.

More recently, further enquiry has elicited the statement that it is the regular practice in many of the countries of Africa to insist on people paying a sum of money if they are to be baptised. A black bishop from Uganda, however, told me that there was no such thing known in his place. Of course the church of Uganda is a good deal older than the church of the Luo. About these more recent missions, it has been explained to me, it was determined 'not to make the mistake we made in the East'—the mistake, that is, of not making the people realise their responsibility for their church. They are thus trained to contribute to it, and, above all, they cannot receive baptism without first paying a certain sum. The purpose of this is that they should manifest their good disposition: 'Just as if someone will not give up concubinage he cannot be baptised, so equally, if he will not manifest his disposition to support the church by contributing a sum of money according to the local discipline of the church, equally he cannot be baptised.' I put this into quotation marks because, being greatly struck by it, I wrote it down in the presence of a witness and checked with the speaker that I had got it right. He was the editor of the magazine in 1975, preaching on behalf of the A.P.F.* in Cambridge.

The Gospel for that day was the story of the sending out of the seventy. 'Freely you have received, freely give.' In the translation actually used it ran: 'You have received without pay, give without pay.'** This Gospel must sound like a pretty bad joke to the African congregations, who are probably made sensitive to the matter by the actions of Gaudencia Aoko.

So apparently it is and has long been the custom in various African countries for priests to refuse baptism except on payment of a sum of money to them. This is simony.

They deny this. They say that they are not making the people 'pay for' the sacrament of baptism. They are 'requiring the manifestation of a disposition to support the Church'. Of course Christians must support the Church!

A sum of money must be handed over to the priests or they will not baptise you, even though you are an instructed Christian believer and you ask for baptism. This act, they suppose, is made *not* to be an act of simony by *thinking* of it as not 'payment for' something. Something, indeed, that they will give to people sufficiently instructed once the money is given them. And will not give otherwise.

Their motives are good! They wished to teach these people their duty of supporting their church. Naturally it is right to teach people that duty. How could it be denied? And so, in some parts, after baptism, everyone who wishes to be a 'Catholic in good standing' will subscribe his little sum every month—say a shilling out of earnings of five pounds—a hundredth of his income; in so small an income, a significant amount, more, much more than if I gave a hundredth of my much larger income. He will have a little book in which it is recorded, month by month, that as far as support of the Church goes he is entitled to be considered a 'Catholic in good standing'. —Should we object to *this* practice?—Not that I know of or will suggest here. I mean: one would have to know more about it, to know whether to object to it. For it is true that we have a duty to support the Church.

* The Association for the Propagation of the Faith, an organization within the Catholic Church in England and Wales which exists to provide material support for the Church in missionary territories.

** *Matthew* 10. 8. The reference is to the story of the sending out of the twelve apostles, not to the sending out of the seventy (or seventy two) disciples.

But it is another thing altogether that one of the considerations on which someone may be baptised is his payment of a sum of money.

It has been known in this country in this century that people (no doubt deemed otherwise also suitable) have obtained peerages through handing over sums of money to party funds, to Lloyd George's chest, to various people who were in a position to get them peerages. What is it always called? It is called the sale of honours. Someone who said 'They were not paying for peerages, they were making a contribution' or the like—well, no one that I ever heard of ever did have the impudence to talk like that.

St Peter seems to have missed his opportunity. When Simon Magus offered him money, of course he could not accept it straight off. But all he needed to do was to give Simon Magus a lesson in semantics: 'You are to understand', he should have said, 'that I will not be conferring spiritual power on you *for* this money; you are not to think of yourself as buying it or paying for it. Such things *cannot* be bought. But since you are making this contribution to the church and you desire this spiritual power, I will confer it upon you. Of course, I would not do so if you did not make the contribution.'

You cannot turn the donation of a sum of money, when it is a consideration without which you will not do something for a person, into something that is *not* a payment for that service, by refusing to *call* it a payment.

This is something that common humanity understands perfectly well. And so the people speak of paying for baptism, of being able or not able to afford baptism, of baptism not being free, but having to be bought.

The *motive* of these priests we understand and have explained. But how were they able to deceive themselves so about what they were actually doing? I believe the explanation lies in this: the nature of your action *does* depend on your intention in performing, say, the physical movements in which it is accomplished. The passage of coins from one hand to another may be all sorts of things, and *what* it is is greatly dependent on the intention with which it is performed.

Quite true: but now, what determines what the intention is? Can you determine it by telling yourself and others 'I am not doing *this*, I am doing *that*'? No, you can't: the facts of the case, the conditions and consequences of your act are mostly enough to determine *what* intentional *action* you are performing, they often declare it very loud and clear, and you cannot make it not to be so by a story you tell or by inviting people to perform some little semantic exercise and *call* something a different name from the name that belongs to it from the facts of the case. For the intention, by which an act is one of making and receiving a payment, or is something different (such as discharging an old debt, for example), is not some adjustment of a private internal mechanism which can be made as you like and then brought to engage with an outward act. If you voluntarily do a certain thing, such as receiving money, it is the whole context that fixes and determines the further description of the kind of act you are performing. It is no use for a politician accused of corruption to say that such and such moneys were paid or gifts made just as a mark of friendship: the judge, if the circumstances are appropriate, will see that the transaction is a *bribe*.

So far as any theoretical considerations have gone into the formation of the leathery consciences of these simoniacs, I suspect that they are connected with this ludicrous application of a doctrine of the 'direction of intention'.

I speak of 'leathery consciences' because, having made the mistake in the first place, these people did not see the red light, were not alerted, halted, stopped in their tracks, by the action of Gaudencia Aoko. On the contrary, they condemned her instead of themselves, because her baptism was 'irregular'; I have even known one say 'it would be ineffectual' because of this irregularity.

It is worthwhile to look up the opinion of St Thomas Aquinas on this matter. It will be a shock even to those who are dismayed at the history I have called to their attention.

> Baptism is the gate of the sacraments. But it is lawful, it seems, in some case to give money for baptism, say when a priest would not baptize a dying child without payment. Therefore it is not always unlawful to buy or sell sacraments ... Reply: In case of necessity, anybody can baptize. And because we ought not to sin in any way, we ought to count it the same thing if a priest will not baptize without payment, as if there were not one to give baptism at all. So whoever has care of a child can lawfully baptize him in such a case, or have him baptized by anybody else. (He could however lawfully buy water from the priest, which is a mere corporeal element.) But if there were an adult who desired baptism, and if he were in imminent danger of death, and the priest would not baptize him without payment, he ought if possible to get someone else to baptize him. If he could not have recourse to someone else, he ought by no means to give payment for baptism, but rather to die without baptism. For what he lacked from

the sacrament would be supplied to him by the baptism of the Spirit.[2]

Objection to making or asking payment of money as a condition of baptism could not be made more strongly than this. One may be momentarily surprised at the extreme form of St Thomas's opinion. Brief reflection shows that it is right. For the crime of simony is not only that of demanding payment, but also (and more originally) of making or offering it. Both parties commit it, who make of the sacraments and spiritual powers things that are bought and sold. Simony itself may not be the negation of faith, disbelief in the power and promises of God; but the *defence* of it will be that.

St Thomas brings home to us the enormous gravity and heinousness of this practice. Across nearly the whole of that continent (and where else?) the Mill Hill Missionaries have instituted this 'discipline'. This is something to tear the heart, to make one first kneel before the altar weeping and crying 'Lord, how was this possible? Why did you allow *this*?' For it is worse than anything that has ever been in the Church.

I may seem to exaggerate. But think about it. The Church in *so huge an area* has been poisoned in its incipience. These people have been damaged in their entry into it, have been given a contaminated Christianity in its origination in each person. Not just here and there by an unfortunate degeneration, a sad lapse into venality. Not by an outbreak of worldly wickedness, which everyone knows is that. Nor is it a case of the high authorities of the Church conscientiously and from little faith engaging in what are really betrayals. Those are the three principal types of wound which continuing members of the Church have been accustomed to inflict upon her.[3] But this is different from all of these. It may seem no different; it may seem merely to be a mixture of the first and the third, to be merely very extensive. But here greatness of quantity makes a change in quality. For where are the victims and poor accomplices, the people, to learn, in what are they to know the Church and Christ?

---

[2] St Thomas Aquinas, *Summa theologiae* 2a 2ae, q.100, a.2, first objection and reply.

[3] In the late 1960's there was a row in the English [Catholic] Church because the national press picked up and made news of a reference to 'corruption' of the Church by the Editor of *Blackfriars*. He was following my friend Michael Dummett, who however remarked that if there should be something theologically incorrect about speaking of 'corruption' he begged to be understood as saying whatever it was correct to say in referring to certain facts. The sentence here flagged supplies, I think, the alternative way of speaking of which he obscurely felt the need.

And, secondly, how painful, how almost unspeakably painful it is, to think of the missionary priests themselves. They must so many of them have been moved by generosity in giving their lives for this work; and it has proved a trap to them.

When young men in training for the priesthood are taught about the requirements of obedience, they are of course taught that it can never be one if what they are ordered to do is to commit a sin. Example: 'As', the lecturer laughingly says, 'if I were to order you to commit fornication'—and everybody smiles. Well, here is a better example. 'As', the lecturer should say, 'if your superior should require you to exact a money offering as a condition of baptism'. The example given ought to be a known, a real, possibility.

Here in England the news of what has been done in Africa is likely to be a shock to many people, to many earnest supporters of the Missionaries. Let me warn them that approaches to the authorities who have been concerned produces no satisfaction, only smooth words such as I have quoted. Some people may be placated by such words, or easily confused by a bit of the twisty thinking that sometimes passes for moral theology. Others will remain perturbed. Our own clergy would never dream of making such exactions. It may in some places be common practice to make an offering to the local church when you are baptised or when you bring someone for baptism. If so, it is not widespread enough among us to appear as a necessary condition. And it is unimaginable that our priests should say 'No offering, no baptism'. Let them, if any are reading this, just try to imagine it! They *know* they could not do it. They would not want to do it.

Our priests are even becoming sensitive about mass stipends, and when one raises my present subject, this is the first comparison that is made. Now as to that matter, I have no very strong conviction, it may possibly be an undesirable practice—but such conviction as I have is that there is absolutely nothing wrong with mass stipends. Nor should we shilly-shally about what it is to give a mass stipend. One is paying for a mass to be said for a *particular* purpose that one has at heart. It is bad, indeed, if one can't ask a priest to say a mass for a particular purpose without paying a mass stipend. And if a priest would never say mass at all if he did not get a mass stipend for it, he would be a bad priest. He would certainly not be a possible parish priest, or any that has a care of souls. We need priests to say mass; we need the sacrifice to be offered. That is the main reason why priests are (modestly) supported. Imagine a state in which all were like St

Paul in earning their living at manual labour, but, having the power of saying mass, were usually too busy and could be got to do so only upon request! The offering of mass and the administration of the sacraments is the work for which they are maintained in a general way. Thus, that mass should be offered for the Christian people is *not* something for which any *ad hoc* payment for each one is appropriate.

But that is all. It is no simony to pay for a particular purpose to be prayed for with the prayer of the mass. If the priest wouldn't give one communion when he said mass, if one had not made a payment —that would be simony.[4] (And similarly for any sacrament and any spiritual jurisdiction.)

So I say to the English clergy: do not allow yourselves to be confused or made uneasy, given a false bad conscience, by the fact that you, or many of you, receive mass stipends. Do not let it cloud your recognition of the horror of simoniac baptism of the Catholic converts in Africa. *Ecrasez l'infame!* Throw the weight of Christian opinion against this practice, so that it may cease as soon as possible. It won't stop unless it is perceived for what it is.

---

[4] I once heard an entertaining story—surely American?—of a little dispensing machine to make a sanitary issue of unconsecrated hosts by the depression of a lever; thus what you got wasn't contaminated by the touch of a fellow communicant. The next trick was to have the dispenser worked by the insertion of a small coin. But here authority interposed. This could not be allowed.

24*

Philosophers and Economists: Two Philosophers' Objections to Usury

To demand usury is defined as demanding interest, high or low, on the mere strength of a loan. To share the profits on a productive investment for which you have put up the capital is, according to rabbis and Christian theologians, though not according to Muslims, not to take usury. (Muslims equate usury and interest and forbid usury, hence difficulties about capital investment in Pakistan.)

But what is the objection? Call it rent: this at any rate is St Thomas's picture, and it seems reasonable: you pay for the hire of something, a house, say, and yet have to restore the house intact to its owner at the end. So why not the same for money?

Aristotle's answer is that there's something perverse about it: money is the medium of exchange, and can't itself be made the commodity bought or sold without, so to speak, going against its nature.** This is rather interesting, as after all, money, in the sense of definite weights of gold or silver, presumably started as a commodity. Some people say that coined silver got into circulation through being found tremendously useful as a medium of exchange, though in the first place the stamp was just a guarantee of weight and purity by the people who were exporting it simply as silver. I don't know that this is entirely plausible, since weighed amounts of silver and gold, in small enough amounts to be perfectly useful for small trans-

* Paper presented at a General Seminar of the Faculty of Philosophy, University of Cambridge, 4 November 1970. Unpublished.

** Aristotle, *Politics* 1258b1-8.

actions, are mentioned for fixing workmen's wages and fines as long ago as the Code of Hammurabi, which is four thousand years. Stamped pieces are just a mark of technological advance and I doubt whether it is sensible to hail their appearance in the sixth century in Lydia as 'the invention of money'. A propos, St Thomas says that if you are genuinely hiring coins as *objects*, for display, say, there is nothing wrong with both having to pay a rent for them and having to return them. Text-bookily, money is called a standard of value (or unit of account), a medium of exchange, and a store of wealth. We can see it doesn't make sense to speak of rent on a unit of account; Aristotle's objection seems to be that you can't really speak of rent on a medium of exchange; but someone might say: Why not of rent on a store of wealth?

St Thomas expressed the objection in a more fundamental way.* If you lend a consumable good, you can ask for the equivalent back (that, after all, is what lending is) but you cannot ask for payment for the use of it as well, because you are recompensed for the use of it you let the person have, in getting back the equivalent; and a consumable good is not anything over and above the use of it so that you can both ask for the equivalent back and for payment for use. It is clear, then, that he would object to 'taking interest' as *Exodus*** calls it, of any consumable goods, such as bread; and in *Deuteronomy**** the prohibition on usury explicitly mentions other consumables, not merely money.

The argument is not an easy one. It would have been easier if it had run: if you lend a loaf you can charge a (reasonable) hire on it while it is being used, but you can't ask for it or its worth back again, because using it is *using it up* and you've already been paid for that in being paid for its use. But of course nobody charges hire on a thing like a loaf; and hire on money, which meant you did not have to repay the money, would not be called hire but piecemeal repayment, possibly plus an addition. However, I think we can see St Thomas's argument if we imagine hire on a loaf of bread, and say that if you pay that you can't also be expected to repay the equivalent of the loaf itself, for what you were paying for was the use of it, which is precisely *using it up*; if therefore someone proposed such a contract he would be demanding to be paid for something he had already been paid for, and that would be fraudulent. (We might actually consider the case

* St Thomas Aquinas, *Summa theologiae* 2a 2ae, q.78, a.1c.

** *Exodus* 22.25.

*** *Deuteronomy* 23. 9f

of a consumable good of a kind that lasts for a long time but does get worn out in the end, like a wireless set or a vacuum cleaner: it would be iniquitous to be asked both to pay hire on the thing and to supply a new one or its price at the end of the period of hire which had been long enough to exhaust the life of the machine.)

Now St Thomas says that money is a consumable good, which is 'used up and dispersed' in being spent; i.e. you are not to consider '*the*' money that you lent as existing once someone has spent it, any more than a loaf once someone has eaten it. This enables us to answer the objection: why not rent on a sum of money as a store of wealth? The answer would be: money as a store of wealth is comparable to seed as a store of crop-life. Seed, like money, can be kept for a long time and used at any time; but if the seed is used—i.e. planted to grow a crop, it dies and does not exist any more. So you could ask for a share in the crop; or a greater amount of seed if it is used to make more seed; but if it was just a loan of so much seed, all you can ask is the same quantity back.[1]

It is interesting that those philosophers, to whom money was certainly physical gold and silver, should have refused to regard it as a permanent commodity but said that 'it' was no such thing, concentrating on the character in regard to which it is an abstraction, whereas we, to whom money really is practically nothing but a mental construction, should be so clear that it is a permanent commodity!

Now how is it that the Catholic Church, which condemned usury in unretractable terms as late as 1745,* should have fallen silent about it; and further, how is it that to all economists, apparently, the objection to it makes complete nonsense? The interest of these questions led me to do some slight research, not high class: mainly, I fear, secondary or tertiary sources of which I will give the results.

First, as to the economists. Keynes tells us, in the appendix to the *General Theory*, that he was brought up to regard the medieval objection as obvious nonsense, and their attempts to distinguish getting a

* Benedict XIV, Encyclical letter *Vix pervenit* to the Bishops of Italy, 1 November 1745. [Denzinger-Schönmetzer, *Enchiridion Symbolorum Definitionum et Declarationum de rebus fidei et morum*, editio XXXVI, 1976: §§2546–2550.]

[1] An economics tutor at Oxford (with the advantages of a philosophical training) has explained to me that I have got it all wrong: interest on money but not *hire* of money. It is payment *for having something now instead of later*. This, however, does not seem accurate, as after all I pay to have something now any time I buy something. One may of course pay now for something one is to have later, or pay now when one might pay later, and demand a discount.

return on investment from getting interest on a loan as Jesuitical evasions of the consequences of an absurd position. He came to think, however, that there was more in their theory than he had supposed: namely, that they were feeling after the distinction which he formulated, between the 'rate of interest and the marginal efficiency of capital'.* Now I will confess that this does not seem very plausible to me, because his concept of the marginal efficiency of capital appears to me to be a rather usurious one, at least in spirit.

'It now seems clear', he says, 'that the disquisitions of the schoolmen were directed towards a formula which should allow the schedule of the marginal efficiency of capital to be high, whilst using rule or custom or the moral law to keep down the rate of interest.'** Now I assume that by this he meant that the object was to get people willing to lay out *more* capital for *less* profit. I doubt whether theologians had any economic policy; that however might be a fair way of stating what their teaching came to economically. I don't think, however, that Keynes's conception is free of the spirit of usury, which the schoolmen would have wished to combat. For he defines marginal efficiency as the rate of discount which would make the value of the prospective profits equal to the supply price, or cost of replacement. And the term 'rate of discount' rather strongly suggests e.g. paying £90 now to get £100 later on: that is a 10% discount. Suppose, then, to state the point in an extreme way, that you lay out £1000 now on something that is going to yield £5 a year for 20 years and will then be quite used up. I disregard complications about compound interest and so on: then £1000 now has yielded £100 over the years; if therefore we speak of a rate of discount here, we must call it a rate of discount of 90%. If this is allowed by Keynes's language, and I think it may be if we take it strictly, then that is all right; but it is not just the first thing one thinks of if one talks about rates of discount. And *any* interest, if it is lawful to take interest, is a better bargain than this. And yet it would be false to say that doing this would not be getting *a* return on your money. And if all sorts of things in a society—law, custom, your status and its obligations—conduced to make this the absolutely obvious thing for you to do with that money (although someone else may be laying out £1000 on part of a merchant cargo which will bring him in £3000 when the ship comes home, and such differences strike no one as odd), it might be that you would do it

* John Maynard Keynes, *The General Theory of Employment, Interest and Money* (London: Macmillan & Co. Ltd, 1936), pp. 351–2.
** *op.cit.*, p.352.

without regarding yourself as a philanthropist or a loser; and isn't it almost certainly the case that a lot of things that need money laid out on them might be something like this? Houses, for example. An interesting light is thrown on his attitude by his praising the people who tried to keep interest down, even invoking the moral law to do so; he obviously thinks of morality as a sort of force that might be invoked for any purpose you had in mind.

Nevertheless Keynes does seem to have had a rather destructive effect on the old conception of interest, and economists who were still a bit classically minded complained that his explanation of interest amounted to this: that there is interest because there is interest. For Keynes's explanation is in terms of liquidity preference, and liquidity preference has motives which are all concerned with what you expect to happen in the markets, and therefore partly with what you expect to happen to the rate of interest. Thus, as it was complained, interest seems to be something that pulls itself up by its own bootstraps, and as Joan Robinson put it, people seemed to have an awful horror of bootstraps. But, as both she and Mr Harrod have pointed out, there really is no particular objection to bootstraps, here; why should not Keynes have had the rights of the matter?

Now, though Keynes speaks kindly of the medieval objection, it is clear enough that he didn't grasp it at all; and we get further light on this from some consideration of Mr Harrod's. He tells us that he once had an awfully good idea, namely that the objection to usury went with land's being unmarketable and inalienable; however, his medievalist friends assured him that this was only a pretty picture, as there never was a time when this was so; he therefore had to resign himself to the fact that the medieval theory did not make sense at all. (I have not been able to determine *why* his explanation would have been one if it had been true.)

I regard it as a great merit in Keynes that there generally is no ethic in him and a sign of poison in an economist that he puts in an ethical justification for a payment's being made—such as 'the reward of waiting' or 'the reward of abstinence'. Professor Robinson made short work of these considerations, pointing out that there really is no particular reason why a person should not pay *more* now to have *some* later (this in fact is what any clearheaded person is doing who at present 'saves', i.e. buys National Savings Certificates); and so for the abstaining, that is usually inflicted on other people than those who propose to get the 'reward'. But I observe that to her—and reasonably enough, I believe—the distinction between a return on money through ownership of debts and through ownership of shares in some productive venture did not appear a very significant one. Reasonably, because in the present if you lay out money to get a return, you probably look only at the market's display of possibilities and have not the slightest real interest in or connection with the companies in which you invest. Further, productivity is itself measured in terms of money making, but it often happens that a venture is 'productive' by driving some other product off the market and in *no* other way.

I remained perplexed by the utter failure of economists to see any point in the objection to usury. For it appeared to me that *I* could understand well enough the distinction between investing in a capital venture, with a view to sharing the profits *if* it should succeed, and demanding interest on the mere strength of a loan. I therefore went back to older texts: in particular, to Ricardo; and here at last I thought I saw light. For Ricardo describes how, as soon as in a new country second quality land (which will produce 90 quarters per acre per annum) comes into cultivation, first quality land (producing 100 quarters) acquires a *rent* of 10 quarters. For otherwise the *same* capital outlay will be producing a *different* rate of profit. And now at last I got an inkling: the cardinal principle of economic science is this, that the same capital outlay must produce the same profit. This is of course not in accordance with the facts; but differences in fact are explained partly by things like time lags, contributing to friction, and partly by *calling* differences 'rent'.

If we contemplate this principle, I think we can see it has, so to speak, two faces. In one way, it is just a practical point: if two adjacent shops sell visibly identical articles, they probably can't charge different prices. So, if you are thinking of farming, in the situation Ricardo describes, you clearly won't pay rent on second quality land, if you understand how things are; and will pay rent of 10 quarters on first quality land. That is, other things being equal. I will call this the 'shop-window aspect' of the cardinal principle. It has another quite different aspect: namely that it is required if economics is to be a formal science at all.

If anyone expressed doubt of the principle, it would be presented in its shop-window aspect. As a formal principle, it is very lacking in the power to describe any reality unless things have, so to speak, *got into* a shop window. But that is exactly what they have done by the creation of stock markets and money markets. And that money just as such should command a rate of interest is an important part of the works. The essential condition, however, is that there should be a vast amount of business simply concerned in laying out money with a view to making more money, and providing a picture in which the obvious thing to do with any money was to lay it out to make as much more money as markets allowed; anything else would be conscious extravagance or conscious philanthropy, etc.

Whereas, it would seem to me proper to think that if you had spare money you might in fact be able to do something with it that notably enriched you, but most probably not; and that while it might take religion or esteem of learning or desire for the repute of one or the other to make you spend it on building a church or founding a college, it would be reasonable to do something else, like building a house, just because a house was required in this place, and it was part of your function, when you had the disposal of some spare money, to do that sort of thing with it. Houses, in fact, are a very interesting case. I should be inclined to think that it is reasonable to build a house and let it to someone, just because you know the house is a useful thing; and that it is reasonable that your rent should yield you some small profit: but that the reasonable rent of a house is not to be calculated in terms of return on capital outlay in building the house compared to every other possible return on outlay of the same capital; it should be enough to pay for the *permanent upkeep* of the house if that is not left to the tenant, and I suppose give the landlord *some* profit besides. But in face of a system in which everything is in a money- and stock-market shop window and you can always lay out your money to get a return, *such* a conception of the business of building a house becomes totally out-of-date—until the wheel comes full circle and the tax on profits (unless a farmer, say, chooses to build a few cottages) is so great that he decides to build some because he might as well—and farmers think it a great joke that the madness of the time and the proceedings of the government are such that a man might as well build a few cottages because his profits won't be any good to him anyway and he'd as soon do that as put it into the government's pocket! For the reserved idea of 'a fair return on capital', a phrase we become very familiar with in connection with rent bills for example, is: a return on capital which is much the same as you would get from some other investment.

* * *

My other enquiry was: how did the Catholic Church come to lose its grip on this question? It is quite an interesting story, of which I have a few salient fragments.

In the late medieval times, there were firms dealing in the transfer of money from one country to another. Clearly, if they had the job of transferring both ways, they would have no need of actually shipping coin, except for the balance of traffic one way over another. As shipping coin was expensive, they adjusted their charges for the services in order to tend always to equalise the traffic, partly directly, partly be way of encouraging the flow in the required direction, discouraging it in the other. The rates of course could not rise so high that the expense of arranging a transfer through them was actually greater than that of shipping coin; that was the upper limit. It is clear that this was a legitimate business from the point of view of the strictest theologian.

However, it seems to have been one of the things that led to the prohibition on usury's becoming a complete dead letter in the following way: I want to borrow £100 from you. So I give you a bill on myself in some foreign place, and you give me the £100; I have no coin in that foreign place, but, when the bill falls due, draw a bill back on myself at home, as from that place, with which to meet the first bill. I then meet the second bill at home. (The transaction might even be a genuine foreign exchange transaction in the sense that what it actually costs me depends on the fluctuating rates for transfer of money.) Now I don't know whether this might not have been condemned as a form of the famous Mohatra contract[2], but it is pretty clear that we are at a stage when it is excessively difficult to distinguish, to say what is legitimate and what is not, on the old principles.

Modern banking is apparently founded on the highly successful dishonesty of the goldsmiths in late medieval times. Their receipts for coin deposited with them circulated as money: they made loans, perhaps in the form of chits, backed by this coin; they could, further, lend out the coin again. The success was determined, so we are told, by the actual need for money in circulation in the expansion of trade, which the existing coin was totally inadequate to cope with.

---

[2] The Mohatra contract was this: you ask to borrow £80. I say 'I'll sell you this little box for £100; you needn't pay me now, but I'll buy the box straight back for £80'. It was condemned by Innocent XI as a dodge for extorting money without seeming to. A modern theologian just says blandly 'It is not now unlawful'.

And with that I come to the only thesis that I can put forward about interest. But before I propose it, I will draw attention to one other grave consequence—as I suppose it to be—of the confused state of mind about interest into which theologians fell. Not every payment or service in connection with money lent was excluded: the essential thing was that there should be a 'reasonable title' other than just the loan. If, e.g.. making you the loan deprives me of something I ought to have, as St Thomas puts it, I can ask you to make it up to me as a condition of the loan. I take it that what he has in mind is that e.g. you might need £50 urgently which is all I have to live on this month; I then say 'All right, I'll lend it you, but I'm afraid you'll have to feed me, as I've no other means'. Now 'a title other than the mere loan' seems to have become a magical formula, and someone invented the title 'risk'—a monstrosity, I should say. In 1645 an enquiry came to an unimportant meeting of a Roman Congregation—I mean one whose decisions were not regarded as solemn ones—whether the Chinese Christians could lend at 30% interest, in accordance with Chinese law; title: risk. The permission was given. Among the Chinese in this century the reputation of the Catholic missionaries was that of cruel usurers to their defenceless tenants whom they could punish at will in private courts; and in view of the story of that permission, the reputation may perhaps have been deserved. It is in such an example as this that we feel what I suppose is the *popular* objection to usury: that a man might have paid interest to the value of the whole original loan several times over and still be deeper in debt than he ever was before. Isn't he robbed? Yes, but why, unless he is robbed anyway if interest is demanded on an unproductive loan.

My thesis, which I will put up for examination, is this: the existence of the automatic right of money to bear interest is something that essentially goes with a stock market; and further is something that must go against prosperity unless trade and productivity are continually expanding. For if interest is paid, then either there must be a real increase of productivity, or there must be a flow of the country's money into the hands of the people who already have money (to them that have shall be given) or there must be inflation. The second tendency might of course be counteracted by taxation.

An important thing to notice is that the surplus that productive work produces cannot indefinitely go into more and more capital ventures to make more and more money. Where then should it go? Keynes, who in the 1930s thought sheer expenditure was necessary to counteract depression, thought that the fact that Ancient Egyptians built pyramids and the Medievals sang dirges and built cathedrals was conducive to prosperity, or at least preventive of depression. Better 'dig holes in the ground and fill them up again' than not spend. His own praise of 'valuable human activities' such as cultured people will promote if they have the money to do so, has that indescribably tinny early twentieth century Cambridge thinness (intrinsically good experiences and all that) which marks him when he is not being strictly professional. I understand that the same problems do not exist now, rather the contrary; but I imagine that there is always a question what a fairly prosperous society puts its surplus into, and in our case I suppose the answer is easy enough: mainly into atomic research, space travel and 'defence'.

These considerations appear to me to throw some light on the necessity of communism, as I might call it. The capitalistic system—to put it in a nutshell—necessarily leads in the end to things like a housing shortage: that is an epitome of its consequences, which I will leave to your imaginations to expand in accordance with my thesis. (It should be needless to say that I do not suggest that actual communist societies don't have things like housing shortages!)

I also suppose that it is idle to speculate how society might possibly have developed if it had been marked by respect for the anti-usury law, assuming it not hamstrung by lack of money in circulation. By a society so marked I do not mean one in which there are not people breaking the laws. In any society it can be safely predicted that quite a lot of people will do so. Thus in every society there will be murders; and in every society that has money as an institution—and before, probably—there will be usurers. Further, it can be safely predicted that in any society the people who are not usurers—we'll suppose that this is regarded as an evil occupation—will most of them *not* act generously as far as concerns making loans from their surplus. For this reason usurers are actually necessary and useful, as St Thomas insists, since there will be people needing loans who can't get them otherwise. It might seem to follow that in a highly developed mercantile society interest must assume the dominant role it has in ours. I do not think that it does follow. So I do not exclude the possibility of a high mercantile and industrial development in which usury—i.e. the demand for interest on the mere strength of a loan—is indeed to be found, but *is not the king-pin of the whole system.* But what that would have looked like and how it might have grown up instead of what did, it is fairly idle for me, perhaps for anyone, to try and imagine. (I'm not thinking of it as an 'ideal' society; it might easily be marked by an addiction to ritual murder, for example.)

25*

On Wisdom

There is an ancient Greek saying, πολυμαθίη νόον ἔχειν οὐ διδάσκει, 'Much learning doesn't teach you sense', the truth of which is fairly obvious. This, in spite of the fact that you need to have a fair—often, a considerable—amount of intelligence in order to be justly counted as having a lot of learning. The Greek word νόος, which I have translated 'sense', might be translated 'intelligence', but I think 'sense' is better because what the author of this maxim was thinking of was obviously that much learning doesn't make you wise. Wisdom is something beyond technical intelligence. You might say: One needs wisdom to know when and how to exercise one's technical intelligence well; and sometimes to know that one needs a particular technical intelligence to deal with some matter, and hasn't got it.

This is of special relevance in considering the topic of the future of higher education. There has developed in this century, if not before, a certain deadly fault in the exercise of the still higher education that some have received. It is connected with the great esteem that accrues to learned and clever people if they leave their mark on a subject. This may be achieved by successfully insisting that a commonly held assumption or opinion is mistaken. No doubt this is sometimes right. That butter is better for one than margarine may be an example. I don't know if some original cardiologist made his name by surprisingly denouncing butter, only that cardiologists tend to be hostile to butter now; and they may be entirely correct. The general field of what may be bad for you is so prominent that it has become rather a joke, but that doesn't mean that a cardiologist's disapproval of French fries as a frequent item of diet is as mistaken as it is likely to be ineffective.

* Tex t of a lecture delivered during the 25th International University Congress, Rome, 13–14 April 1992. Published in *Acta Philosophica* 2 (1993), pp. 127–33. The present printing restores emphases in the original typescript.

I want, here and now, not to attend to sound and unsound opinions and practices in eating and drinking, but to concentrate on a quite different field of possible, or even frequent, misbehaviour. It is that of translations of the Scriptures.

I have been startled by some things here, in ways which have convinced me that these were cases of misbehaviour. I have heard readings at Mass which have made me jump and think 'Can that be right? It doesn't sound like what I've been used to.' One time was when I heard a reading from St Paul's letter to the Galatians, chapter 1, where he said he spent fifteen days seeing Peter in Jerusalem. The reading went on 'I did not see any other apostle. I saw James, the brother of the Lord.' Hearing this I hurried home to look up the Greek, which seemed to say 'I did not see any other apostle *except* James the brother of the Lord', which was how I remembered the passage. The Greek is ἐι μὴ two words which taken together mean 'unless' but which form a very usual way of saying 'except'—the way, indeed, that the older translations I looked at take them. Being myself in Jerusalem a few months later, I consulted François Dreyfus OP,* who took me to look at Lagrange's commentary. Here the matter was discussed, Lagrange mentioning one or two places where it doesn't look as if ἐι μὴ meant 'except' but concluding that it pretty surely does mean 'except' in this text of St Paul. I wondered why on earth this new translation had been foisted on us, and concluded that what had been at work to start with was the ambition I have mentioned, to make one's name by introducing new and different translations. The particular matter was not of very great importance, but I noted it as an example of the various kinds of things that seem wrong in the readings of the Scriptures that we hear at Mass. The punch line in a story is left out, e.g. some things never read, like what St Paul wrote about 'Israel according to the flesh'—i.e. the unbelieving Jews who did not join in that formation of the early Church almost entirely by Jews. To this I might add a fault in the English translations which is not new but very old. It is especially noticeable in translations of St John's Gospel, where it is repeatedly said that the Jews wanted to kill or otherwise get rid of Jesus, that he was warned that the Jews were after him, and so on. These passages are quite incomprehensible when you remember the facts; they make a per-

* François Paul Dreyfus (1918–1999); a convert from Judaism who became a Dominican priest and biblical scholar; Professor of New Testament Studies at the Dominican House of Studies, Le Saulchoir, 1957–1969; Professor of Biblical Theology at the École Biblique et Archéologique Française in Jerusalem, 1969–1990.

verted sense to later non-Jewish Christians. They'd become intelligible if the word given was 'Judaeans' (meaning the authorities of the main people living in Judaea) and not 'Jews'; the Greek and Latin do not make a difference in the word for 'Jews' and the word for 'Judaeans' and hence the unintelligible translation in languages that do.

I encountered something much more serious last year. We were discussing what our Lord meant when he said to Pontius Pilate 'Those who are of the truth hear my voice'. Who were, or are, 'those who are of the truth'? I reminded the man who was talking with me of what it says earlier in St John's Gospel, chapter 1 verse 9: 'That was the true light, that enlightens every man who comes into the world'. My interlocutor said he had not heard of that sentence, and he looked it up in the 'revised version', I in some other text I happened to have with me. In both cases it ran: 'The true light, which enlightens everyone (or: every man), was coming into the world.' That is quite different and destroyed my explanation of what Jesus said to Pilate. I had recourse to the Greek text, and found that there was no question of a variant reading, but that because of a peculiarity of Greek grammar, you *could* take 'coming into the world' as a phrase agreeing with 'light'. You just *could*; it was harsh Greek, for reasons I will not bother you with. But I thought 'Aha!—the same thing again—someone decided to offer a new translation just because it occurred to him as grammatically possible.' I then learned that everyone, from the earliest times, and from Augustine and Jerome and subsequent Christians, including Luther and Calvin, had taken it in the way I was used to—right up to the nineteenth century translation my friend happened to have with him.

This was not a trivial matter at all. It had been anciently thought and taught that in the eighth chapter of the *Book of Proverbs*, where Wisdom speaks, that Wisdom is the Word of the Father, the divine Wisdom, the second Person of the Trinity. This is earnestly argued, for example, in St Athanasius's writings against the Arians. And, without knowing *that* fact, I had taken it as true that here was a case of the 'greater', as St Thomas calls them, among the Hebrews having some knowledge of the Holy Trinity in the times before the Messiah was born incarnate into the world. The Wisdom in *Proverbs* 'was life, and the life was the light of men' (*John* 1.4). Thus those who remained true to it—such were the people 'of the truth' of whom Christ said 'They hear my voice'—i.e. the voice of him incarnate as a man who spoke to them in a material voice. You see in this how grave an error was involved in the rendering 'The light was coming into the world'. He was already in the world, and the world was made through him, and his delight 'was with the children of men'—'*deliciae meae esse cum filiis hominum*'. Furthermore, this Wisdom says 'The Lord had me in the beginning of his ways, before he made any beginning of things' (*Proverbs* 8.22). I am told that the word I render here as 'had' is the Hebrew word also for 'begot'. Also: 'before the abysses were made, I was conceived' (*Proverbs* 8.24).

That the divine Wisdom is the source and cause of human reason and speech in its essential working seems to me to be the truth, which a wise intelligence will perceive. But I have a confirmation of this by a highly intelligent present day philosopher who nevertheless has not perceived it.

This philosopher is Willard Van Orman Quine, an American logician, for a long time professor at Harvard. His many books include some not concerned with technicalities of logic alone; he knows many languages and has thought much about problems of translation and communication, of how we know what a piece of language says. His handling of these problems gives occasion for enunciating a famous formula, which expresses a doctrine largely sound and clarifying, but which raises a fundamental difficulty for his this-wordly philosophical programme, by which all possible knowledge should fall within the bounds of 'science' (in the word's usage in English and also in French and Italian). Science so conceived is 'natural science' and is thoroughly materialistic. Quine's famous dictum is: 'To be is to be the value of a variable'. I should offer a brief explanation of this. In modern logical notation we have sentences which can be read 'For all x, x is F'. To give an example, a true proposition of this form would be 'For some x, x is an even prime', i.e. 'Something is an even prime number'. The 'x' in these notations is called a variable, and in a logical system it is likely to be said what the variables, x, y, n and so on 'range over'. n is the most usual letter to choose when you are talking about numbers. Thus we would be most likely to find e.g. 'For some n, n is an even prime' and it would be obvious that the variable n ranges over numbers. There is only one even prime, the number 2, but that doesn't mean that the only possible substitution for n in the 'open sentence' 'n is an even prime' is 2. It is the only substitution for it which results in a *true* sentence: '2 is an even prime', but as the variable n ranges over numbers, you could produce a well-formed but false sentence by substituting 7 or 10 or any other numeral.

Now when Quine said 'To be is to be the value of a variable' he meant that to be is to be a member of the class of things that a variable *ranges over*. Thus, if numbers are what the variable ranges over, numbers are being reckoned to exist.

This brings us to a further idea that Quine has: that of 'ontological commitment'. Your ontological commitment is to the things that your theory *says* there are. That is, you must now not choose *false* sentences like 'There are 3 even primes', but rather true ones like 'There are just five primes from the number 1 to the number 10'—true if 1 itself is allowed to count as a prime number. This proposition implies that there are numbers, and so your adoption of a variable whose values are numbers shows that you have an ontological commitment to numbers.

It is of course possible to criticize this account of existence, but there are many things that are very interesting about it. One of these is that it seems to be a matter of choice what variables you are going to accept in your system. This may not seem correct when the example is 'numbers'; after all, how can you avoid admitting that there is just one even prime number, and *therefore* that for some n, n is a number? This last is rather unlikely to be a theoretical statement that you will find yourself making, but it does seem to be one you'd have to assent to if you granted that 'to be is to be the value of a variable' and that you can express arithmetical truths by using formulae in which the variable n occurs, which ranges over *numbers*. To say you have an ontological commitment to numbers is to say that your theory says that numbers exist, inasmuch as it uses a variable ranging over numbers to say that there are numbers with this or that property.

I now come to a peculiar difficulty which Quine has, though he does not let it bother him to the extent of giving up his thesis. It is that we can find no properly scientific account of *intentional verbs*. If we are strict with ourselves, we shall eschew them. That is to adopt as our own the 'severe' muse of 'science'. But we cannot easily do this, and Quine doesn't want to forbid us e.g. to speak of someone as believing or saying such and such. In his big book *Word and Object* he does indeed find a way of construing sentences to the effect that someone believes something, which allows him not to speak of an intentionality apparently involved in them.

To explain 'intentionality' quickly: a verb like 'believe', indirectly governing a sentence, as in 'James believes that Tom is a thief' might be true of a particular James who knows a particular Tom. But it might nevertheless be false to say 'James believes that his mother's cousin is a thief', even though he believes that Tom is one and *also* Tom is in fact his mother's cousin, but he doesn't know the relationship. Hence the occurrence of 'Tom' is not 'purely referential', since another perfectly true way of referring to Tom can turn a true sentence into a false one. This is the characteristic of intentionality in our verbs of attitude etc. Quine manages to devise a way in which he can take 'believes' *not* as a *term*, but only as part of a longer expression which has not got this characteristic.

But—and this is what I've been leading up to in telling you of Quine's philosophy—he has not found a way of sterilizing the expression 'says that' as it occurs in speaking of what a theory says, so as to make it appear as part of a construction that is innocent of the objectionable characteristic of intentionality. To repeat, he doesn't want to forbid the use of such expressions as have that characteristic—but he does want, or need, to have a possible analysis in the background to which he could retreat. In the case of 'says that' he hasn't got such an analysis. What then becomes of his conception of ontological commitment to what one's chosen theory, or conceptual apparatus, *says* exists?

'Such and such—or so-and-so—says that'—this remains a locution which Quine knows he can't forbid. But his philosophy insists that it *ought* to be forbiddable, because he is in some odd sense a materialist. I say 'in some odd sense' because after all he believes e.g. that *numbers* exist and they are not material. Yet he does not hold that if he followed his conceptions of the scientific, he would have to strive after an analysis involving no mention of numbers. Intentionality however is unacceptable.

If I have any lessons for you in what I have been saying, they are two: (1) beware of modern translations of ancient texts, when the translators may be inspired by the spirit I spoke of. Alas, it has even infected the translators of the Scriptures into Latin. The revised Vulgate perhaps corrects errors of St Jerome; but concerning verse 9 of chapter 1 of St John's Gospel, it *corrects* him where he was not only right, but all importantly so. His text—and the Greek one—say that Jesus was the light that enlightens every man who comes into the world. This leads to (2), for it means first of all that developing humans become able to express, or at least realize, that something *is so*. Quine's fancy here is that there are primarily 'stimulus sentences'. They may consist of just one ejaculation, e.g. 'Rabbit!'. (He makes up the word 'Gavagai'.) We observers discover what stimulus this is a response to by e.g. trying it as a response and seeing whether it itself evokes signs of assent or dissent on the part of the people to whose language it seems to belong. If it evokes assent, we *may* learn that it is a stimulus response to what *we* were trying it as a response to.

This is wrong in so far as it assumes that a primary stimulus response can be regarded as something *saying that* such-and-such is present. But think: one may say 'Mmm' in response to the song of a blackbird. If someone else has a response of the same kind, that may show that their utterance is a suitable translation of our 'Mmm'. It would not show e.g. that anything has been named or said to be present.

Saying what is so, or is to be so, is the act of a word. Not indeed of just any word. (Counter-examples are easy to find.) Not yet indeed always of a word that *can* have that role. Sometimes a gesture, not even a conventional one, can be a word. But if there is a saying that something is or is to be, this is done by some sort of word that says it.

Quine's marriage to what he counts as the 'austere muse' of the strictly scientific prevents him from being able to give any account of 'saying that ...' He cannot legitimately accept the lack of 'transparency', the unavoidable 'referential opacity' of intentionality. He does something to avoid it for the verb 'believe'; but his effort at an account of 'says that' only uses what looks like, but he says is *not*, direct speech after 'says'; it remains 'referentially opaque'. This he calls an advantage, as indeed it must be if the account is to succeed. For though in 'A says true 'B is an F'' he allows substitution of equivalent terms, he cannot allow substitution of alternative designations which merely happen to designate the same. Thus he deserts his 'severer muse' and grants that one must do so as a matter of convenience. But what has become of 'ontological commitment'? How can a man in his position so much as speak of this as if it belonged in a 'scientific' account? We are left wandering in a desert waste of subjectivity.

Let me now return to the fact that 'saying that ...' is the act of a word. If there is a linguistic utterance which is a 'saying that ...' then it is a sentence, even if it consists of only one 'printer's word', or is a complex sentence with subordinate clauses. There are indeed plenty of sentences, of one word or many, which do not 'say that' anything. Consider the following:

Help!

Fire! (imperative)

Fire!

Fiat lux.

When I bang the table you will leave the room.

Lovely.

Going, going, gone.

Of these, the third could be a 'saying that'. The last is the utterance of an auctioneer in a sale. His performance makes it the case that the bidding for an item is finished. The fourth '*Fiat lux*' (in English 'Let there be light') is taken from *Genesis* telling of the creation: 'God said "Let there be light" and there was light'.

The similarity and the contrast between this and the case of the auctioneer are interesting. The bidding in the sale of the item is finished because that is the rule in an auction. By contrast, in the *Genesis* story light is made to come into existence by the creating will which the human writer symbolized in the word '*Fiat lux*'. That creating will is the thought whose occurrence or existence is the occurrence or existence of the created thing. The act of creating intelligence is indicated by logical and mathematical calculi being usefully applicable in exploring phenomena. Cf. Newton's feeling of 'thinking God's thoughts after Him'. He was apparently seeing what was *so* in the universe.

We utter words of many kinds. Often they are sentences, and among sentences some are 'sayings that ...'. These we perhaps call 'propositions', which in turn are of many varying kinds. The 'saying that ...' by many propositions is what gives them their enormous importance. This lies in the extremely usual peculiar connexion between a saying that ... and a reality. Where there is this connexion, it exists whether the proposition is true or false, for a false proposition is converted into a true one by negating it, and negation introduces no new feature.

Not every saying that ... has this characteristic; that some utterance is a saying that ... may merely be a mark of its surface grammar, the form of words that makes one call what is said 'an indicative statement'. In doing philosophy we should beware of being misled by this into pointless searches. Galton found that many people have coloured visual images in connexion with numbers.[1] He did not find out or (I believe) try to find out 'what having such images *is*'. The

[1] See his *Enquiry into the Human Faculty*.

reports were 'sayings that' in their grammatical form, but not reports where truth was anything other than not pretending.

Here we may note that Quine's test, by observing assent and dissent on the part of users of a language we are trying to understand, would have no application in this case. If A says the number five is yellow and B says it is purple this is not a relevant sense of 'dissent'; nor would it be assent on B's part if he too said it was yellow. Quine in fact has no account of assent and dissent which will serve to characterise a bit of language as a 'saying that'. Sympathy with a cry of fear, for example, or response to a call for help will not give us examples.

The power of thinking *what is so*, even wrongly, is created in men, giving them language that can express it. 'Being so' is the first thing to get into the nascent human intellect, the beginning of knowledge which is not wisdom but is its background.

Index

Order Form

Name . . . .
Email . . . .
Address. . . . .
. . . .
. . . .
. . . .
Home Telephone . . . .

Carriage Charges

Inland (UK) post: 1-2 books: £1 per book; 3 or more: free of charge
Overseas (airmail): 1-2 books: £2.50/$5.00 per book; 3 or more: free of charge

Please send the following:

☐ *Values, Education and the Human World*, £17.95/$29.90 (pbk.)
☐ *Philosophy and Its Public Role*, £17.95/$29.90 (pbk.)
☐ *Relativism and the Foundations of Liberalism*, £30.00/$59.00 (cloth)
☐ *Human Life, Action and Ethics*, £17.95/$34.90 (pbk.)
☐ *Institution of Intellectual Values, £14.95/$29.90 (pbk.)*
☐ *Life, Liberty & the Pursuit of Utility*, £17.95/$34.90 (pbk.)
☐ *Distributing Healthcare*, £17.95/$34.90 (pbk.)
☐ *Liberalism, Education and Schooling*, £17.95/$34.90 (pbk.)
☐ *Landscape of Humanity*, £17.95/$34.90 (pbk.)
☐ *Faith in a Hard Ground*, £17.95/$34.90 (pbk.)
☐ *Subjectivity & Being Somebody*, £17.95/$34.90 (pbk.)
☐ *Understanding Faith*, £40/$80 [2009] £17.95/$34.90 (pbk.)
☐ *Rethinking Bus. Management*, £40/$80 [2009] £17.95/$34.90 (pbk.)

Postage (free for 3 or more books) . . . . *Total* . . . .

☐ *Cheque enclosed (pay 'Imprint Academic') — £UK (drawn on London)*

☐ *Visa* ☐ *M/C* ☐ *Amex* ☐ *Switch* ☐ *Delta.*

Card # . . . .
Expiry Date . . . *Sec.Code/Issue No. (Switch)* . . . .
Signature. . . . .
All credit cards charged in £UK and converted by the card issuer.

ORDER OFFICES:

Imprint Academic
PO Box 200, Exeter EX5 5YX, UK
Tel: +44 (0)1392 851550, Fax: +44 (0)1392 851178
Email: sandra@imprint.co.uk

Imprint Academic
Philosophy Documentation Center
PO Box 7147, Charlottesville, VA 22906-7147, USA
Tel: 800-444-2419, Fax: 434-220-3301
Email: order@pdcnet.org

imprint-academic.com/standrews